# Good Planting

# GOOD PLANTING

## Rosemary Verey

PHOTOGRAPHS BY ANDREW LAWSON

FRANCES LINCOLN

HALF–TITLE PAGE
A subtle spring planting of a band of blue grape hyacinths and deep crimson primulas whose velvet-like petals echo the emerging stems of the peonies. This border is cleverly planted for successive interest – alliums, delphiniums and lilies follow in summer.

FRONTISPIECE
Lilies, dianthus and roses are an old fashioned and romantic trio; the rose associates perfectly in colour and shape with the dianthus and the lily contributes its pink buds, which will develop into waxy white blooms later. Dianthus make an excellent underplanting for roses, the scent of the rose wafting on the air and the dianthus fast with its bounty (when you bend or pick it, you will also discover its clove-like perfume).

CONTENTS PAGE
A perfect colour echo – the double yellow poppy bringing out the matching yellow splash on the iris fall.

*I would like to extend my special thanks to Andrew Lawson – not only for his wonderful photographs, but also for sharing with me his vision as a painter and his invaluable knowledge about colour; and to Katherine Lambert who has unsparingly helped me both to gather my ideas together and to put my thoughts into words. R.V.*

Frances Lincoln Limited
4 Torriano Mews, Torriano Avenue,
London NW5 2RZ

Good Planting
Copyright © Frances Lincoln Limited 1990
Text copyright © Rosemary Verey 1990
All photographs © Frances Lincoln Limited 1990 except those on pages 9 left, 13, 14 bottom, 15, 17, 21 top right and bottom right, 23 top right, 26, 35 top left, 36 top left and bottom left, 40 top left, 42, 43 right, 46, 48, 49 bottom, 50, 52 top, 54, 59 bottom, 60 right, 61, 63, 70, 73, 74, 77, 78 left, 79, 81, 84 top left and centre, 85, 86, 88, 94, 95, 97, 99, 101, 102, 109, 110, 111, 114, 115, 117 left, 118, 122 top, 123 top, 125, 126, 127 right, 130, 131, 132 bottom, 133, 136, 138 bottom left and bottom right, 140, 142 top right and bottom, 143 bottom, 145, 147, 148 bottom, 149, 151 left, 153 topright, 156 bottom right, 159 right, 161 left, right and bottom, 162 right, 163 © Andrew Lawson 1990

**British Library cataloguing in publication data**
Verey, Rosemary
Good Planting
1. Plants. Cultivation
I. Title
631.5

ISBN 0-7112-0606-6

Set in 11/13 Bembo in England by SX Composing Ltd, Rayleigh, Essex
Printed and bound in Hong Kong by Kwong Fat Offset Printing Co. Ltd

# Contents

# Introduction

In Mrs Pugh's garden at Docton Mill in Devon, this planting in her bog garden in June makes a perfect picture of contrasting leaf shapes (especially of lysichiton, iris and hostas), textures and flower colours – the strong purple of the geranium contrasts with the yellows. At first sight one could imagine that the planting had just happened, but on closer analysis it becomes apparent how well it has been thought out, with enough foliage plants to keep the scene beautiful through the spring and summer.

The ideas in this book have been evolving in my mind for several years, as day by day I have walked round my garden looking at the closely planted beds developing through the seasons. I realized that unless I wrote my thoughts down they would remain as fleeting impressions, of little help to me and no help to anyone else. I wanted to analyze why certain combinations of colours, shapes and textures, whether harmonious or contrasting, to me looked beautiful, while others, often just as carefully conceived, did not work – they were too electrifying or simply drab. And though I loved it when friends said 'I was here three weeks ago and the borders look as good now as they did then, but in a completely different way', I needed to explore the lessons to be learned from such a comment. I determined to put my feelings about planting into words and to try and express them so that they would be of practical use.

In life we have five senses – we see, hear, touch, smell and taste. We experience all of them in the garden and all have influenced this book. It is not a new thought: in 1618 William Lawson wrote, 'Whereas every other pleasure commonly fills some one of our senses, and that only with delight, this makes all our senses swim in pleasure . . . What can your eye desire to see, your ears to hear, your mouth to taste, or your nose to smell, that is not to be had in an Orchard?'

In our gardens colour, tone, texture, shape and growth combine to satisfy our eyes and agitate our hearts. While an understanding of them can be taught, it is familiarity with them that will bring the most deeply satisfying response, just as it does in music, poetry and art. Indeed a gardener has always seemed to me closely related to a painter. In some ways his task is more complex, since his palette is composed not only of living colours but also of changing textures, and his canvas is fluid in time – maturing, fading, finally ceasing to exist. Like Penelope's weaving of Ulysses' winding sheet, a garden is constantly being unravelled and re-created. But in other ways the gardener's task is easier than the painter's: a bulb planted to bloom next spring will grow and flower on its own, while the painting relies on the artist for its whole creation.

Good planting skills are not abstract concepts to be learnt solely from books, catalogues and other people. The best way to start is by learning to look, and in looking to see and to see critically. Nothing costs us so dear as a waste of time, said Diogenes. But never think that moments spent walking round your garden are wasted time. In them the seed of inspiration may be sown, and without inspiration a garden may be pretty but lack beauty, interesting but not memorable, and disturbing rather than restful. Ideas take time to evolve and mature, and it is by sitting or walking silently that they can come flooding in. I have special sitting and looking places in my garden where I can absorb the colours and shapes, the masses and textures, and in winter the richness of the bare stems of the shrubs. Then I can create in my imagination new pictures, new combinations.

When you are planning your own pictures and planting schemes, other considerations – the architecture of your house, your immediate surroundings and your way of life – will naturally play a part. Every gardener is blessed, or burdened, with elements which are difficult or impossible to erase – the house itself, existing paths and walls, old trees and established shrubs. From the start your planting schemes will be buttressed

The pictures on this page show good planting for foliage in two quite different sites: a damp shady area, where the plants have an upward movement, and a dry sunny site, where the plants are compact and rounded.

LEFT A streamside planting, mostly with green foliage, again all about contrasts of shape, with iris, ferns, hostas and *Rheum palmatum*. The ferns include ostrich plume fern, *Matteuccia struthiopteris*, and *Osmunda regalis*.

ABOVE This picture, taken in the herb garden at Jenkyn Place, gives an equally pleasing but different feeling, because each of these herbs grows in mounds – apart from the allium, which gives a spiky variety to the group – almost like a landscape of rolling hills.

OPPOSITE LEFT Many shrubs can be brought to life, with flowering climbers growing through them, to extend their interest through the year. Here, the tiny yellow leaves of *Lonicera nitida* 'Baggesen's Gold' provide a host for the dark purple flowers of *Clematis × durandii*, an association which makes good contrasts, both of colour and of shape. They make good companions, too, because the lonicera can be cut hard back in late winter to keep it to size and shape and the clematis, which is semi-herbaceous, requires pruning to the ground – or old wood – at the same time.

OPPOSITE RIGHT This little plant grouping, comprising a series of spikes and globes, can be enjoyed on several levels. Firstly, there is a pleasing contrast in shape between the round globes of *Allium aflatunense*, the spikes of the tree lupin and the triangular shape of the flowers of the *Iris pallida* 'Variegata'. On the colour level the allium and the iris harmonize, with the lupin providing a note of complementary colour. The grey stachys softens the picture while the dark evergreen background enhances the whole effect.

by the architectural and gardening thoughts of your predecessors; you may not like what they have done, but to a certain extent they will dictate your decisions. You may pluck planting schemes from Gertrude Jekyll or the Reader's Digest, but they will have to be fitted into and adapted to your own site. So much the better, for it ensures that every garden is unique. Each garden has its own character, unlike a row of identical houses.

You will also need to think about the amount of time you want or can afford to spend in the garden. Some trees and shrubs need far more attention and energy than others. Climbing roses must be pruned and tied, while an evergreen berberis or a patch of ground-covering pachysandra will look after itself, except for an occasional tidy. The beauty of a plant bears no relation to the amount of work it requires – fortunately perhaps, or we would all use the same ones in our gardens.

You must be honest, too, about whether you are a warm weather gardener. If you are reluctant to step outside from October until March, you will prefer to concentrate on the effect in spring and summer, when you will be walking among your beds and borders, so they will have more elaborate detail, with ephemeral bulbs and exuberant herbaceous plants. That being said, you will still want to make a satisfying winter picture to view from your windows by creating a framework of evergreen shrubs and interesting shapes.

A great part of the art of gardening lies in making the most of those plants which enjoy a particular site and a particular climate. There are plants for every situation. Those that will thrive in a sheltered patio are different from those that will survive on a windswept hillside. If you have a stream you will choose water-loving plants; if you live by the sea they must be wind- and salt-resistant. Although it may be easy to discover which specimens will be suitable – you can look over your garden wall and visit your local garden centre – it is more of a challenge to your imagination and creative intelligence to decide what kind of plants you really like and need. There is an important distinction between buying a plant and then choosing its position, and having a gap to fill and selecting the right plant for it.

When you are composing your borders, you will be thinking about leaf texture, shape, habit of growth, flower colour, and all the other elements which create the character of a plant. As you study each one, you will become aware that your visual reaction is different if you look closely at it than if you stand back and consider the whole plant as a mass or an outline. Occasionally one or other of these perceptions is used on its own – when you want to create impact solely from a distance, or when plants can only be seen close-to, such as in a tub on a terrace. Almost always, however, these perceptions must be combined: if more weight is given to the one or the other, the plant will not be used in its full strength.

Colour makes the most obvious impact in the border – indeed, I think that some people never consider anything else – but comparing and contrasting leaf textures is important if plants are to be good companions. Feathery green fennel and narrow-leaved verbena are too similar in texture for the quality of each to stand

out when they are planted side by side, whereas that same fennel matched with broad leathery leaves of bergenia is quite different in weight, and the two enhance each other, especially as they are of a similar green.

Leaf shape and density must also play a part. Using the same example of fennel and bergenia again, a good contrast is made between the light, tall and upright fennel, and the low, solid and spreading bergenia. Similar rules apply to shrubs: cistus, usually soft and mushroom-shaped, contrast well with spiky iris; the sword-like foliage of yuccas or phormiums makes, I believe, too piercing a contrast for the cistus, whereas the foliage of bergenias or hostas is bold and rounded enough to be a perfect foil to the tall blades of the yuccas.

Think, too, about the outlines of trees and shrubs. Some junipers have arms which protrude horizontally, so occupying more ground space, while others have an upright silhouette. The branches of *Viburnum plicatum* 'Mariesii' grow outwards in tiers from a central stem, whereas *V. farreri* has many branches ascending from ground level; these two occupy an equal space in the border, but the way in which their branches grow creates a different pattern and feeling.

Some trees and shrubs, such as hollies, berberis and choisya, are solid in appearance by virtue of the density of their leaves. Others, such as gleditsia or kolkwitzia, you can see through even when they are in leaf, either because of the small size and scattered nature of their foliage, or because their arching branches give them a light, ephemeral air.

When we think of flowers, we must consider not just the colour of their petals and the shapes of their blooms, but also how they merge and contrast with their leaf frames. They emerge in different ways into their settings: some hold their heads proudly upright; others are downcast. The stems of most roses or dahlias are stiff, offering their blooms boldly for your admiration. Fuchsias and fritillaries stand upright and then hang their heads, still tall enough to be seen, but to enjoy the low-growing hellebores and snowdrops you must turn up their faces.

Some flowers need shining leaves to set them off, particularly, I think, white flowers with green centres. Others, like potentillas, merge into their foliage, the frail petals resting and relying on the soft green leaves. They are so long in flower, blooming throughout the summer, that it is difficult to think of the leaves as being separate from the flowers.

Certain flowers, like magnolias or hellebores, suit their own leaves; others seem to be mismatched with them. Often a planting of gold and grey looks wonderful, but strangely enough I think that in a single plant the combination can be unhappy. I can do without the harsh yellow flowers above the almost turquoise

OPPOSITE These well filled borders at Crathes Castle have always excited me with their original planting. Scottish gardens are usually at their best in late summer, the herbaceous plants all blending and billowing together. Here the shapes – delphinium and buddleja spikes, feathery astilbes and rounded forms of hebes and hostas – make the various greens of the foliage a harmonious but exciting picture. Even the colour of the stone path brings together all the different shades in the borders. Instead of a statue or a fountain, an old arbutus tree acts as a perfect focal point.

ABOVE The same view of a corner of a border in my own garden at different seasons. In early May there are pink tulips among myosotis, and alchemilla leaves coming through. The evergreen *Iris foetidissima* 'Variegata' has a dominant presence in winter and spring, but in the course of the summer it is progressively overtaken. By June the alchemilla and dianthus are in flower. The myosotis and tulips have been taken up and replaced with *Lychnis coronaria alba* and *Penstemon* 'Rich Ruby'. The *Aruncus dioicus* has come into its own with handsome cream plumes.

leaves of *Ruta graveolens*, and in fact always cut them off, just as my preference is for *Santolina pinnata neapolitana* without its yellow flowers, and to my mind the dark crimson flowers of *Spiraea japonica* 'Goldflame' clash unattractively with the orange-red leaves.

Then there are plants, like the nerines, whose flowers appear before the leaves, and so need to borrow a covering of green from another plant. With the alliums, the leaves fade as the flowers emerge, and the dying foliage should be masked by neighbouring growth.

These general impressions are intended as guidelines to help you develop your own preferences and channel your own decisions. While you are doing this you will find yourself looking more closely at plants, considering their outlines as well as their details, in the same way that a painter has to observe his subject on several planes at the same time.

As you become intensely familiar with the minutiae and the mass in your own garden, you will find that it is difficult to see it with a critical eye – in this case familiarity breeds indulgence. If your ideas are not to stagnate and your garden become unprogressive, you must stimulate your imagination by seeking out combinations of colours and patterns wherever you go – even when you are driving through a village, along a country lane, or across a stretch of moorland. Other people's gardens are, of course, one of the best sources of inspiration. As you walk round, you will often be struck by a strong first impression – not necessarily one that is complimentary. You may see colours put together in a way that would never have occurred to you to use, or it may be a contrast of shapes. It is a good idea to write down all these thoughts.

Keep a notebook in your pocket or a camera in your car. I rarely visit a garden without some features sparking off an idea in my mind. I will never forget my first sighting of a James van Sweden grass planting, walking with him one evening through downtown Washington. On this cold night in winter it was the airiness of the grasses, like dancers clustering together and towering over mysterious ghost-like skeletons of perennials, that appealed to me. He plants these tall grasses, for foliage and flowers, amid low-maintenance perennials. I like this idea much better than whole beds of grasses put together without any relief.

A summer visit to David Hicks' garden in Oxfordshire gave me another grass and foliage thought. Running down an allée was a central mown lawn and on each side was a 5-6m/6-7yd strip of unmown grass standing about half a metre tall and in full flower, the stems all bending with the breeze. Behind each of these was a green wall – standard beech clipped as a hedge on stilts; but what gave the originality to the scene was another row

TOP Here is an example of dual performance, the hydrangea acting as a host for the prolifically-flowering double *Clematis viticella* 'Purpurea Plena Elegans'. The paler colours of the unopened clematis petals pick up the pink hydrangea flowers, and the deep red hydrangea flower stems echo the rich colour of the clematis flowers. The hydrangea needs careful pruning in order not to cut off next year's blooms; the clematis must be hard pruned in spring.

ABOVE A delightful, detailed spring planting in which colours and shapes echo each other. Snakeshead fritillaries in both forms – the white and checkerboard – and the *Narcissus cyclamineus* with its striking reflex petals all have hanging heads. While the purple in the checkerboard fritillary picks up the purple of the berberis behind, the clear yellow of the narcissus and soft pale green of the unopened fritillary are shown up by the dark background.

of beech, this time clipped as a conventional hedge. It taught me what different greens, textures and treatments can do.

The well-known group of tall *Calocedrus decurrens* at Westonbirt Arboretum made another impression – a memory of strong verticals and a dark mass close to the light-textured horizontal Japanese maples. I might not have the space to mimic this planting, but I could use the idea on a much smaller scale.

Another memory I carry in my mind is of the mass of wonderful tall delphiniums growing on a raised bed in the late Dowager Countess of Westmorland's garden at Lyegrove near Badminton, Avon. This was truly 'planting in layers', first with lawn, then a stone retaining wall edged with nepeta, and behind this, delphiniums, with climbing roses on the tall backing wall.

And then I remember a Sunday evening at Pyrford Court in Surrey, walking through a garden created by Gertrude Jekyll many years ago. It was the golden garden leading into the blue and green borders and on through the red borders. I can no longer remember them in detail, only in a colour haze, but when we planned our borders here at Barnsley in 1969 they were based on this theme.

Inspiration will come not just from the natural world. Another enjoyable way of discovering associations of colour and texture that please you is to look at decoration in everyday life – in pictures, carpets, furnishings. Almost everything around you has a message. Sometimes it is the shock of the new that will fire your imagination – bright blue or purple with deep orange in a curtain material, or aubergine with mustard in a dress – or it might be the subtle and sophisticated range of fawns and greys, blues and greens in a museum tapestry. These visual memories may resurface for you when you are feeling for an effect in your border.

Remember, though, that the rules for living plants and for stylized decoration are necessarily different; they cannot be translated wholesale. You must try to produce the effect of the fabric you have admired rather than its actual colours. When I look at the bright materials I enjoy, I know that I would not want a shocking pink petunia beside a flaming red rose in my garden – even kept apart by their own green foliage.

Another experiment I have tried when making a new scheme is to take different coloured wools, a rainbow range of flowers or a selection of leaves, and spread them out in a tapestry of my own, remembering always that in the garden the flower colours will be distanced and may be enhanced by the many shades of green, gold and grey of grass or foliage. Try it for yourself: new combinations of colours and textures will occur to you as you move the clippings around, and you will be tempted to try them out in your borders.

Achieving a garden which looks satisfying at every season and

ABOVE In a planting scheme where the colours are reduced to green and white, the shapes and textures take on a greater significance. Earlier flowering spring bulbs have here been covered by the spreading *Clematis × jouiniana*, a very sweet-smelling, small-flowered variety that makes effective ground cover (and which needs pruning very hard each winter). The sword-like leaves of the *Crocosmia paniculata* make a good contrast of foliage shape, and help to support the long arms of the clematis. The silver 'pennies' – honesty seed heads – match the white clematis while their papery texture is foil to its more waxy flowers.

The photographs on these pages show three different, equally good, plant associations, where colours, shapes and textures all play an important role.

Seen here – above and left – are two equally effective monochrome schemes where the contrast between shapes and sizes becomes very important.

ABOVE LEFT The fluffy, full flower heads of the 'Iceberg' roses are repeated on a much smaller scale in the small flower umbels of the annual *Ammi majus*. Every inch of ground is covered; the felted grey leaves of the stachys harmonize with the monochrome effect.

LEFT The shining red of the autumn-flowering *Schizostylis coccinea* is reflected in the red berries of the cotoneaster growing behind. As the rhizomes take up little space, it would be a perfect combination for a narrow bed in front of a wall.

Above and opposite are two high flying double acts in which each partner shows off the other.

ABOVE RIGHT The pink and green in the leaves of the *Actinidia kolomikta* in summer are taken up by the *Clematis florida* 'Sieboldii', whose double white flowers have dark pink staminodes and pale green stamens. This is a brilliant combination.

OPPOSITE *Itea ilicifolia* makes a perfect host for climbing *Tropaeolum speciosum*. The itea is best planted against a south- or west-facing wall as its evergreen leaves can be harmed by hard frost. The long tassel flowers, which hang and lengthen elegantly from July until late autumn, have a musky fragrance. The scarlet tropaeolum is difficult to start, especially in an alkaline soil, but once established it is completely hardy and will increase in vigour each year.

which retains quality and excitement as it evolves through the year is the summit of any gardener's ambition – all and more that he or she can aim for. To try and describe how to achieve this is an almost superhuman task. I cannot hope to satisfy every gardener in every type of soil and every situation; I can only lay before you the thoughts which have developed and the convictions which have grown in my mind during the thirty years of my gardening life, in the hope that they will strike a chord with others.

The thought that lay uppermost in my mind as I wrote this book was the same as the one which governs the planting of my borders. I always try to plant so that one effect follows on from another – crocus, daffodils, tulips, early herbaceous material moving through to the wonders of July and into late summer as the colours become more autumnal, with a fling of late chrysanthemums, asters, rudbeckias and the last of the annuals, then finally to winter with its magic of strong but sparser colour and the wonder of the emergent bulbs. As well as thinking about planting for year-round interest, I have also tried to think about planting in vertical layers, encouraging a climber to billow out over a shrub, or herbaceous plants to push through spreading ground cover.

It is this never-ending cycle, from one season to the next, from one flush of colour to the next, from one surprise to the next, that makes me want to go on gardening. It becomes like reading an exciting novel or climbing a mountain – I want to discover the end of the story or the view from the top. In the garden there is always next season, next year to anticipate. Indoors, you may cook a wonderful meal and then it is eaten and remains only in your memory – and that fades. Your curtains and walls gradually become worn and old, but your garden is quite different. A few snowdrop bulbs will multiply into a whole drift, a cutting you took from a friend's garden may grow into an important feature. As long as you are willing to spend time nurturing your plants, your garden picture will mature and develop each year, giving you the same satisfaction that an artist has when his picture takes shape on the canvas.

Just as there is a plant to suit every situation so there is a style to suit every gardener. If this book does anything to help you realize your own style, I will be well pleased. Most importantly, of course, it is up to you. Renoir relied on his instinct when he created a picture. Asked if he followed some special rational method, he answered: 'No, I don't; that is the procedure of an apothecary, not of an artist. I arrange my subject as I want it, then go ahead and paint it, like a child . . . I am no cleverer than that.' It is excellent advice for the gardener, too.

# Colour, Shape and Texture

**A**s you walk into any garden the immediate impression you have is of colour. This is true whether the garden is a medley of bright flowers with green, a single colour with green, or a gentle gradation of green, some in shade and some in sunlight. Most gardeners use a combination of these elements and it is the way in which the colours are blended that creates the atmosphere – exuberant, depressing, muddled, startling or peaceful.

The colour which surrounds us affects our whole mood. Luckily we all respond differently – if we all liked the same colours, our houses, our clothes and our gardens would lack variety. When I was nineteen I loved to wear bright red dresses; if I wore a pale one it had to have a vivid sash. Our ideas change, and today there is not a single red garment in my wardrobe. They are all quieter tones – mauves, blues and autumn colours, but no drab browns or greys.

We cannot avoid colour – we wake to a grey day or to golden sunlight – and I see a relationship between colour and the seasons. Winter is brown and green, shot through with bright red and yellow, all intensifying according to the quality of the light. Spring is golden, white and pale green with crocuses, daffodils, euphorbia, pools of blue grape hyacinths and a medley of tulips against the young growth on herbaceous plants and trees bursting into leaf. Summer starts with soft colours – pinks and mauves – with roses, lavender and penstemon, and then turns to hotter colours, with bright reds, orange and the strong yellows of dahlias, marigolds and the sunflower tribe. Autumn must be glowing tints, from the vermilion of maples through the softer reds and yellows of Japanese acers, sorbus and beech.

But the changes we see in the garden are more mercurial than that. We say, 'The air is so clear', colours seem brighter, more translucent than usual. In the moments after a rainstorm, when the sun bursts out and raindrops are hanging from bare branches or lodged in leaves, they reflect every colour in the spectrum, like soap bubbles in the bath although they themselves are colourless.

Colour sends us a clear message – red fruit is ripe and ready to eat. It also causes an emotion – a rainbow and a dramatic sunset excite us just as a medieval stained glass window with the sun pouring through it.

Colour can even control the pace at which you walk through your garden and the direction in which you are led. Shady green trees make you pause (they do me), while a fountain, a pool of bright light or some brilliant planting will make you quicken your pace to discover what is glittering, and the distant eye-catching trunk of a silver birch will draw you towards it. Any strong colour – red, orange or yellow – stands out and advances towards you, while the shady colours – blues, purples and greys – recede, both in the border and into the distance.

Thinking about colour and discovering how it affects you personally can help you in designing your garden and planning your planting. You will become aware of the nuances of colour echoes, how colours change in morning and evening light, and of shadows and strong contrasts. If you are a painter or work in industrial design, then your knowledge of colour must be raised to a technical level, but for gardeners it is enough to be aware of colour tones and contrasts and to plant instinctively according to personal feelings.

An artist paints a picture and then its colours become static, altered only by a surrounding frame or the position in which it is

hung. Gardeners, unlike artists, have to compete with a constantly changing scene – the wind blows, the flower petals fall, leaves change colour, plants die, they follow their life pattern. The total effect is evolving and then fading. They must experiment and make their own changes.

Leonardo da Vinci saw a direct relationship between colour and the elements: yellow for earth, green for water, blue for air and red for fire. Monet's understanding of colour was instinctive and became increasingly profound through his long life. As gardeners we need only think back to our first mixing of colours.

A truth we discovered in the schoolroom when playing with our paintboxes or crayons, and which I believe we should rediscover when we are considering ideas for our borders, is that there are three primary colours: red, yellow and blue. To the painter these colours are readily available in their purest form, and may be used to make pure and obvious statements. For the gardener, however, there are only a few flowers which actually fall into these definite categories. Some tulips are indeed pillar-box red, but even they have markings to their petals which tone down

their brilliance as you look at them closely. Of the two other primaries, a true blue can be found in *Salvia patens*, a true yellow in winter jasmine and forsythia.

In most situations these primary colours do not mix well. I do not like to see blue salvias with vermilion phlox or 'Paul Crampel' geraniums. In my garden yellow daffodils and scarlet tulips definitely do not go well together; but in a cottage garden with a medley of flowers they look natural, just as poppies and yellow coreopsis, mingled with green as the co-ordinating factor, become a perfect spectacle in a wild garden. Planted in small groups, these bright primary colours can become agitating to the eye, but a whole sweep of any one of them used alone (remember Wordsworth's host of dancing daffodils) looks spectacular and creates a unity which is surprisingly soothing, essentially softened by their green leaves.

Fortunately, the vast majority of flowers is on the periphery of the primary colours, edging into secondary – orange, violet and green, each made by mixing two of the primaries. In the garden, green is ubiquitous, and so our eyes are accustomed to seeing it

OPPOSITE Mrs Frank's cottage garden at Steeple Aston, Oxfordshire, has a dazzling but successful mixture of primary colours in spring, using scarlet and yellow tulips and blue grape hyacinths. The co-ordinating factor is the element of green. By early summer there is a complete change to a medley of white and mauve *Campanula persicifolia*. The bulbs are left in to flower again next year.

LEFT The two yellows of *Argyranthemum maderense*, pale petals and dark eye, are complementary with the deep purple of *Heliotropium* 'Princess Marina'. The latter is best treated as an annual and the former as a tender perennial wherever there is winter frost.

RIGHT Orange and blue are complementary colours and so make a strong contrast. *Anchusa italica* 'Loddon Royalist' is a rich shade of true blue, the anthemis a mellow orange. Yellow and blue, being closer together on the chart, would make a less startling combination.

RIGHT A simple colour chart shows the three primary colours (red, yellow and blue), and the three secondary colours (green, orange and violet), which are mixtures of the primaries, together with the colours that link them. The colours which are opposite each other on the chart are complementary: this means that they provide the strongest contrasts. To choose colours which are harmonious, select those which are close together on the chart. The colours of the flowers in these pictures are all primaries and secondaries, and they show how complementary colours can be used in the garden.

RIGHT Use complementary colours to make strong contrasts. The vivid vermilion of the oriental poppies will always stand out in a border when seen against green foliage.

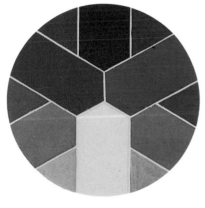

in conjunction with every other colour and to accepting it as the perfect partner for every one of them.

The other secondary colours, orange and violet, associate well together, although not in such a vibrant way as the primaries yellow and blue. Think of some particular combinations you enjoy. In spring I like deep blue-purple grape hyacinths with bright orange *Fritillaria imperialis*. Later the flowers of *Lonicera* 'Dropmore Scarlet' go well with *Rosa* 'Veilchenblau', low campanulas with orange rock roses, or tall bell flowers with orange heleniums or *Gaillardia* 'Mandarin'.

You can also successfully mix a primary colour with the secondary colour immediately opposite it on the colour circle: blue with orange (orange is a mixture of red and yellow), for example: blue forget-me-nots and orange tulips; red with green (green is a mixture of blue and yellow), for example: *Salvia fulgens* and its own green leaves; and yellow with violet (violet is a mixture of red and blue), for example: yellow irises and violet aquilegias.

These contrasting colours, far apart in the rainbow, are in opposition but are pleasing together. They are strong colours, carrying equal weight, and you will notice that the secondary colours, particularly the orange and violet, will look much more intense if matched with the primaries than if two secondary colours are paired together.

Intermediary colours are those on the fringes of the primary colour segments, and vary in hue according to the proportion of each primary colour used: orange-red, orange-yellow, yellow-green, green-blue, blue-violet and violet-red. You need to be wary of combining intermediary colours belonging to the same primary colour: yellow-red (tangerine or marigold) with violet-

red (pink), orange-yellow with yellow-green, green-blue with blue-violet. Again, translate this thought into the plants you know: imagine a nasturtium with a pink geranium, or helichrysum with *Alchemilla mollis*, or forget-me-nots with purple iris. I know they would not appeal to me.

Your garden can be full of colour mixes, but pause and consider what you really like. You can make this discovery by consciously taking in the effect colours have on you. I have a small glass bowl which is a wonderful strong violet colour, and I love to fill it with yellow primroses or chartreuse euphorbias and *Alchemilla mollis*. The primroses can have blue grape hyacinths with them, but the grape hyacinths need the yellow primroses in order to make a harmony with the violet glass. You can learn so much from picking flowers and bunching them together.

Sometimes it is satisfying to have a colour theme of a gradation of tones, at others a contrast of secondary colours. As I write, there is a deep blue tumbler on my desk filled with flow pens. The orange one looks wonderful with the blue – and in my garden I can translate this mixture into marigolds and nasturtiums growing round delphiniums or polemoniums. Remember that there is a high proportion of green in the garden and that the flowers will have a gradation of blue and of orange, unlike the glass and the pen, both of which have a solid colour.

The pink pen, on its own, looks very mellow in the blue glass. In the garden, where pink and blue look equally good together, I would want the pink flowers to be more important than the blue – pink roses underplanted with blue violas or campanulas, pink *Verbena* 'Silver Anne' with pale blue lobelias, pink *V.* 'Sissinghurst' with blue *Felicia amelloides*, *Anemone × hybrida* 'Lady Gilmour' with *Hydrangea aspera villosa*, *Sidalcea malviflora* 'Rose Queen' with *Nepeta* 'Six Hills Giant', *Penstemon* 'Evelyn' with *Viola* 'Belmont Blue'.

## Shape and texture

To create a successful scheme, gardeners must have a natural or an acquired feeling for colour as well as, of course, some horticultural knowledge; but they also need the aesthetic sensibility to incorporate shape, texture and scale successfully. It is impossible to divorce colour from shape and texture. In borders of one colour with green and grey foliage, the shapes of leaves, flowers and whole shrubs immediately stand out as important. For instance, in a green and white planting of *Hydrangea paniculata* 'Grandiflora' with a green juniper, grey-leaved *Eryngium giganteum* and the fern *Polystichum setiferum divisilobum*, the textures and shapes would predominate. If you substituted a ground cover with a red, gold and green leaf for the fern, then it would stand out as a main feature and you would lose the importance of the texture of the hydrangea leaf in juxtaposition with the juniper.

Texture is not naturally a dominant feature but once you start to notice this you will appreciate it. A simple example is the feathery foliage of *Santolina chamaecyparissus* next to the felted leaves of *Stachys byzantina (S. lanata)*. Here, colour is played down but the subtlety of texture is highlighted.

You can also play down colour to allow full appreciation of contrasting or reflecting shapes. Round bushes of *Hebe rakaiensis* can be surrounded with horizontal grey *Stachys byzantina (S. lanata)*, upright grasses, *Iris foetidissima* 'Variegata' or quite simply with summer-flowering nicotiana. In a blue theme, the spikes of delphiniums and monkshood would contrast with rounded forms of *Salvia nemorosa* 'East Friesland'. In these examples the round contrasts with the spikes; but if you added *Allium aflatunense* or *A. christophii (A. albopilosum)* you would create another rounded shape, the whole in harmony. In a more detailed picture, if two or more flowers of the same colour are grouped together – for instance, in an all-pink planting of dianthus and phuopsis or *Allium aflatunense* and *Polygonum bistorta* – then your attention will be made to focus on their shapes rather than on their colour.

The lesson is that shapes become increasingly significant as the colour scheme is simplified. This is especially true in all-green themes. Imagine fennel and angelica in front of an upright

The pictures on these pages all bring out the same point: in a monochrome planting your attention is drawn to shapes and textures.

OPPOSITE If these plants were brightly coloured, you might not notice the contrasts of texture between the velvet leaf of *Hydrangea sargentiana*, the spiky seed heads of *Eryngium giganteum* and the delicate filigree of the fern. The grey-green of the eryngium is echoed on the undersides of the juniper in the background.

RIGHT ABOVE Erect stems of verbascum contrast well with the flat round heads of the white daisy, *Leucanthemum × superbum*.

RIGHT BELOW A clever combination of white and cream variegated leaves: *Iris pallida* 'Variegata' with the annual *Euphorbia marginata*, and behind them, the half-hardy variegated abutilon.

FAR RIGHT ABOVE In Anne Dexter's tiny Oxford garden the white hydrangea 'Lanarth White' stands out beside the narrow pathway, which leads to a false door.

FAR RIGHT BELOW In February white Dutch crocus grow through a carpet of *Stachys byzantina*, which surrounds an old plant of *Santolina chamaecyparissus*.

cypress, and it immediatcly becomes obvious that the angelica, with its large fingered leaves, stands out boldly, while the fennel would become lost. Thinking on this theme, the large leaves of *Rodgersia pinnata* or *Ligularia dentata* 'Desdemona', with its handsome purple leaves, would be splendid neighbours for the conifers; just as effective would be *Euphorbia characias wulfenii* or *E.c.w.* 'Lambrook Gold'.

The more you consider leaves, with their highly individual shades, textures and shapes, the more important they become in your planning. Each leaf has its own shape – long, pointed, round, oval, fingered – and the mass or density of a shrub will depend upon the quality of its leaves. Some leaves are tough and shiny like holly and box; others are solid like bergenia, hard and matt like garrya, or light and airy like gleditsia or fennel. As you become more conscious of shapes and textures, you will find their associations just as rewarding as colour combinations.

## Colour, Shape and Texture

Here are four good examples of the use of nearly monochrome treatments of pink, emphasizing the contrasts of shape and texture.

BELOW LEFT The rose associates perfectly in colour and shape with the helianthemum.

BELOW RIGHT The fragile-looking faces of annual cosmos make a good comparison with the much firmer spikes of lythrum.

BOTTOM LEFT The globe-shaped flower clusters of *Phuopsis stylosa*, about 4.5cm/1¾in across, provide an interesting contrast of shape to the dianthus with their jagged edges.

BOTTOM RIGHT Pink *Diascia rigescens* stands firmly above *Cistus* 'Silver Pink', a variety which is ideal for the front of the border. Not only do the pale pinks harmonize with each other, but the yellow eyes of the cistus match the yellow centres of the diascia. Diascias have understandably become extremely popular in the last few years, but as they are not reliably hardy it is essential to take cuttings – which root easily – in late summer and to overwinter them in a cold frame or frost-proof house.

# Colour, Shape and Texture

Interesting pictures can be made with almost any monochrome colour scheme if there is enough contrast of size and shape.

BELOW LEFT A successful combination arrived at by chance. The *Campanula persicifolia* has seeded itself between the spikes of *Stachys byzantina*. The flower stems of this stachys can be picked, tied and hung up to make useful dried specimens for winter. If the dead flowers of the campanula are taken off regularly, new buds will develop and increase the colourful life of the stem.

BELOW RIGHT A tub of blue winter-flowering pansies and *Hyacinth* 'Bismarck' planted by Andrew Lawson in his garden at The Gothic House in Charlbury, Oxfordshire.

The hyacinth is identical in colour and provides fragrance as well as an intriguing difference of shape.

BOTTOM LEFT A path winds between cream to yellow borders with *Phlomis russeliana* in the foreground, beside *Anthemis tinctoria* 'E. C. Buxton', the rose 'Maigold' and *Argyranthemum* 'Jamaica Primrose'. The *Elaeagnus pungens* 'Maculata' gives height and winter colour and is excellent for picking.

BOTTOM RIGHT If santolina is left unclipped it will become a mass of small round flower heads. The lemon-yellow tones perfectly match the *Lilium* 'Sterling Star'.

All these pictures show the inspiring effects of foliage associations. As seen on the previous pages with the monochrome use of flowers, placing leaves together emphasizes their diverse textures and shapes.

OPPOSITE ABOVE LEFT In his remarkable garden in Oxfordshire, David Hicks relies on texture, shape and contrast of leaves for many of his effects. *Angelica archangelica*, with its red stems, has been allowed to grow up almost through the tree peonies. The round leaves of the *Alchemilla mollis* tucked in underneath echo the round angelica heads. Golden hop, *Humulus lupulus aureus*, is appearing behind and will soon be over the wall.

OPPOSITE ABOVE RIGHT Bronze fennel makes a soft and enticing background to shiny hosta leaves and young sedum foliage.

OPPOSITE BELOW LEFT A vignette of different pale greens and dots of red. Softly variegated *Salvia officinalis* 'Icterina' with matt-felted leaves looks perfect encircling *Euphorbia cyparissias*.

OPPOSITE BELOW RIGHT I like *Lamium galeobdolon* for its fresh yellow nettle-flowers in spring and its silver-splashed leaves which get a purple tinge in winter. Here in the border it is growing with *Artemisia abrotanum*, southernwood – a contrast in texture, colour and shape.

TOP FAR LEFT A haphazard but interesting effect has been created with *Milium effusum aureum*, Bowles' golden grass, and the soft pewter-blue leaves of *Potentilla anserina*. The grass is wonderful for lighting up shady corners; everything about the plant is bright yellow, including the flower heads.

TOP CENTRE LEFT In the herb garden the golden sage, *Salvia officinalis* 'Icterina', has the best form of curly parsley as neighbour.

TOP CENTRE RIGHT *Salvia officinalis* 'Kew Gold' is growing here with *Holcus mollis* 'Albovariegatus'; the variegations add another dimension to the contrast in leaf shape.

TOP FAR RIGHT *Euonymus fortunei* 'Emerald Gaiety' has beautiful silvery and green variegated leaves, which make a superb contrast to golden hop and an artemisia.

ABOVE LEFT Young leaves of *Trachystemon orientalis*, still pale as they emerge, push through common cow parsley. Colour, texture and shape of these all mix well together.

ABOVE RIGHT A softly rounded mound of variegated balm, *Melissa officinalis* 'Aurea', with its irregularly variegated leaves, is growing beside the spears of *Molinia caerulea* 'Variegata', whose striped leaves show up well in summer, and are effective even in winter.

## Colour harmonies and associations

No one understood colour effects better than Monet. At his house in Giverny, in France, he planted the western edge of his garden with brilliant orange, gold, bronze and even pink wall-flowers to catch and reflect every last ray of the setting sun. This fiery horizon which he created for the end of the day was a counterpoint to his planting of clear blues and salmon pinks at the eastern frontier to emphasize and symbolize the magical, misty light of early morning. The sense of distance and mystery was strengthened by concentrating the clearer, crisper blues and stronger pinks in the foreground, leaving the more shadowy tones to recede into the background. Monet combined the vision of the painter with the instincts of the gardener – Giverny is unique and is a lesson in colour themes.

A garden which made a lasting impact on me when I visited it one August is that created some sixty years ago by the great land-scape designer Beatrix Farrand in Maine. You walk through shady woodland and through a moon gate into a green garden with cool water. Turn, and straight away you are astonished by the colours beyond. On your right, facing south, is a long hot border, dominated by reds, golden yellows and orange; on your

LEFT All the colour schemes in the garden at The Priory have been carefully thought out by Peter Healing. Here the cooler colours – pinks, purples and creams – are used in the island bed and, glimpsed beyond the lawn, in the middle of his long herbaceous border, are the warmer colours – yellows, oranges and reds. In the island bed, which is planted for summer and autumn effect, dark blue salvia is growing in the foreground, with a clump of *Lobelia* 'Vedrariensis' just behind. The spikes of both act as a perfect foil to the rounded shape of *Sedum spectabile*. Further back are dahlias, lavatera and *Verbena bonariensis*.

These four pictures opposite demonstrate the effective use of a mixture of harmonious colours within the range of rosy pink through purple to blue.

OPPOSITE ABOVE LEFT Dark purple spikes of *Salvia nemorosa* 'East Friesland' are planted with *Lamium maculatum roseum* and an allium which starts white and opens to pink.

OPPOSITE ABOVE RIGHT Foxgloves and roses are a good association in a place with dappled shade. Here *Digitalis purpurea* mingle with a pale pink rose and *Meconopsis betonicifolia*. The pure blue of the poppy subtly echoes the latent blue in the purple foxgloves.

OPPOSITE BELOW LEFT Sometimes the camera will catch what the eye may miss. The highly fragrant *Dianthus* 'Loveliness' is perfect in colour, shape and texture with *Nigella damascena*, a hardy annual which can be sown directly into the border in the autumn, and *Borago officinalis*. Borage flowers are like blue stars on red stems, the leaves coarse but attractive.

OPPOSITE BELOW RIGHT We usually think of planting clematis to climb through another shrub, but the idea of growing two clematis together is good if the colours harmonize, especially when they flower simultaneously. Here pink *Clematis* 'Comtesse de Bouchaud' and mauvy-blue *C.* 'Perle d'Azur' are entwined.

left, cool colours – blues, greys, lilacs, pink, pale yellow and, of course, green – are massed together. Both borders make a wonderful tapestry, perfect in their own colour schemes. The lesson I learnt from these borders is the electrifying effect hot colours have and the calming influence of the cool, pastel shades.

Within each range of colours we all have our favourite combinations and associations. I think that I would list mine as:- pink with grey, blue with yellow and yellow with itself. In the first, the grey will be foliage, and you can have a wide choice of height, shape and leaf size. Grey is a splendid colour to experiment with, and comes in varying degrees of intensity and texture. I believe it brings out more strongly any colour with which it is associated, although I do not like the very strong tonal contrast of grey with darkest burgundy-red verging on black. The texture of the leaves of the curry plant is a good and complete contrast to the fleshy leaves of *Aeonium* 'Zwartkop' (*A.* 'Tête Noire'), but I feel that the colour of the aeonium is too strong and makes the grey look washed-out. However, put the aeonium with a vivid shiny green and the effect would be rather challenging (you can try this in your vegetable garden by planting ruby chard next to annual spinach).

Most grey plants look at their best in summer and sunlight. Some must be cut hard back in March or April. Useful grey shrubs 50-75cm/20-30in tall include *Santolina chamaecyparissus, Senecio* 'Sunshine', *Artemisia* 'Powis Castle' and *A. absinthium* 'Lambrook Silver', lavender, *Lotus hirsutus (Dorycnium hirsutum)* and *Helichrysum italicum*. Rather smaller in height are *Hebe pinguifolia* 'Pagei' and *H. topiaria, Artemisia stelleriana* and *A. pedemontana, Cerastium tomentosum* and *Convolvulus cneorum*, which

For me red borders create a definite mood, perhaps unsettling when very intense, giving a shock, a surprise. I can relax in a red room – this suggests warmth – but I would not choose to sit quietly beside a red border. However, I greatly admire the three plantings opposite, realizing how hard it is to use only hot colours – those that are adjacent on the colour wheel – with such success. The result is very stimulating.

OPPOSITE FAR LEFT Peter Healing has planted rudbeckia beside dark red nicotiana, bright red dahlias and *Crocosmia* 'Lucifer', backed with the bold leaves of *Ricinus communis* (treated as an annual), and *Cotinus coggygria* 'Atropurpurea'.

OPPOSITE ABOVE In the red border at Hidcote the spiky leaves of *Cordyline australis purpurea* grow between *Dahlia* 'Bishop of Llandaff' and the brilliant red *Crocosmia* 'Lucifer'.

OPPOSITE BELOW In his own garden near Cirencester, John Sales, chief gardens adviser to the National Trust, has the purple-red *Cotinus coggygria* 'Notcutt's Variety' growing between and through heleniums varying from vermilion through orange to yellow. Their black centres and turned-back petals are a feature.

itself has pink flower buds opening to white. *Teucrium fruticans* has pale lavender flowers which combine well with pale pink.

You can make a mix of pink and grey with *Verbena* 'Silver Anne', a non-stop flowerer through summer and autumn. The round heads contrast well in shape with *Artemisia arborescens* and *Senecio vira-vira (S. leucostachys)*. The pink Japanese anemone, flowering in August and September, looks well growing behind *Artemisia* 'Powis Castle'. The diascias, all with a slightly different pink, associate happily with *Stachys byzantina (S. lanata)* and santolina. *Diascia vigilis* will scramble through the cotton lavender, giving it a pink flower instead of the yellow buttons, which you can discourage by pruning the santolina hard in spring. *Helichrysum italicum* is one of the most satisfactory low shrubs. In front of a sunny, well drained wall it will luxuriate and smell deliciously of curry. The annual spider plant, *Cleome hassleriana* 'Pink Queen', flowers late in the year and likes the same warm position as the curry plant. Or you could have *Penstemon* 'Evelyn' or *P.* 'Hidcote Pink' with the grey. *Sidalcea malviflora* 'Rose Queen' has elegant spikes of mallow-like flowers in late summer. It would look good planted in groups between the white daisy-flowered, grey-leaved *Anthemis punctata cupaniana*, which blooms in early summer. Pink tulips would mix well with this planting; they can also be used successfully in spring as a foil to *Rheum palmatum* 'Atropurpureum' and the emerging leaves of *Cynara cardunculus*.

Pink roses must be treated with respect, using soft colours around them or a contrast of green or grey foliage. The hardy geraniums are constant standbys from June through to August. *Geranium pratense* 'Mrs Kendall Clark' cover the ground where early bulbs have flowered, and their leaves look good against bergenia and fennel. Our *G. sanguineum*, with magenta-purple flowers, and *G.s. striatum (G.s. lancastriense)*, with paler rose-pink flowers, have hybridized and seeded themselves into cracks in the paved path and have produced some attractive children. When we gathered and sowed the seeds there was a very poor germination, so we allow them to seed naturally and then divide the progeny. These geraniums are growing in the border with grey *Artemisia ludoviciana* and *A. canescens*.

Add another colour in harmony with the grey and pink. Mauves and deeper purple combine well with the grey and pink in May: nepeta and lavender, *Veronica gentianoides, Geranium* 'Johnson's Blue', *Campanula persicifolia* and *Erigeron* 'Darkest of All' (60cm/24in) and lavender-blue *E.* 'Adria' (75cm/30in). Lilac-blue delphiniums will bloom in the height of summer and back a vignette of *Cistus* 'Silver Pink' with furry grey leaves, *Artemisia ludoviciana* and pink astrantia, diascias or astilbe. *Erysimum* 'Bowles' Mauve' with pink penstemon and the firm leaves

Pure grey, which is made in painting by mixing black and white, could be called a 'non-colour', and so it acts as a neutral background for any other hue. It is particularly effective with pink, I find, possibly because pink can be such a difficult colour to associate with others.

LEFT ABOVE Peter Healing has *Rosa* 'Lavender Lassie' growing round the foot of *Pyrus salicifolia* 'Pendula' in his garden. Both are set off beautifully by the dark yew hedge behind.

LEFT BELOW The delicate pink flowers of *Lychnis coronaria oculata* make a happy combination with the juvenile grey foliage of eucalyptus.

BELOW RIGHT The fast-growing *Helichrysum petiolare* is one of the most useful half-hardy grey shrubs for summer bedding and for using in containers. Here it is mixed with *Verbena* 'Silver Anne' and *Sphaeralcea munroana*, another very good subject for pots and tubs. They both flower without ceasing throughout the summer and autumn; they can be left to cascade down or given minimum support can become quite tall. As with many grey foliage plants, they will survive the winter when given a sheltered, very well-drained situation.

OPPOSITE LEFT Grey works equally well with deeper pinks and purples. At Upton House in Warwickshire, *Linaria purpurea* has slender erect branches which are densely clothed with narrow leaves and bluish-purple flowers in long racemes. This is an easy plant which will thrive in shade and dry soil. Toadflax, as it is commonly known, will seed itself into cracks in paving and even into walls. Here it is overhung by *Picea pungens* 'Glauca'.

OPPOSITE RIGHT ABOVE A brilliant bedding scheme in Holland Park, London, using the half-hardy *Tanacetum ptarmiciflorum* with *Verbena rigida*. The lace-like foliage of the tanacetum contrasts well with the firm flower heads of the verbena. The grey cools the bright pink of the verbena but also makes it stand out strongly.

OPPOSITE RIGHT BELOW A grey and purple colour scheme for bedding out at Hidcote uses the cherry-pie *Heliotropium* 'Lord Roberts' as a ground cover around *Artemisia* 'Powis Castle'.

of *Hebe pinguifolia* is a good combination, and another effect can be made by using the dark green *Hebe rakaiensis* as a contrast in shape with the spikes of the penstemon and in leaf texture with the cheiranthus.

For a pink and grey section in a border, *Artemisia ludoviciana* or *Senecio* 'Sunshine' would provide a good grey backing, with pink *Diascia rigescens, Euphorbia amygdaloides rubra* and *Astrantia major*, alternating with the grey foliage of dianthus and *Veronica cinerea*, and *Aconitum hyemalis* 'Ivorine' adding a touch of cream.

These are all colour harmonies using pale colours with the grey. White flowers will also stand out, using white and grey *Spiraea* 'Arguta' as a background to delphiniums, digitalis, *Clematis* 'Marie Boisselot' and artemisia in front.

I like the effect of the velvet leaves of *Stachys byzantina (S. lanata)* with *Artemisia canescens*, and the wiry branching stems of *Lychnis chalcedonica alba* used in combination with blue campanula, golden-leaved feverfew and the variegated snowberry. The feverfew leaves help to pick out the yellow markings on the symphoricarpos.

True blue and yellow are both primary colours, and using them together is too strong a contrast, even with a generous infilling of green – I would not like rich blue delphiniums with *Ligularia* 'The Rocket'. But often the combination of mauvy blue and a less strident yellow can be effective. The young leaves of *Philadelphus coronarius* 'Aureus', cowslips and forget-me-nots or *Viola labradorica purpurea* is a good spring combination, and so is another of *Geranium pratense*, mauve Dutch iris and bold heads of *Euphorbia characias wulfenii*. This chartreuse yellow is sensational with blue grape hyacinths and also with fresh leaves of purple sage, or with the perennial wallflower *Erysimum* 'Bowles' Mauve'.

Euphorbias are invaluable plants. The rather spreading *Euphorbia cyparissias* is wonderful in spring with *Spiraea japonica*

In painter and photographer Andrew Lawson's garden at Charlbury in Oxfordshire, this bed under a west-facing wall has my favourite combinations of chartreuse-yellow and mauve-blues. It also has the quality of fullness – no bare earth leaving you with a feeling of frustration. *Geranium* 'Johnson's Blue', bright with flowers through the summer, and *G. magnificum* fill the ground where bulbs were blooming in spring, and there is a patch of *Ajuga reptans* 'Atropurpurea' at the front of the border. The back is dominated by the giant heads of *Euphorbia characias wulfenii* and the bearded iris. *Spiraea japonica* 'Goldflame' makes a brilliant splash of colour in the centre. This spiraea, very easy to propagate, has recently caught the fancy of garden designers, but it must be used with tact. In spring the leaves are bright gold and flame-coloured but by August it becomes drab.

'Goldflame', *Viola cornuta* and *Polemonium caeruleum*; or use other euphorbias, *E. polychroma* with pale blue chionodoxas or the low *E. myrsinites* with grape hyacinths.

I love yellow when it is very bright, almost a primary colour, but used with a secondary colour rather than with another primary in order to take away the too vibrant glare. For instance, *Coreopsis verticillata* 'Grandiflora' is a very strong yellow, and I would put it next to the purple-brown leaves and ivory-white flower spikes of *Cimicifuga ramosa* 'Atropurpurea'. The cimicifuga dominates through its elegant stature and the coreopsis through its brightness; neither overshadows the other.

Our yellow Welsh poppies are now established in many odd corners in the garden, and I try to keep them under control, growing round the old yew trees. They are just as strong in colour as the rich violet form of granny's bonnets, *Aquilegia vulgaris*, but neither is quite a primary colour. We save the seed of these and they are one of my favourite spring flowers. They are lovely with the poppy and with the foliage and flowers of epimediums and ferns coming through.

The theme of soft yellow, lime or chartreuse together with purple going towards paler mauve and also to bronze is one which carries on through the year, and can be exciting in the border. Cowslips should have bronze fennel growing between them – the first flush of fennel foliage is spectacular, and you can always cut down the flower stems as they appear.

My most striking early June effect is created by the mass of round-headed *Allium aflatunense* which have increased many-fold since I first planted them twenty years ago under our laburnum walk. This is a strong clear yellow and pale mauve picture, interspersed with plenty of green; the magic is that they are both at their best for the same two or three weeks. I can claim credit for choosing the alliums, but not for the fact that, being darker in tone than the laburnum, they act almost as shadows, with the laburnum as the lighting overhead. (If you were to reverse these colours, with purple wisteria above and yellow alliums beneath, the glow would be lost.)

Similar colours can be used to make other good garden pictures. *Clematis macropetala* growing through golden privet, *Viola cornuta* associated with the young leaves of *Spiraea* 'Goldflame', and the same viola with golden lonicera and golden marjoram. A background of golden weigela can have a wide planting of *Campanula persicifolia* and *Oenothera biennis*. You can make a whole strip of border wonderful in August by using 'Old English' lavender, *Nicotiana langsdorfii* and lime-green nicotiana, *Agapanthus* Headbourne Hybrids and the pale yellow *Argyranthemum* 'Jamaica Primrose'.

The same colour theme – of purples and golds – occurs in foliage associations as well as flowers. *Ajuga reptans* 'Atropurpurea' can grow round tufts of *Molinia caerulea* 'Variegata' or clumps of the useful *Iris foetidissima* 'Variegata'. Your group of iris can extend on and have *Pittosporum tenuifolium* 'Purpureum' to back it. The pittosporum leaves open green and soon become deep purple. Another contrast would be with the very slow-growing *Weigela florida* 'Foliis Purpureis', whose dark leaves need a paler background to show them up; they almost merge into the colour of a rich dark soil and also into a dark green background. The soft yellow leaves of *Acer shirasawanum* 'Aureum' (*A. japonicum* 'A.') make a good foil for the weigela or the pittosporum – but remember it is best grown in a degree of shade, and that you must buy a specimen branching from ground level.

If you wish to continue the golden and purple foliage scheme on the other side of your group of *Iris foetidissima* 'Variegata', there are several low to middle-height shrubs with golden variegated leaves. For the front, *Spiraea japonica* 'Goldflame' would also introduce flame-red in its leaves. The same effect of leaf colour happens with *Salvia officinalis* 'Tricolor', but the texture of the leaves of the sage and spiraea is quite different – the one smooth, the other almost rough. The leaves of *S.o.* 'Purpurascens' are wonderful in spring in colour, texture and freshness, and a circle of the variegated strawberry, *Fragaria × ananassa* 'Variegata', combines green, creamy-white and purple in equal strengths. I have this strawberry as ground cover round *Ilex aquifolium* 'Silver Queen', whose young shoots are deep purple.

For an upright shape behind the rounded purple sage, a semi-circle of *Pleioblastus auricoma* (*Arundinaria a.*), only 1m/40in tall, makes a lively splash of colour with its bright yellow leaves, striped thinly with a green margin. Cut it down each spring and you will find the colour of the new leaves is even brighter. The line of low bamboos can be carried on round the sage to the front of the border with *Carex oshimensis* 'Evergold', a graceful low grass with a central yellow-creamy stripe. Too solid a golden mass might be startling and unrestful, but a leavening of green, such as *Alchemilla mollis*, with its round, frilly leaves and lime-green flowers, will achieve the right effect.

Other useful golden-leaved shrubs are *Philadelphus coronarius* 'Aureus' and *Sambucus racemosa* 'Plumosa Aurea'. (You can be as drastic as you wish with this elder to keep it to your required size.) As a backdrop for this grouping of shrubs plant the purple-leaved *Acer platanoides* 'Crimson King' for an alkaline soil, and *Acer palmatum* 'Atropurpureum' on acid ground. The golden hop, *Humulus lupulus aureus*, would scramble through either, but I would start it off through a wooden tripod; the hop is herbaceous and is cut to the ground each winter, so the tripod would be easily renewed.

I repeatedly use the contrasting colours purple and yellow, but do not always follow the rules, and I find blue and yellow almost as satisfying.

ABOVE LEFT Cowslips merge with the young leaves of *Philadelphus coronarius* 'Aureus', and blue myosotis completes the picture.

LEFT The blue flowers of *Clematis* 'Madame Edouard André' hang their heads above pale yellow *Potentilla* 'Elizabeth'.

RIGHT ABOVE At Barnsley House mauve *Campanula lactiflora* is separated from the golden lemon balm (*Melissa officinalis* 'All Gold') by the starry white flowers of *Astrantia major*. The background tree is *Gleditsia triacanthos* 'Sunburst'.

RIGHT Golden privet makes a fine shrub on its own, but it is also useful as a host for mauve *Clematis macropetala* – which later forms feathery seed heads.

ABOVE LEFT A raised bed and pathway at Edinburgh Botanic Garden, where *Lavandula* 'Hidcote' planted on the top of the low wall billows down and makes a contrast to *Senecio* 'Sunshine' behind the seat.

LEFT A lovely soft contrast using *Euonymus fortunei* 'Emerald 'n' Gold' and *Geranium* 'Johnson's Blue' with luminous blue flowers which continue for most of the summer. The weight of these colours together is perfect.

RIGHT ABOVE Low-growing *Lysimachia nummularia* 'Aurea' covers the ground around *Viola* 'Huntercombe Purple', and the *Allium moly* adds sparkle to the picture.

RIGHT The same effect is achieved here as in the picture above it, but on a different scale. The golden hop, *Humulus lupulus aureus*, which has brilliant yellow leaves and is a most useful herbaceous climber, is used with purple violas at its feet.

In the spectrum yellow moves on to orange, or it can be toned down to a primrose or yellowy lime-green. Mixing these different shades together to make a yellow garden can be a compromise between having a regular flower garden and only having foliage. A lesson in this is the yellow garden at Crathes Castle in Aberdeenshire.

Yellow-leaved trees to use as a background to shrubs and herbaceous plants include the deciduous *Robinia pseudoacacia* 'Frisia', *Gleditsia triacanthos* 'Sunburst', *Acer pseudoplatanus* 'Worleei' and some of the golden conifers – I have *Chamaecyparis lawsoniana* 'Lane' with golden-yellow foliage planted in front of a dark green yew hedge to set it off. In the middle ground there are many golden-leaved shrubs to choose from – some require sunshine, others a modicum of shade to keep their colour. Among my favourites are *Philadelphus coronarius* 'Aureus', *Weigela* 'Looymansii Aurea', *Elaeagnus pungens* 'Maculata' and *E.* × *ebbingei* 'Limelight'. Other reliable yellow-leaved evergreens include *Lonicera nitida* 'Baggesen's Gold', various hollies (my choice is *Ilex × altaclerensis* 'Golden King'), *Euonymus fortunei radicans* 'Emerald 'n' Gold' and the golden-leaved privet, *Ligustrum ovalifolium* 'Aureum'.

Golden leaves often look at their freshest in spring, and I like to use the lonicera and the golden privet in several situations. The small leaves of the lonicera contrast successfully in colour with a dark green ivy and in size and texture with a golden ivy grown round its stem. You can do many things with your secateurs and grow the lonicera as a ball on a single stem or make it into a pyramid. For edging, where box would take two or three years to achieve a positive shape, lonicera will assume a definite character in a year; in your herb garden try golden thyme surrounding a low standard of 'Baggesen's Gold'. Golden thyme and herbs with golden leaves and markings, such as *Salvia officinalis* 'Icterina' or *Origanum vulgare aureum*, can also play an important part at the front of the border.

For yellow flowers on shrubs in the summer you can have coronilla, genista, kerria, hypericum and phlomis; other yellow flowers have been suggested earlier in combination with blue flowers.

In a monochrome scheme, shapes and textures are, as I have said, as important as colours. Just because you call it your yellow garden, do not spoil your picture by refusing to include another splash of colour if you feel it is needed in a particular spot. I like grey and gold in combination as long as they are woven together, not used in little pools that become intrusive to the eye. A long border I admire, created by Peter Coats, is backed by a wall and the front is in sweeping scallops, with gold marjoram, thymes and hostas alternating with grey artemisia, santolina and *Stachys byzantina* (*S. lanata*).

Grey in contrast to green is easy to achieve – it is the size and texture of the leaves which is important. Soft-textured rue looks lovely framed by shiny, solid box edging, and so does *Senecio vira-vira* (*S. leucostachys*). The combination of *Stachys byzantina* (*S. lanata*), *Santolina chamaecyparissus* and a dark juniper is perfect. *Hosta sieboldiana* 'Elegans' and other glaucous-leaved hostas are spectacular beside green leaves such as epimediums, dicentra, euphorbia, acanthus, tellima, upright ferns and spikes of iris or crocosmia.

We must move on from the pinks, blues and yellows to the stronger oranges, reds and purples. The deep purple *Salvia × superba* 'East Friesland', though not spectacular, is interesting when in flower and later when the bracts keep their colour. It is useful in front of the border beside spikes of yellow *Asphodeline lutea* and golden-leaved hostas or *Hemerocallis* 'Canary Glow'. Daylilies are so wide-ranging in their variety that you really

The three pictures opposite demonstrate the vivid use of foliage, and show how the theme of purple, yellow and green can be as effective in foliage as it is in flowers.

OPPOSITE ABOVE LEFT *Robinia pseudoacacia* 'Frisia' stands above *Berberis thunbergii* 'Rose Glow' and green foliage.

OPPOSITE ABOVE RIGHT *Gleditsia triacanthos* 'Sunburst' makes a good contrast to the dark purple leaves of a cotinus, while *Hydrangea paniculata* adds another shape of leaf as well as its white flowers.

OPPOSITE BELOW The herb garden at Barnsley House has a framework of box infilled with herbs. Green *Buxus sempervirens* 'Suffruticosa' associates dramatically with *Origanum vulgare aureum* and more soberly with purple sage.

The two pictures on the right show how grey, green and gold can be very satisfying when they are woven together.

RIGHT ABOVE A simple composition with *Alchemilla mollis* and *Artemisia ludoviciana* as the main planting, with golden feverfew adding another touch of yellow.

RIGHT BELOW Green leaves and chartreuse-yellow flowers of *Euphorbia polychroma* contrast with the grey leaves and flowers of *Ballota pseudodictamnus*.

should see them growing before you buy. They are essentially a minimum-upkeep plant, and in January and February have the virtue of pushing through the soil with their new leaves, a refreshing pale green in satisfactory spikes.

A well balanced group using orange and red can include a soft orange, cactus-flowered dahlia with dark foliage, *Helenium* 'Moerheim Beauty', orange to red kniphofias and *Crocosmia* 'Emily McKenzie' (60cm/24in tall) in front, and old-fashioned antholyza behind. Lobelias are at their best in August and September, and the various hybrids of *Lobelia cardinalis* – 'Queen Victoria', with deep red flowers, and 'Dark Crusader', an even deeper red – would complete this rich picture. Another grouping of hot reds could include *Cordyline australis* 'Atropurpurea', a scarlet rose, *Fuchsia* 'Thalia' and two annuals, species poppy and red nicotiana.

An unexpected but happy relationship of hot colours happened by chance in my border. I put *Cotinus coggygria* 'Atropurpurea' in the front to contrast in summer with *Cistus* 'Silver Pink', but for three weeks in autumn it contrasts wonderfully with its neighbour, *Acer palmatum* 'Atropurpureum'. I cut the cotinus hard back in spring just before new growth starts, and the acer is just kept shapely. Sometimes the most spectacular union of hot colours happens in an herbaceous border. I have already extolled Peter Healing's use of hot primary colours at The Priory, Kemerton, where the aristocratic *Dahlia* 'Bishop of Llandaff' jostles with ruby chard and red penstemons. Experiment yourself, on any scale.

As well as thinking about colour harmonies, we should bear in mind the dramatic effects that can be made by colour contrasts, and especially tonal contrasts – that is, contrasts of darkness and light, which are often created by using dark leaves with light flowers or vice versa. I have already considered the combination of almost black aeonium and palest grey helichrysum. This would be smart in a dress, but does not work in the garden, especially under grey skies. Quite close as a combination is *Cosmos atrosanguineus* with *Artemisia* 'Powis Castle', the deep red flowers coming through the grey foliage, but the flowers and leaves are better balanced in size and texture and the composition achieves a harmony which the other does not.

Reversing the roles, to set dark flowers against light leaves, the poached-egg plant, *Limnanthes douglasii*, can have a backing of purple-leaved sage, or the yellow-and-white daisy flowers of *Anthemis punctata cupaniana* the companionship of bronze fennel. *Berberis thunbergii atropurpurea* is a useful background shrub. In spring the paler pink *Tulipa* 'Mariette' would reflect the freshness of the berberis leaves, and later the silvery-blue bracts of *Eryngium giganteum* would make a strong tonal contrast.

The plant groupings on these two pages demonstrate effective contrast of tone – of darkness and light.

ABOVE The silver leaves of *Artemisia* 'Powis Castle' make the dark red flowers of *Cosmos atrosanguineus* stand out dramatically; against a dark foliage the cosmos would become virtually invisible. (This cosmos is a tender perennial – it can either be dug up and potted in the autumn or the roots well protected.)

OPPOSITE ABOVE LEFT White anthemis flowers with yellow eyes stand out strikingly against the dark filigree leaves of bronze fennel.

OPPOSITE ABOVE RIGHT The backdrop of the dark yew hedge makes the white and silver plants seem even lighter and brighter. This theatrical setting in Mr and Mrs David Hodges' garden uses *Spiraea* 'Arguta', white delphiniums, grey artemisia, white chrysanthemums and foxgloves, and *Clematis* 'Marie Boisselot'.

OPPOSITE BELOW LEFT Foliage lasts longer than flowers and often can be just as effective. Brian Halliwell in his bedding schemes at Kew Botanic Gardens used the dark purple and bright green forms of Swiss chard to create contrast in tone.

OPPOSITE BELOW RIGHT A dark curtain of berberis makes the distinctive shape of the eryngium flower heads appear almost illuminated in Anne Dexter's garden.

Dark and light flowers make a strong impact too – white osteospermum with deep purple *Nepeta × faassenii* have an added touch of sophistication created by the purple centres of the osteospermums echoing the nepeta flower spikes.

Nature herself is a perfect guide to colour combinations, often in a single flower. For example, purple Dutch irises have yellow markings on their falls, and the yellow can be picked up by Welsh poppies. The more you actually look face to face with your garden flowers, the more fun you will have picking out a particular colour and matching it with another. The red stems of ruby chard match red nicotianas; the creamy stripe on the variegated leaves of *Iris foetidissima* can be echoed by the bracts of the annual *Euphorbia marginata*. The interesting *Clematis florida* 'Sieboldii', with its wine-coloured stamens, is spectacular growing through the green and red leaves of *Actinidia kolomikta*, and a lovely effect is made by underplanting standard *Salix integra* 'Hakuro-nishiki' with *Euphorbia griffithii* 'Fireglow'. Dark crimson Barnhaven Courichan polyanthus match the young stems of herbaceous peonies, and the small lime-green flowers of *Nicotiana langsdorfii* reflect the wide bands of cream on the leaves of *Symphytum × uplandicum* 'Variegatum'.

Look at your violas and pansies with their huge variety of markings and pick out one of the colours to echo in a leaf or flower beside it. It is easy to find echoes in leaves too. I love the combination of Bowles' golden grass and *Helleborus foetidus* in the early spring. Colours that are too similar can sometimes kill each other, but the gold of the grass and the lime-green of the hellebore flowers are made perfect together by the interruption of the deep green of the hellebore leaves. Melissa with golden markings catch the yellow in *Hosta* 'August Moon' and the golden grass *Milium effusum aureum*. *Houttuynia cordata* 'Chameleon' lives up to its last name, the leaves combining green, yellow, bronze and red. You can enjoy echoing any of these colours with your own inspiration. Some of the echoes are bold and obvious, others are subtle and merit a close look.

The same is true of colour through your whole garden. Sometimes you may paint in abstract style, using colour in bold sweeps; at other times you will follow the Impressionists' example, with dots of colour mingling with green.

I have discussed colour more specifically in spring and summer, but the other half of the year has its own importance.

In the mixed border, the leaves of several of the herbaceous plants assume lovely shades. Hosta leaves as they age have a week or two when they change in texture and become a glorious golden straw colour. *Geranium sanguineum* foliage develops amazing crimson tints lasting a long while, but the leaves of *Bergenia* 'Abendglut' change from shining green to a deep red and

The photographs on these two pages show how the use of echoing colours can make highly effective and pleasing combinations.

OPPOSITE ABOVE LEFT At Hadspen House, the almost black tulip 'Queen of Night' picks up the purple leaves of the sage, while the grey *Stachys byzantina* echoes the handsome cut-leaves of *Cynara cardunculus*. Soon the cynara and sage will take over the ground where the tulips were blooming.

OPPOSITE ABOVE RIGHT Another perfect echo, but this time the blue-purple flowers of *Nepeta × faassenii* pick up the dark purple centres of the *Osteospermum ecklonis*.

OPPOSITE BELOW LEFT A low-growing blue veronica echoes the blue centres of *Osteospermum* 'Pink Whirls'.

OPPOSITE BELOW RIGHT A pale pink form of *Geranium sanguineum* is a good match with the pink flowers of *Lamium maculatum* 'Beacon Silver'. (Once the lamium has flowered you should cut the stems to the ground to encourage new fresh growth, which will come up a shining silver.)

RIGHT ABOVE Ruby chard, usually found in the vegetable garden, is grown by Peter Healing in his flower bed of hot reds, the brilliant red stems finding an echo in the flowers of the red nicotiana. (Both are best treated as annuals, the seed sown indoors in March or April and the plants put out in May.)

RIGHT BELOW Autumn provides an opportunity for warm red combinations. At Batsford Arboretum the red berries of *Sorbus pohuashanensis* hang over the brilliant autumn leaves of *Acer palmatum heptalobum*.

The visual impact made by juxtaposing red and green is achieved because the two colours are diametrically opposite each other on the spectral wheel. This has the optical effect of exaggerating the difference between them.

LEFT Signs of autumn at Barnsley House as the *Photinia davidiana* on the right in the background and the *Cotinus coggygria rubrifolius* start to turn colour, and the beech hedge takes on a tawny tone. The contrast of leaf colour of the variegated holly and the golden privet remains good through the whole year, and the rounded treatment of the holly against the straight sides of the beech is effective.

OPPOSITE LEFT ABOVE The tall *Crocosmia paniculata*, growing to 1.2m/4ft and more, makes ample support for the Japanese wineberry, *Rubus phoenicolasius*. The fruits of the rubus ripen as the crocosmia flowers in August and September, making an arresting combination. (This wineberry is a useful plant in the borders as its fruits are often eaten by the birds and they drop the seeds about. In winter its arching stems with red furry bristles stand out attractively and on frosty days they become covered with rime.)

OPPOSITE LEFT BELOW In autumn, as the leaves of *Parthenocissus quinquefolia* gradually turn a brilliant red, they make an exciting contrast to the ivy, *Hedera colchica* 'Dentata Variegata', which grows through them. (Both are strong growers and can be clipped back every year in early spring.)

OPPOSITE RIGHT Autumn brings its distinctive hues to the mixed border at Barnsley House. *Acer palmatum* has turned a fiery red to match the purple-red leaves of *Cotinus coggygria* 'Notcutt's Variety'. Each spring, just before the leaf buds form, we cut this cotinus right back to the old wood at 25cm/10in from the ground in order to keep it low (about 1m/3ft). This also seems to produce especially large and well-coloured foliage.

stay like this all winter, even through frosty weather. Astilbe leaves are attractive whether green or coppery, and last well into the late autumn. they create a good contrast to the foliage, green striped with cream, of *Iris foetidissima* 'Variegata'. The plain-leaved form of this iris has huge pods which burst open in winter to reveal orange berries – I would like to have it growing through the evergreen *Houttuynia cordata* 'Chameleon', whose leaves, all through the year, are an amazing mixture of yellow, green, bronze and red. Among my favourites for winter green are the narrow leaves of *Asphodeline lutea,* which make handsome clumps increasing year by year. In the mixed border chapter are suggestions for coloured winter stems, such as the dogwoods and willows, and also ideas for berries.

Autumn may burst into an explosion of colour; winter is the time when shapes and skeletons stand out and evergreens become important, so in your planning keep places in your borders to make autumn and winter full of interest. Foliage can be the framework as well as the background of your border. In winter, a mixed border can look like a well designed tapestry of brown, green, gold, silver and grey. The brown is the bare earth, made even browner by your top dressing of peat or leaf mould; the dark green and gold are broad-leaved evergreens, choice conifers and a few herbaceous plants which keep their leaves in winter, silver comes from variegation on leaves, and grey from those evergreens that have grey foliage. Most of the smaller grey-leaved plants look drab in winter, but santolina and *Senecio* 'Sunshine' make effective round mounds and *Stachys byzantina (S. lanata)* remains a grey carpet. To create a foliage effect in winter you should have just enough, not too many evergreens. Looking along your mixed border, there should be enough in-cident for you to enjoy the scene without anticipating the early bulbs pushing through.

# Bulbs

In April the lilac-pink buds of *Magnolia × loebneri* 'Leonard Messel' open on leafless stems. The petals, pure white within, reflect the white of the *Narcissus* 'Actaea', whose strong yellow eye, margined red, makes a bold impact in the grass. Before planting magnolias, make sure that the ground is well prepared. This magnolia, a cross between *M. kobus* and *M. stellata*, is lime-tolerant. The narcissus, one among several different narcissi planted here at Marwood Hill in Devon, is sweetly scented and lovely for picking and will naturalize when grown in grass.

The reawakening of the garden early in the year is always a moment of wonder. All good things come to an end; gradually the muted browns, fawns, greens and greys of winter and the framework of the leafless deciduous trees standing out as individual patterns are overlaid and brought to life as other colours and shapes slowly obscure the bare earth and tracery of naked branches. Bulbs push through the soil, wallflowers and forget-me-nots fill out, herbaceous leaves appear. It is a slow, almost imperceptible process, until suddenly winter is overtaken by spring and then by summer, when the garden becomes full of flowers.

Spring is the start of the gardening year, its exuberance, in part, the reward for our diligence the previous autumn. Spring bulbs are the curtain-raiser, stealing the scene when the garden is fresh and young, and continuing to create the brightest effect from February right through until mid-May. There follow the delights of summer lilies, gladiolus, acidanthera, crinums, nerines and the summer hyacinths, *Galtonia candicans*; then the delicate flowers of autumn-flowering cyclamen and crocus.

Bulbs are among the most reliable sources of pleasure in the garden. When you buy them you know that they have an incipient flower bud waiting to emerge in due season; they have the great strengths of resilience and annual reappearance without our help; and they come true to colour, size and shape.

Bulbs are particularly important for their colour in spring when they have little competition at ground level. Their rivals are tree and shrub blossoms – prunus, malus and forsythia – and fresh young foliage, especially of the golden-leaved shrubs. Many of the bulbs that flower later in the year are taller, more dramatic, holding their own in the well-filled border and making bold statements. They feature as individuals – think of a stand of lilies outside a cottage door.

Throughout the year, planning your bulb planting can well be an object lesson in learning to combine colours in harmony, to contrast sizes and even shapes, and to create an overall scheme in which they are the focal point; sometimes with each other and sometimes growing between and through the emerging or evergreen leaves of hardy plants, ground cover and shrubs.

## The colours of spring

In spring the garden is much more open than it is in summer. You can see through borders, often beyond them, and you are afforded a wider panorama at a glance. For this reason you must co-ordinate the colours of your spring bulbs as a whole picture, perhaps keeping the brightest reds and vividest pinks to places where you come upon them unawares.

Think about the impact of bulbs on a garden and you will realize that it is achieved by the pure and delicate strength of their colours. Generally speaking, I do not like strong primary colours together in a border, but springtime has a feeling of fiesta and awakening, and a bright, startling effect may appeal to the imagination. Scarlet and yellow tulips, blue grape hyacinths and white daffodils may mingle together, provided they are amply framed with green foliage.

To me, spring is mostly yellow, with blue and white mingling with the pink and white of tree blossoms and the fresh green of young leaves. One of my favourite colour combinations at every season is blue and yellow. In spring there is a wide choice of both

OPPOSITE A mown grass path leads up to the clock house at Bramdean House, Hampshire. The blue of the door gives a memorable effect to this spring scene, where massed daffodils have naturalized and flowering cherry trees come to maturity. On either side tall Irish yews provide strong, pencil-slim, vertical lines in contrast to the round heads of the trees and the white cupola.

ABOVE LEFT The Cyclamineus miniature narcissus are wonderful naturalized in grass and under trees. Here the clusters of buttercup-yellow N. 'Tête-à-Tête' are growing with *Scilla siberica* 'Spring Beauty' and the paler blue *Puschkinia scilloides* (syn. *P. libanotica*). This patch of early bulbs was planted at least seven years ago, and opens as a herald of spring. Later the ground is covered by *Clematis × jouiniana*, and the combined planting makes a trouble-free area.

ABOVE RIGHT *Anemone blanda* with Cyclamineus narcissus 'February Gold' piercing through them, each golden trumpet surrounded by a lemon-yellow perianth.

colours: yellow ranging from cream to strong deep gold, from pale primroses to rich daffodils and tulips, taking in, almost in passing, the subtly acid yellow of *Euphorbia polychroma (E. epithymoides)*; blue ranging from deep violet and mauve through azure, sky and cobalt. The large-flowered Dutch crocus come in both these colours – pure yellow and pure purple – and they look marvellous planted under deciduous trees where the sun will reach them to open their petals, or in large drifts in the border between herbaceous plants (their dying leaves will be hidden by the material growing up).

Look out for flowers with petals combining blue and yellow too – you will be surprised by their number, not among tulips and daffodils, but among lower growing, modest bulbs. Chionodoxas, well named 'the glory of the snow', have delicate yellow hearts to their blue petals, re-emphasized by their yellow stamens. The falls of several of the *Iris reticulata* hybrids have yellow markings, and the species crocuses, so exciting to examine at close range, often have yellow throats, centres and stamens setting off their blue, violet or striped petals. No wonder they are the centre of attraction for bees in search of pollen as they open in the February sunshine.

Blues are always more difficult to associate together than yellows. As Gertrude Jekyll warned, you should not mix purple blues with gentian blues – the first has red in its composition, the second a hint of yellow. Equally, a deep blue will kill a paler one, although I do like the strong combination of the pure yellow miniature *Narcissus* 'Peeping Tom' with the bright blue *Scilla siberica* and chionodoxas in the same, but paler, strain of blue.

Scillas, chionodoxas and puschkinias create a blue spring carpet and, if you plant then under deciduous shrubs, the dying leaves of the bulbs will be hidden as the new leaves of the shrubs form a canopy over the ground. *Scilla siberica* flowers in March and increases each year; *S. mischtschenkoana (S. tubergeniana)* opens its pale porcelain flowers earlier still, in February. Blue scillas and blue *Anemone blanda* make a lovely effect under a March-flowering *Magnolia stellata* just before its leaves appear. The more modestly coloured *Puschkinia scilloides*, closely related to scilla and chionodoxas, are probably better suited to the alpine house

ABOVE Grape hyacinths, *Muscari botryoides*, line a Cotswold stone path at Barnsley House. The leaves die down in summer, reappearing in autumn, so allowing space for summer annuals – poppies, eschscholzias or nasturtiums. Two weeping cherries, *Prunus × yedoensis* 'Shidare-yoshino' (syn. *P. × y.* 'Perpendens'), are in bloom; and beyond them, the limes (*Tilia platyphyllos* 'Rubra') are coming into leaf. This is an important vista in the garden, leading from the pond garden through the lime and laburnum walk.

than to the garden, but I have a small clump protected and overhung by *Symphoricarpos orbiculatus* 'Foliis Variegatis'; the flowers, pale blue with a darker streak down the centre of each petal, are carried on 10cm/4in stems.

Many spring bulbs have their white forms – tulips, daffodils, crocus, iris, scilla, fritillaries. While the white flowers of summer help to cool and refresh borders which, by July may be almost oppressive in their richness, in spring they play a quite different role: white bulbs and blossoms stand out vividly in their own right, set against the brown earth and leafless branches.

The white grape hyacinths and scillas are less well known and less popular than the blue varieties. I am still trying to analyze why I prefer blue to white muscari. I think that one reason is perhaps because the white is not strong enough in colour to suit the pale spring sunshine; another is that the total effect of the white muscari is solid and heavy. White bluebells overcome this drawback by their natural habitat in dappled shade under deciduous trees, and other white spring bulbs, snowdrops, for instance, or the late-flowering *Anemone blanda* 'White Splendour' always look invitingly modest. It is also a question of neighbours: snowdrops look marvellous growing through ivy leaves, and anemones under dark yew or box, but where would white muscari look best? After they have flowered their leaves get progressively larger and more untidy – I think I like them best growing thickly in a black container for a brief moment of drama.

Snowdrops are perhaps the best known and the best loved of all the spring bulbs, a miracle of fragile determination at the severest time of the year, appearing often when the ground is still white with snow. There are many different varieties, all of them lovely. Under trees they will naturalize in drifts, but the shining purity of their colour stands out in the border, visible from afar; it is rewarding, too, to lift their heads and look closely into their faces, each variety differently marked with splashes of green.

Together with snowdrops, daffodils are truly the heralds of spring. Of all the daffodils I think that the most beautiful are the pure white, multi-headed *Narcissus* 'Thalia'. They are, without doubt, my spring favourites. Other lovely whites are the long-cupped *N.* 'Desdemona' and the trumpet daffodil *N.* 'Vigil'. A truly double-flowered variety, *N.* 'White Lion' is basically white, with the centre petals shading to soft pale yellow. It has multiplied in our borders. It may be grown alone or mixed with others with which it blends well: choose *N.* 'Canasta', a butterfly narcissus 36cm/14in tall, with a pale yellow scalloped corona almost, but not quite, as wide as its petals. Then perhaps add, carefully placed for height, the 30cm/12in *N.* 'Marie José', whose white corona is painted with a deep yellow star.

Some tulips come along before the daffodils are over; others

ABOVE A spring border at its best in Andrew Lawson's garden. Elegant lily-flowered tulips, *T.* 'White Triumphator', stand above the soft pale pink and white double *T.* 'Angélique'. Forget-me-nots and *Primula* 'Guinevere' line the edge of the border. Seedlings of last year's *Silybum marianum* are developing large green and white rosettes before sending up their typical thistle-like flowers in summer. The shimmering impression of this scene is enhanced by the bark of the silver birch and the white margins of the variegated climber on the wall. When their leaves die down, the tulips will be dug up and the bulbs stored ready to replant next autumn. The cycle of plant life continues, and in the summer perennials will come through to take the place of the bulbs.

RIGHT Snowdrops are beautiful in any situation. Here they create a green and white carpet with the bold, shining leaves of *Bergenia* Ballawley hybrids. Ivy also makes an ideal backdrop for snowdrops.

Kaufmanniana tulip 'Heart's Delight' blooms in March and April. *T. kaufmanniana* is a native of Turkestan and often known as the waterlily tulip, as the narrow petals reflex wide in the sun. The hybrids introduce a subtle combination of colour as well as an unusual wide-open shape. The mottled, striped or spotted foliage inherited from *T. greigii* makes a picture as they lie flat in a spring border.

remember to keep yellows away because they spoil the scene.

There are two double-flowered pink tulip varieties that we leave in the herbaceous border to reappear year after year: the early *T.* 'Peach Blossom', only 30cm/12in high, which opens in mid-April and may be associated with deep red Barnhaven hybrid primulas, and the late-flowering double *T.* 'Angélique', whose delicate satin-pink petals look well near the dark green foliage of acanthus leaves. For me they are among the most beautiful of spring bulbs – at a distance in their full-blown voluptuousness they may well be mistaken for peonies. Double tulips have a rather different effect from the upright singles – they are often more graceful, the very weight of their heads making them lean and bend.

The truth is that tulips are so divergent and exciting in both form and colour that time spent getting to know them at flower shows and specialist nurseries and money spent experimenting with new varieties in different positions in your garden are time and money well spent.

There are, for example, the bi-coloured tulips many of which incorporate white and another colour in their petals. You must be careful how you plant the white-and-red varieties; the early-May-flowering Triumph tulip 'Garden Party' is often recommended for bedding out, but unrelieved masses of these white flowers with carmine pink edges remind me of lollipops on sticks. This is not subtle gardening, it is a wanton use of colour. Treated more sparingly, perhaps growing through deciduous shrubs, they can look exciting, and the striped effect may be softened by mingling them with the violet-purple 'Attila' or the creamy 'Kansas'. On the whole I find the creamy-white varieties whose petals are tinged with violet-rose on their edges more appealing – the lily-flowered 'Elegant Lady' and May-flowering 'Shirley', which is similar in shading but more rounded in shape.

Some tulips open in the sunshine to reveal petals which are a completely different colour on the inside. I am thinking of the dwarf *T. kaufmanniana*, which flowers in March or April: when closed, the three outer petals are carmine-red outside, then as the flower opens out, it shows off the white insides of these petals as well as its three white inner petals. You need only a few of the beautiful early-flowering species tulip *T. clusiana*. Closed, their flowers are pointed and burgundy-red, and you imagine they are red through and through; open, they become creamy-white stars with dark centres. Plant these tulips among *Helleborus orientalis* – both prefer to be left undisturbed and are happy in the shade. They also look marvellous planted around *Rheum palmatum* 'Atrosanguineum': they will come into bloom as the rheum leaves emerge, and later, as the rheum leaves grow, they will take over and cover the ground.

take on the major role a little later. We plant the double white early-May-flowering *Tulipa* 'Mount Tacoma' in our white, grey, blue and mauve border beside the laburnum walk, where they come through *Senecio* 'Sunshine' and forget-me-nots, following on from early white crocus and blue chionodoxas.

The lily-flowered *T.* 'White Triumphator', with their marvellous reflexed petals, need to be associated with quiet blues and greens – forget-me-nots or mertensia; I dislike them either with strong-coloured wallflowers or alone and unrelieved. They are splendid with arching sprays of Solomon's seal bending over and behind them, using a dark purple honesty to frame the picture. They also look elegant in tubs, but again need a background of green. Most years we have standard 'Silver Queen' hollies as the central feature of our terrace tubs and incorporate white narcissus and a few of these lily-flowered tulips as their companions; the petals echo the white margins of the holly leaves.

The pinks of spring – in bulbs and blossoms – are sparkling in their freshness and can match and combine well together. The tall, lily-flowered *Tulipa* 'Mariette', a beautiful rose-pink with reflexed petals, is growing in my garden between the 75cm/30in stems of *Prunus tenella*, a shrub which suckers quite gently, and in front of the darker purple leaves of *Berberis thunbergii atropurpurea*. These three make a fine spring picture, but I have to

A lovely mixture of pure white and checkerboard purple snakeshead fritillaries, *Fritillaria meleagris*, are growing in rough-mown grass at Abbotswood. These are British native species, easy to cultivate in grass, peat beds, damp borders or between shrubs. If the grass is not mown until after the fritillary seeds have ripened they will have the chance to increase each year. Fritillaries all hang their heads – you should turn them up and examine the beauty of the insides of their petals. This is an old garden, but these fritillaries are not expensive and a hundred of them will immediately make a show and forever increase.

## Subtle shades and shapes

Bulbs need not be strong or startling in colour to make their mark. Many offer subtle shades and mixtures of shades, and ravishing shapes: fritillaries, species crocus and parrot, lily-flowered and fimbriated tulips, conjured straight from the palettes of Thornton, Rory McEwen or the early Dutch painters.

Most of us will have seen the single-colour Dutch crocus bedded out by the thousand in public places. When you become familiar with the species crocus, you will realize what a wealth of tones they encompass: cream and buttercup, lavender and lilac, stripes and featherings, with their vivid saffron stamens apparent as the petals open. Some of the crocuses, too, open from one colour into another. *Crocus chrysanthus* 'Blue Bird' starts off as pearly blue, *C.c.* 'Ladykiller' as purple-blue, but then, as their petals flatten out, the inner white predominates. Most of the species crocus are two-coloured, even if this is only hinted at in delicate stripes and feathering. I love all the species crocus, and every year enjoy experimenting with new names. They can be tucked into so many corners – in fact the quality of their colours emerges more clearly when they are grown in exclusive numbers in chosen spots in the garden rather than in the carpets so characteristic of park and woodland.

I do not think of crocuses as particularly good companions to other plants, in part because many of them flower so early in the year, but they do share the ground well with later-flowering plants. *Crocus tommasinianus* are by far the best spreaders for naturalizing in grass; other species crocus can be grown through a low ground cover like ajuga or a small-leaved saxifrage. In the border, once the leaves have faded, you can fork over the ground and use their space for summer annuals.

Fritillaries, with their distinctive markings, also present themselves for use in subtle combinations. All fritillaries hang their heads and, unless you look inside, you will be unaware of their individual and exciting interior markings – bestowed by nature as an attraction for insects to enter, receive a reward of nectar and in so doing pollinate them. We tend to buy them in smaller quantities than tulips or daffodils, not least because of their cost. The exception is the snakeshead variety, *Fritillaria meleagris*, which will naturalize given time, and may be allotted a grassy space in which to spread; it needs at the very least a background of grass as a framework, giving an illusion of support to its fine stems. In both its purple and white forms it combines beautifully with April-flowering white narcissus; it also looks natural growing through low grey-leaved sub-shrubs, such as rue, which bring out its beautiful checkerboard markings, varying from green through pinkish-lilac, reddish-purple to deep chocolate. As the shoots push through the ground in spring, you must be careful

LEFT Forget-me-nots and pink tulips make a perfect carpet in this spring border at Barnsley House. The view is framed by clipped hollies, *Ilex × altaclerensis* 'Golden King', and in the distance the evergreen shrub *Viburnum rhytidophyllum* is in full flower. It is a fast-growing shrub, ideal as a wind and a sound break. The large leaves are prominently ribbed, white felted underneath and the flowers will be followed by a crop of red berries which turn black in winter.

LEFT BELOW A pool of white mixed with occasional blue *Anemone blanda* creates a natural setting round the tree trunk and makes an easy transition to the wild area beyond, giving the illusion that the sheep might almost wander and graze in the garden.

not to weed them out, for their narrow greyish leaves can easily be mistaken for coarse grass.

Many of the other varieties of fritillary look better in small, carefully placed groups in the border. Unless they are grown as specimens, probably in pots in a frame or alpine house, their normally wiry stems and narrow leaves look more attractive interspersed with other fresh spring plants to act as a cover through which they will emerge. The maroon flowers of *F. assyriaca* can have primroses or dark red Barnhaven hybrid primulas at their feet or be interplanted with white drumstick primulas; they also make good contrasting companions for low-growing, early-flowering narcissus. Turn up their nodding heads and you will discover the gold-bronze linings of their petals. One of the smallest varieties, the 18cm/7in *F. michailovskyi*, whose roundish, reddish-purple bells are tipped with bright yellow, looks well growing through the dark purple leaves of *Ajuga metallica* or *A. reptans* 'Burgundy Glow'.

All these fritillaries are for the front of the border, but one of my favourite species, *F. persica* 'Adiyaman', named after a town in Turkey, can stand farther back. It is 90cm/36in tall, with grey lanceolate leaves growing densely up its stem and dark purplish flowers clustered above in ordered profusion. Just three or five of these fritillaries planted together make an interesting accent in late April and May. The only danger is that their young shoots may be frosted as they come through in early spring, so give them the protection of a hedge or wall, or of low shrubs such as santolina or lavender.

With *F. imperialis* in both its yellow and red forms we are getting back to the primary colours of the bulbs I mentioned first of all. I preserve with pleasure two memories of these superb crown imperials. One is the sight of them growing luxuriantly around the trunk of each tree of an avenue of limes at Bampton Manor; the other is a completely different treatment in a cottage garden, where their heads were peering into the road over the top of a Cotswold stone wall. They are so dramatic that they never go unnoticed – some of the other fritillaries I find more beautiful, but admittedly more modest too.

All fritillaries should be planted when you are tidying your beds in the autumn, for during the winter months they will be making roots preparatory to sending up their flowering shoots in spring. Once planted, they should not be disturbed, just given a feed of sulphate of potash in autumn and again in spring.

## Bulbs in drifts and carpets

Spring bulbs are so versatile and may be used in so many different ways: in grass, in woodland, under deciduous shrubs and trees, in borders and, of course, in containers. A mass planting may be breathtaking in its impact, but I would leave the really large drifts, in woodland or in grass, for bluebells, snowdrops or daffodils. Tulips, although they look wonderful in grass, their colours standing out boldly against the green, do not naturalize there – in fact they will disappear within two or three years. Catalogues which show photographs of bulbs (especially of tulips) taken in conjunction with an interplanting and background of other plants are helpful when you are planning. A whole block of one variety of tulip can be wonderful, but my preference is for associating them with other bulbs, or with early biennials, perennials and shrubs with good foliage.

In the borders bulbs may be used to create pools or ribbons of colour and movement. I enjoy making ribbons of the large-flowered single-coloured crocuses down the centre of my borders, and this year we have planted the white 'Jeanne d'Arc' in profusion; maybe it is my imagination, but the birds seem less attracted to them than to the yellow or mauve varieties. In small numbers they become vignettes, bringing incident to the corner of a bed or enlivening the ground at the base of a wall or beneath deciduous shrubs. Brightly coloured tulips, to my mind, should not be planted too thickly in beds and borders – they look better in smaller groups, as often happens in informal or cottage gardens, allowing for plenty of green between them. I like them as a surprise for visitors when they round a corner.

I believe that if you want a blazing carpet you should use a single colour or two colours very close together in the spectrum: for example, *Tulipa* 'Beauty of Apeldoorn', creamy-yellow overlaid with orange, would go well with the dark golden-yellow *T.* 'Golden Apeldoorn', of the same height, shape and flowering time in mid-April. Another interesting group of tulips can be made using the salmon-orange 'Temple of Beauty' and buttercup-yellow 'Hocus Pocus' alongside 'Blushing Beauty', which holds together the various hues of the primary colours, red and yellow, in its orange-pink and yellow-orange petals. These three lily-shaped tulips, all newly introduced by the Dutch firm of Van Tubergen, are about 60cm/24in tall and May-flowering.

When buying bulbs one tends to think of a number and then double it – I know I do. I can hear myself saying to my gardener Andy, 'Don't be mean, put them closer together.' But although this massing may be the traditional way to plant bulbs there is another approach. Pause and weigh up your thoughts, then plant so that you achieve the effect of just enough bulbs, not too many but not too few. Avoid a mean, bitty look, because most bulbs, by their very nature, require to be close to their own kind – a single grape hyacinth standing alone looks pointless, whereas several groups of as few as five or seven along a border look

LEFT A special spring moment at the end of April at Barnsley House when the Darwin tulip 'Yellow Dover' comes into flower. These are majestic tulips, bold and colourful, dwarfing in size and impact the cowslips planted between them. Blue grape hyacinths, *Muscari armeniacum* 'Blue Spike', add a cooling touch of blue. Beyond, the unusual orange and red *Tulipa* 'Prinses Irene' are echoed in the border under the house. Tubs are filled with tall lily-flowered tulips. The key to a successful spring planting of tulips is not only to use them in a mass but also to echo their colours in subsidiary planting and cover the ground with perennials which infill every spare space to give a feeling of luxuriance and anticipation. The leaves of the shrub – *Euonymus fortunei radicans* – climbing beside the doorway also echo this golden theme, creating a feeling of exuberance.

OPPOSITE The same border seen from the other end: in the foreground *Tulipa* 'Prinses Irene' blooms and blends with *Primula* × *polyantha* Gold Laced. Beyond, cowslips grown from home-gathered seed are increasing in vigour in the good garden soil. *Helleborus foetidus* and Barnhaven hybrid primulas are backed by a stand of *Erysimum* 'Bowles' Mauve'. The yellow archangel, *Lamium galeobdolon*, is kept in check by cutting the flower spikes immediately after they fade and never allowing it to spread. Once the bulbs are over, the ground is taken over by hardy geraniums and tradescantia.

planned, intentional. Avoid, too, swamping a bed with bulbs of one variety, or drama will turn to excess.

In our borders we treat our bulbs after flowering in one of two ways: either leaving them in, or digging them up and then storing them until the next autumn. If you leave them in the ground, it is essential to make notes of their whereabouts so that when you add new ones you keep to the same colour scheme. These will be areas of low maintenance, for the bulbs will be occupying ground between herbaceous plants which do not need to be divided annually. Very early bulbs can stay in the ground and be allowed to multiply for years under deciduous shrubs: scillas, chionodoxas, crocus and the like will bring colour under philadelphus, viburnums, magnolias, all of which tend to have a fairly clean, bare base. Aconites, *Eranthis hyemalis*, flower in late January and February, and will increase happily for years under deciduous trees or even under old yews which have lost their lower branches.

Another approach, which creates a different effect and demands more maintenance, is to use a specific area of a border for 'bedding out'. We started this twice-yearly routine in borders which had unpleasant weeds and which needed repeated digging to keep clean. The turning of the soil in spring and autumn finally defeated the ground elder and bindweed, but we have kept up the practice and it has now become part of our routine. The summer bedding which replaces the bulbs is always an annual or half-hardy perennial which is easy to propagate in quantity.

The pleasure of treating bulbs in this way comes from the changing look it gives the garden – a two-season interest and an opportunity for us to ring the changes year by year. Tulips can be planted between forget-me-nots or wallflowers and then taken out and kept for the following year. If you decide on wallflowers, do choose colours which suit you and your garden. I like the pastel shades – they fit in with my idea of spring and with our Cotswold stone – but in a garden with red brick walls, hotter colours

This view at Barnsley House changes through the year. In winter it is the architecture of the laburnums that stands out. The colour scheme changes too: in spring it is white and red, with *Leucojum aestivum*, white-flowered honesty and bright red tulips; by May the broad grey leaves of the *Allium aflatunense* form a carpet through which their pale purple heads rise up and open in early June when the laburnum also comes into flower. The pathway under the laburnum tunnel is made of pebbles brought from beaches in Pembrokeshire and set in cement. The focal point, which stands out in all seasons and in all lights, is an old stone pillar with an inscription, from an unpublished work by John Evelyn, incised in metal by the sculptor Simon Verity: 'As no man be very miserable that is master of a Garden here; so will no man ever be happy who is not sure of a Garden hereafter'.

might be more appropriate. Never be nervous of copying ideas remembered with pleasure from other people's gardens. I have a happy memory of Peggy Munster's pink, rose-coloured and pale lemon yellow wallflowers at Bampton Manor. Although you may have to search for the seed of these pastel wallflowers, once you have them you can save your own. Forget-me-nots are so easy: they seed themselves, can be thinned out and make ideal companions for tulips of any colour, playing second fiddle because of the relative size of their flowers.

## Summer and autumn bulbs

While spring bulbs play a leading role in the garden by virtue of the lesser amount of leaves and an almost complete lack of other competing flowers, the bulbs that flower in summer and autumn tend to blend into a well developed scene. They are equally beautiful, but in a different way – as if aware of the need to show themselves off, many are tall, strong in shape and rich in colour.

Known as 'summer snowflakes', white Loddon lilies, *Leucojum aestivum*, have the same delicate air as snowdrops. In my garden they stand 50cm/18in tall and, with the green tips to their petals, make good companions for white honesty with variegated leaves, flowering at the same time.

Alliums, though not as beautiful as lilies, can be as dramatic. You will find them in the autumn catalogues, for they like to be planted then, allowing time to make a good root system. They are an enormous family, containing perhaps a thousand species, and range in size from dwarf to giant and in use from herbal to ornamental. Chives are alliums too, of course, and a border of them can make a change from lavender or parsley in your herb garden. I am told they keep aphids off the apple trees, so you could plant them as a ring round their trunks. Most of the alliums are self-seeding. I like them in quantity, for although the flower heads cannot be described as beautiful, in a mass there are few plants which make such an impact. They are upright, soldierly

and reliable, and deserve to be carefully placed to reflect their qualities and characters. Earliest to flower and so useful at the front of the border are *Allium karataviense*. The leaves, broad and blue-grey mottled purple, come one pair to a bulb and lie flat against the ground; the flowers, growing in dense umbels, seem almost too large for the 20cm/8in stems. They are pale purple-pink and make fine bedding bulbs which can be grown with later-flowering herbaceous plants. We have them in a corner of a mixed border with hardy *Fuchsia magellanica* and *Lysimachia ephemerum*. A point to remember in your planning is that the leaves of all the alliums disappear as the flowers develop.

The pale mauve *Allium aflatunense*, flowering in late May and June, look splendid with golden flowers and foliage: laburnum, Welsh poppies or golden privet. In my garden they have seeded themselves among a patch of *Polygonum bistorta* 'Superbum' (now correctly *Persicaria bistorta* 'Superba'), whose spiky flowers of the same hue make a pleasing contrast with the allium balls.

The darker purple *A. sphaerocephalum*, which flower slightly later, definitely need a covering at their feet to set off their flowers on their 50cm/20in stems. I like to see them pushing through grey foliage such as *Artemisia* 'Powis Castle' or *Santolina chamaecyparissus (S. incana)*.

One of the most dramatic of the alliums is *A. christophii* (syn. *A. albopilosum*) which has round heads 25cm/10in in diameter, covered in star-like flowers of an exciting metallic violet colour. Dried, the seed heads are useful for flower arrangements. These alliums make good companions for hostas, epimediums, in fact any plant with striking leaves which will create ground cover around their bare stems. They bloom in June, so there is plenty of choice for flower companions, but try to pick up the silvery or purple sheen. The best ideas I have are *Erysimum* 'Bowles' Mauve', *Heuchera* 'Palace Purple' or *Geranium* 'Johnson's Blue'.

Lilies are among the aristocrats of our July-September flowering bulbs. They add a touch of elegance wherever you grow

In these three pictures you have first harmony, then almost clashing colours and also an example of tonal contrast.

ABOVE LEFT Alliums are among the most useful early summer-flowering bulbs. They are mostly reliable, often seeding readily. The purple-pink *Allium aflatunense* is growing up between *Polygonum bistorta* 'Superbum' (now correctly *Persicaria bistorta* 'Superba'). The contrast of pale pink flower spikes of the polygonum and the globes of the deep allium make an unexpected and rather special impact. Later the polygonum will turn a darker pink, almost carmine red, and the alliums will become straw-coloured seed heads.

ABOVE RIGHT Another satisfactory combination of *Allium aflatunense* with *Centranthus ruber*, the red valerian we see growing out of limestone walls in May and June against a thick line of lavender. The lesson to learn from this successful planting of the allium is quantity – there must be enough to be effective.

LEFT The same allium, *A. aflatunense*, growing through white-flowered honesty, *Lunaria annua alba*.

BELOW In this sheltered corner of John and Caryl Hubbard's garden at Chilcombe in Dorset, the colour theme is a satisfying white, pale and dark purple, green and grey. The boldly massed group of *Lilium regale*, with their yellow centres, makes a strong statement in the middle. The colours are in harmony and the shapes in contrast, the spikes of the delphiniums and the distinctive shapes of the lilies standing out above the rounded shapes of the herbaceous plants. This is an ideal place for lilies, and they contribute their graceful form and strong scent to a satisfying composition.

LEFT White *Lilium* 'Sterling Star' are the aristocrats of this group in the perennial border. The shape of each individual lily flower is matched by the smaller flowers of Miss Willmott's ghost, *Eryngium giganteum*. Beyond the lilies, blue spires of campanulas also ask for attention.

ABOVE LEFT The only reliably hardy nerine, *N. bowdenii*, requires well-drained soil at the foot of a south-facing wall. Here they are growing in ideal conditions on a raised bed and are good companions with the soft grey *Santolina chamaecyparissus*.

ABOVE CENTRE *Iris sibirica* in full flower in June reflect the blue of the iron gates at Barnsley House. Their season of interest continues through the autumn, when the seed heads ripen.

ABOVE RIGHT *Galtonia candicans* has flower stems up to 1.2m/4ft tall in late summer, so is a good choice for growing through slightly shorter herbaceous plants, or through rounded shrubs such as senecio, lavenders or hebes.

them – in borders, among shrubs in grass and in pots on your terrace. Good drainage is essential to lilies, so if your soil is waterlogged or poorly drained then you must lighten it by adding a generous quantity of leaf mould, sand or peat; equally, remember not to plant them under a south-facing wall as this will be too hot and dry.

Consider your soil type. If this is alkaline you must make a careful selection. Among those that are lime-tolerant, I suggest *Lilium henryi* which flowers in August and September on tall 1.5-2m/5-6½ft stems; the deep orange-yellow blooms are nodding and look well standing behind *Spiraea japonica* 'Goldflame' or *Hemerocallis* 'Golden Chimes'. The dramatic and sweetly scented *L. regale*, 1-1.2m/3-4ft, so hardy and easy to grow, is a stem-rooting lily, so should be planted deeper than the usual 14-20cm/6-8in. Five or seven of these under a west-facing window could take over from the vanilla-scented *Philadelphus* 'Manteau

d'Hermine'. The lovely Turk's cap lily, *L. martagon*, 1.25m/4ft, is dark pink to purple and will blend well in your pink and grey border. For a really rich red try *L. amabile*, 60-90cm/24-36in, which likes partial shade – as do *L. regale* and *L. henryi*. The Asiatic Harlequin hybrids are a lovely strain with pendant flowers, each petal recurving. They vary in colour from pink through lilac, rose, red, tangerine to yellow, and are 1-1.2m/3-4ft tall. I would plant these among early-flowering shrubs – forsythia and lilac – or evergreens – *Viburnum tinus* and holly. The trumpet hybrid *L.* 'Bright Star', 1-1.2m/3-4ft, is a good garden plant, another choice for a lime soil. The silvery-white petals, which open flat, have contrasting orange centres and mix well with nasturtiums.

There is a much wider choice for gardeners with an acid soil. An ideal place for lilies is in a woodland where there are rhododendrons, azaleas and camellias. Drifts of white narcissus between these shrubs can be interplanted with July drifts of Asiatic and trumpet lily hybrids, keeping colours grouped together. For a grand display the 1-1.5m/3-5ft *L. regale* 'Royal Gold' will pick up the colour of *Hosta* 'Gold Standard', *H.* 'Piedmont Gold', or others with a yellow gleam in their leaves.

Some lilies may be too aristocratic for the woodland – too good, even, to be lost in an herbaceous border. 'Green Dragon', 'Limelight', Pink Perfection and Mabel Violet deserve a bed of their own (combined with spring bulbs). Others, such as *L. candidum*, do well in pots: stand these round your terrace or pool, where they can be reflected in the water. Use a loam-based compost with equal parts of loam, peat and coarse sand; cover the bulbs with 7cm/3in of compost, keep them cool until the stems are 5-7cm/2-3in tall and never allow them to dry out.

Nerines and bearded iris like to be in full sun, and not overlaid with other plants, to allow their roots a summer baking. These two – and you must have irises for their passing beauty and nerines for their October flowers in your garden – really need patches of their own, where, before and after they flower, your eyes will be taken elsewhere. Bearded iris, I think, should be planted in narrow strips – perhaps as a border beside a path, so that you can enjoy the beauty of each individual bloom. They do need to be looked at carefully, not from a distance. Later, your attention might be caught by July-flowering roses planted behind them. Nerines are best under a wall, so give them a rose or clematis to flower above them earlier in the year. *Iris unguicularis* likes the same conditions as nerines (including a soil that is not too rich), and will give a third season of interest to this bed. The only practical problem is that both roses and clematis need a richer soil and so should be given their own feeding.

*Iris sibirica* flower in June and make perfect plants for moist beds round a pond. Many first-class new varieties have been raised and introduced, ranging in colour from blue, purple and wine-red through to pink, white and cream. I use them to follow on from the golden marsh marigold, *Caltha palustris*; when the flowers are over we remove only the dead petals, leaving the seed heads to develop and prolong their decorative life.

Other bulbs or corms with the same useful upright habit as nerines and summer-flowering iris are the hardy arum *Zantedeschia aethiopica* 'Crowborough', and the white summer hyacinths, *Galtonia candicans*. Both look attractive growing between the leaves of herbaceous peonies or in clumps in front of delphiniums and, with their drooping inflorescences, they might also be grown through and between hardy fuchsias. Flowers on stiff stems often make good border plants and may be used to provide an element of discipline.

Autumn-flowering cyclamen and crocus are great standbys. Of the crocus, *C. laevigatus* var. *fontenayi*, the most fragrant of all species crocus, rosy-lilac inside and brown-feathered outside, is my favourite. Apart from the cyclamen and crocus, there are two stylish plants which are useful to give an uplift to the autumn borders: the sweetly scented *Gladiolus callianthus*, frequently offered in catalogues by its old name of *Acidanthera murielae*, and the Kaffir lily, *Schizostylis coccinea*. By September many of the leaves of the standby herbaceous plants will have become jaded and tired, so the fresh green of these two plants, with their sword-like foliage, becomes more important than it might have

Scented *Gladiolus callianthus*, until recently named *Acidanthera murielae*, likes well-drained soil with leaf mould or old manure dug in. The deep reddy-chocolate blotch at the base of each petal matches the flat flower heads of *Achillea millefolium* 'Cerise Queen'.

been in high summer. The gladiolus is white with a dark purple basal blotch, so will blend well with any of the asters and the 'Coltness Gem' dahlias. Grown from a corm, it is not reliably hardy with us, so must be dug and dried after flowering; the lily, grown from a thick, fleshy root, will increase in a rich, well watered soil. The schizostylis are much brighter than the gladiolus, ranging from the rosy-pink *S.* 'Tambara' to the pale pink *S.* 'Viscountess Byng'. The Viscountess flowers so late – even into October – that she reflects the colour of the turning leaves, reminding us that our garden year, which began with white snowdrops and Christmas roses, will soon be coming full circle and our thoughts turning to next year's projects.

As I think about the spring- and summer-flowering bulbs I have mentioned – and some I have not – I am struck by just how many things there are in their favour. Several are sweet-smelling, most are versatile in the positions and companions chosen for them, and many will naturalize in grass or increase in the borders. They have the freshness of annuals with none of the labour, and when they have disappeared for a while below ground it is always a happiness to see them reappear. I relish the feeling that nature is working subterraneously to produce this annual show.

# Herbaceous Borders

*C*oming across a mature, well filled herbaceous border at the height of its flowering time is like seeing the Niagara Falls: you just must stand and stare, taking in the whole effect. Such herbaceous borders are not, however, as fashionable today as they were during the early years of this century, in Gertrude Jekyll's time. Things have changed, for logical and practical reasons. Our gardens are generally smaller and we have less professional help, often making do with a jobbing gardener instead of a permanent one – if indeed we are lucky enough to have a pair of hands other than our own. To be successful, 'pure' herbaceous borders – those planted with just non-woody perennial plants – require many hours of committed labour; and since today people naturally want to try and cut down on the work, they tend to cover a certain amount of the ground with permanent plants which need the minimum upkeep – small trees, shrubs and ground cover. As well as being labour intensive, herbaceous borders are interesting for such a relatively short period; in smaller gardens we all want to have shape and incident – if not always bright colours – throughout the year, especially in those areas that can be seen from the windows.

A true herbaceous border is thus rare indeed these days. You may find one which at first sight seems purely herbaceous, only to discover as you look closely that perhaps roses, summer-flowering bulbs and shrubs, such as spiraeas, santolinas and potentillas, are all part of the scene. Today the spectrum of borders tends to range from those in which the occasional specimen adds weight and winter incident to those heavily planted with shrubs – the mixed border.

All herbaceous borders are designed to make a great effect, but that effect can be extremely varied, according to the choice of plants and the way they are grouped. At The Priory, Kemerton in Hereford and Worcester, Peter Healing has carefully carried out the Gertrude Jekyll and William Robinson theories on the use of colour to best effect. His long herbaceous border, which is planned for July–September and has plenty of depth, begins with grey foliage plants, some of them sub-shrubs: *Perovskia atriplicifolia, Senecio* 'White Diamond' and *S. vira-vira (S. leucostachys), Artemisia splendens* and *A.* 'Lambrook Silver'. These are interplanted with white flowers, such as *Lysimachia ephemerum, Eupatorium rugosum (E. ageratoides), Artemisia lactiflora, Leucanthemum × superbum (Chrysanthemum maximum),* and with a few annuals and white nicotianas, cosmos and petunias.

From grey shrubby leaves mixed with white and creamy perennial flowers, you progress to pink and deep pink with mallows, penstemons, *Anemone × hybrida* 'Queen Charlotte', *Monarda* 'Croftway Pink' and *Sedum spectabile.* Mauves and purples then start to appear: *Lobelia gerardii ×* 'Vedrariensis', *Monarda* 'Prairie Night', lilac-blue *Penstemon* 'Catherine de la Mare', the biennial *Salvia sclarea turkestania* and *S. pratensis haematodes* and tender heliotropes.

The colours increase in strength all the time and you have a feeling of excitement as you come towards the centre of the border. Deep yellows and bronze bring it to a crescendo: the 60cm/24in *Anthemis sancti-johannis, Achillea filipendulina* 'Gold Plate' and *Heliopsis helianthoides scabra* 'Golden Plume' – both of which are over 1.2m/4ft tall – and the shorter *Achillea* 'Moonshine'.

Golden rudbeckias, including the annual *R.* 'Marmalade', *Sedum telephium maximum* 'Atropurpureum' with deep purple

foliage, and metallic orange cannas are dropped in between the herbaceous plants. All these make patterns of glowing embers which burst into flame as yellow and bronze turn into bright reds with flowers of *Crocosmia* 'Lucifer', wonderful red lobelia spikes and a selection of kniphofias. These perennials are backed up by less hardy plants, such as *Dahlia* 'Bishop of Llandaff' and dark red begonias. From the centre the colours start to dwindle in heat and intensity, moving in reverse order back to grey and white at the far end of the long border.

The drama here is achieved by using every colour in the spectrum, set in bold groups interspersed with sufficient green. Whereas borders of shades of one quiet colour or a limited range of colours give you a feeling of peace, this border keeps you alert. You are aware of moving through constantly changing colours; yet they are harmonious with one another in a positive way for, used in this manner, each shade is close to its neighbour in the rainbow.

There are, of course, other successful ways of planning an herbaceous border. Using grey, white, pink, mauve and stronger purple, Peter Healing has made another border which is at its best from June until August; again, although it is not strictly herbaceous, since a few shrubs, climbers and annuals are included, it is so in spirit.

Here there are mounds of plants as soft and inviting as their colours, with grey *Artemisia stelleriana* and *Helichrysum fontanesii* as low background. White is always important and refreshing in a quiet colour scheme, and for extra height Peter has used *Artemisia lactiflora, Anemone × hybrida* and *Phlox* 'White Admiral', together with two white roses, *R.* 'Everest' and *R.* 'Dimples'. Pinks include *Penstemon* 'Evelyn' and *P.* 'Hewell's Pink', *Lavatera kashmiriana* and *Monarda* 'Croftway Pink', with annual lavateras and cosmos. He incorporates other annuals too – petunias, nicotianas and dahlias, as carefully selected annuals can improve the interest among herbaceous plants. Deeper colours here are mauves and purples. Mauve accents are created by groups of phlox, *Aster × frikartii* and the lovely *Penstemon* 'Alice Hindley'. Pale blue-purple is represented by the echinops, deeper purples by *Salvia nemorosa, Penstemon* 'Rich Ruby', *Lobelia × gerardii* 'Vedrariensis' and violet-purple monardas. A waterfall of *Clematis* 'Etoile Violette' climbs through four round iron stakes forming a column which blooms with the main burst of herbaceous flowers. Pruned almost to the ground each spring, it grows fast, adding extra height in the border.

During the very dry summer of 1989 I noticed that many people commented to me how well this border at Kemerton looked in spite of the drought. Could it be a lesson that where the ground is so thickly covered it prevents evaporation?

OPPOSITE The twin herbaceous borders at Westwell Manor in Oxfordshire also have the occasional shrub rose, hebe and broom, but their glory lies in the masterly use of colour, texture and shape in the choice of perennials that are satisfying from May through to the autumn. At first the borders are pink, mauve and white; in autumn they become a blaze of golden achillea with rich purple asters. Throughout the season there is a leavening of grey and green, good foliage and a rhythm of rounded outlines between spires.

ABOVE A wonderful lesson in the use of colour and shape in Peter Healing's garden. The dramatic spheres of *Echinops bannaticus* create a centrepiece surrounded by dark purple *Clematis* 'Etoile Violette', *Verbena bonariensis* and pink *Malva moschata* with a dark purple buddleja in the background. These colours make a perfect composition.

An arresting change in colour has taken place within only three weeks in this section of the border at Peter Healing's garden, where strong colours are featured. In the background the tall *Achillea filipendulina* 'Gold Plate' and *Heliopsis helianthoides scabra* 'Golden Plume' have increased in volume and are joined by the red *Dahlia* 'Bishop of Llandaff' and bronze-leaved red cannas.

## Height, colour and timing

Analyzing these successful examples, it is clear that you must draw a plan, however rough, before you start making a border, if only to decide on the placing of your key plants. The points you should consider are height, colour and flowering time. Then you must decide how large each clump should be and what shape it will make. Your plan will vary greatly according to the size of the garden. In a small one, where variety is important, the groups will be smaller and also I think the colour scheme should be simplified to avoid those strident contrasts which could well succeed in a dramatic long border. Keep to colours which blend into each other – cream and pale yellows with blue and mauve – or bright colours but do not mix contrasting reds and orange.

Tall plants, especially in a small border, look out of place and top-heavy unless they are grouped close together and in sufficient quantity and have a high wall or hedge as backing.I do not always like a smooth succession of height, from just a few centimetres or inches at the front to two-metre or six-foot crambes or aruncus at the back, for example. I want to be able to see inlets, with lower plants not hidden, but framed, between slightly taller ones. For instance, a patch of 90cm/36in *Anthemis tinctoria* 'E. C. Buxton' and another of 60cm/24in *Achillea* 'Moonshine' could be each side of low-growing *Artemisia stelleriana*. Even delphiniums can come forward, occupying the middle ground and standing out boldly above the green leaves of monardas and asters, which will flower later. In fact you can have waves of height rather than tailored banks running in orderly progression from front to back of the border.

Plants for the front of the border must have a good shape, with leaves well to the ground so that you do not see bare stems or untidy foliage. Avoid border phlox, Oriental poppies, lupins and pyrethrums here for this reason; they should be planted farther back. Good medium-height plants for the front are *Aster amellus*, *Euphorbia polychroma*, several of the grasses, day lilies ( you will then be able to dead-head them daily without treading on the border) and *Campanula persicifolia*. Another beautiful medium-height plant to use in a border is *Doronicum orientale magnificum* or leopard's bane, a spring-flowering daisy; as its foliage is rather heavy I prefer to put it mid-way, even though the flowers are only about 45cm/18in. The leaves can be hidden later by strong foliage plants, such as acanthus, positioned in front of it.

When experimenting with colours and plant combinations, you must always keep your eyes open and either take photographs or make careful notes of the associations that particularly appeal to you. For planning a succession of interest it is important to visit a garden whose borders you admire several times a year and notice how one scene transforms itself into another.

An imaginative and successful combination of scarlet *Lychnis chalcedonica* with deep orange-yellow *Eremurus bungei*. These two colours, the primary red and the orange, are close in the spectrum; although a surprise, they work well together. Were the eremurus a primary yellow, the colours might be in too great a contrast. And if the lychnis were a rose-pink – going towards the blue side of the spectrum – this would create an unpleasant shock.

# An herbaceous border in late summer

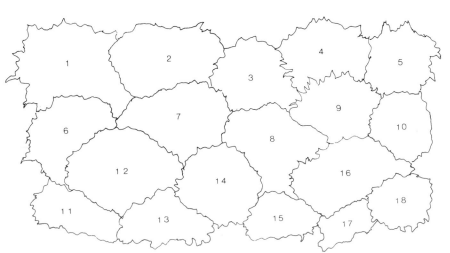

1 *Cimicifuga racemosa*
2 *Artemisia lactiflora*
3 *Anemone × hybrida* 'Queen Charlotte'
4 *Eupatorium maculatum atropurpureum*
5 *Thalictrum aquilegifolium*
6 *Polemonium caeruleum*
7 *Monarda* 'Prairie Night'
8 *Doronicum orientale magnificum*
9 *Aster novae-angliae* 'Andenken an Alma Pötschke'
10 *Anthemis sancti-johannis*
11 *Penstemon* 'White Bedder'
12 *Euphorbia polychroma*
13 *Eryngium variifolium*
14 *Campanula persicifolia*
15 *Penstemon* 'Purple Bedder'
16 *Acanthus spinosus*
17 *Geranium sanguineum*
18 *Sedum telephium maximum* 'Atropurpureum'

In this border of about 7×3 metres (about 22×10 feet) the colours for late summer have been kept to soft mauves, purples, whites and cream, with a shock of bright rose from the aster and the bluey-pink anemone. I would fill it with white crocuses for late winter and with white or yellow narcissus for spring interest. These bulbs should be left as undisturbed as possible.

In one border I know, the main emphasis in June and July is on blues, mauves and whites – a colour scheme I find appealing for early summer. Here I list a few plants you could use in such a scheme. *Baptisia australis* (60cm/24in tall) is beautiful before it flowers for its soft green leaves and after it has flowered for its dark grey seed pods which are also good for dried arrangements in winter. There are many campanulas, mostly 90–120cm/36–48in tall: *Campanula lactiflora* 'Loddon Anna' (pinker than blue) and *C.l.* 'Pouffe' (only 45cm/18in), *C. latifolia, C. latiloba* and, my favourite for its length of flowering, *C. persicifolia*, which forms an evergreen carpet. *Echinops ritro* has colour from June to August with grey-green leaves and steel-blue heads, lovely before the flowers actually open. *Galega officinalis*, or goat's rue, makes a solid clump even on poor soil; its blue pea flowers are always commented upon by visitors and later the seed heads are interesting (there is a good white form as well). Graham Stuart Thomas describes *Eryngium bourgatii* as 'a beautiful plant at all times'. I especially like its stiff flower stems topped with blue-green thistle flowers, standing above the prickly rosettes of leaves. They look so firm planted among less rigid flower stems. The hardy geraniums are real standbys. We cut *Geranium pratense* right down to the ground in mid-July after it has flowered, and then new foliage emerges to look lovely and fresh in August and September. *G.* 'Johnson's Blue' flowers for longer and is a good companion for pale yellows. Finally, I could not garden in mid-summer without *Polemonium caeruleum*. We allow these to seed freely, especially in rather shady areas of the garden; it is essential to have them in a great mass. Again they complement pale yellows to perfection.

I wish that the influential garden at Tintinhull in Somerset, created originally by Mrs Reiss and now guided and cared for by Penelope Hobhouse and John Malins, were closer to me so I could see it every month from March until October. My annual pilgrimage there always proves fruitful. In 1988 it was on 1st August, and I was delighted to find an echo of my favourite theme: mauve, blue, grey and yellow. The border had mounds of Old English Lavender, with its long mauve flower spikes, *Nicotiana affinis* 'Lime Green', round globes of blue *Agapanthus* Headbourne Hybrids and *Penstemon* 'Sour Grapes'. A few half-hardy *Chrysanthemum* (now *Agyranthemum*) 'Jamaica Primrose' echoed the pale yellow-green of *Nicotiana langsdorfii*, with a blue eye to each small flower. The whole scene was completely satisfying. The only truly herbaceous plants in this combination are the penstemon and agapanthus, but the nicotianas make fleshy roots and, if you allow them to remain in the ground and the roots do not get killed by the frost, they will come up next year with greater vigour than ever.

ABOVE Two harmonious colour schemes at Powis Castle: *Aster thompsonii* 'Nanus' with spikes of blue veronica (top); and the deep yellow centres of the white daisy flower, *Anthemis punctata cupaniana*, echoing the mustard-coloured heads of *Euphorbia cyparissias*.

These two pages show studies in hot colours, in gardens created by three famous plantsmen.

LEFT The red border at Hidcote Manor, originally designed by Lawrence Johnston, has as a massive starting point a burgundy-red *Corylus maxima* 'Purpurea', beneath which are spikes of *Lobelia × speciosa* and cascading leaves of hemerocallis. The reds are drawn from both sides of the red spectrum, blue-reds mingling with scarlet and with daylilies that are orange-red.

OPPOSITE ABOVE At The Priory, Kemerton, Peter Healing's choice of reds – from vermilion to magenta – is similar to that used at Hidcote; here there is an equal weight of green, creating a feeling of harmony, and much of the foliage is a strong burgundy, giving richness to the composition of flowers.

OPPOSITE BELOW By contrast to Peter Healing's scheme, in which all the flowers are on the red-to-blue scale, this clever combination – in the garden of John Sales, chief gardens adviser to the National Trust – is on the red-to-orange scale. It is also a marvellous example of colour echoes: the centre of the daylily, *Hemerocallis* 'Missenden', picks up the yellow in the *Helenium* 'Moerheim Beauty', and in both flowers the same rich orange-red occurs. The petals of each, although quite different in shape, size and character – the heleniums reflexing and the daylilies gently trumpeting – are perfectly complementary.

I wish we could get away from the rigid feeling that gardening is only for summer delight – spring and autumn must become part of our palette. By September the garden starts to have impressions of autumn colour, so I like accents of yellow and orange in the borders, with white used sparingly. A combination of selections of *Helenium* 'Butterpat', the coppery-red *H.* 'Coppelia' and the bronze *H.* 'Gypsy' (all about 90cm/36in tall), alongside *Aster linosyris* 'Gold Dust' and golden kniphofias will create a memorable autumn picture.

If the border will take taller plants, especially those whose individual flower spikes do not make a dense mass, among my favourite later flowering plants are the ivory-white *Cimicifuga racemosa* 1.2-1.5m/4-5ft and *Lysimachia clethroides*, a plant with character of which surprisingly little use is made; maybe it is because it appreciates a fairly moist place and flowers late in the gardening year. Other tall plants include the double-flowered *Helianthus* 'Loddon Gold' 1.2-1.5m/4-5ft, *Anemone × hybrida* in its white form and *Rudbeckia laciniata* 1.5m/5ft, which Graham Stuart Thomas recommends planting in association with the creamy-white plumes of *Artemisia lactiflora*.

LEFT Contrasts of shape and texture help to create a pleasing combination with spires of *Campanula persicifolia*, wands of *Lychnis coronaria* and rounded forms of *Tanacetum parthenium aureum*. The colours – white, pale blue, cerise-crimson and lime-yellow – harmonize well and the beautiful grey-green foliage of *Rosa glauca* adds yet another subtle tone.

OPPOSITE These two richly-filled borders at the House of Pitmuies, in Scotland, echo one another in height and shape, but are varied enough in colour and texture to give them enormous visual interest. They are set off by the grass path, which, in summer, has a cooling role and co-ordinates with the greys and greens at the front of the borders. The wrought iron gate serves as a focal point and, being painted white, takes its place in the colour scheme of the borders with their generous quantities of pale colours.

You will find that many of the autumn flowers are compositae, in fact variations of the daisies. Most last well in bloom. To make good compositions, it is preferable to choose sparingly among them, adding flowers with quite a different character. Tall grasses come into their own in late summer and the plumes of miscanthus or *Stipa gigantea* are a good foil for any of the daisy types. Although it does not flower frequently, *Pleioblastus auricoma (Arundinaria viridistriata)* is a lovely bamboo, with rich yellow and green foliage. Another way to achieve late summer and autumn height is to grow a clematis up a metal or wooden pyramid. At Powis Castle this is done to perfection by mixing together various clematis which flower in autumn.

Included in any scheme which flowers from late summer onwards should be some pink and mauvy-blues (by this I mean the blues which have more red than yellow in them, so that they go towards purples). You might choose *Salvia sclarea turkestanica*, the lilac-blue *Campanula lactiflora, Aster novae-angliae* 'Harrington's Pink' and *A. amellus* in variety. Another useful plant for late

flowering is the tall, white-flowered *Chrysanthemum uliginosum* (now correctly *Leucanthemella serotina*), which grows to 1.5m/5ft or more and is a mass of blooms. The Japanese anemones also come into their own in the early autumn; these wonderful plants hate to be disturbed once they are established. All their colours combine well: 'Lady Gilmour', 'Queen Charlotte' and 'Géante des Blanches' will associate particularly happily together. For a background, *Hydrangea sargentiana* is a perfect foil for the anemones, and if you have sufficient space to fit them in, then a clump or two of *Acanthus spinosus* would add further interest.

Much the most satisfactory way to choose herbaceous plants such as Michaelmas daisies and hardy chrysanthemums, which come in such a wide range of colours, is to visit a specialist nursery in early autumn when you will see them growing in profusion. Remember my advice to take notes and photographs as you go around. Many of the later flowering herbaceous plants are better planted in the early spring, so this will leave you plenty of time on a winter evening to draw a plan and order the plants.

# Climbers and Wall Shrubs

Some climbers, like some people, benefit from a partner. Clematis can twine through climbing roses, and the autumn-flowering Texensis clematis 'Gravetye Beauty' looks wonderful in late summer growing through *Vitis vinifera* 'Purpurea'. Other climbers have a fuller personality and stand better alone, unencumbered by any twining neighbours – I am thinking of the common *Pyracantha atalantioides* and *P. rogersiana* in their various varieties, with white flowers and brilliant autumn berries, and also of the evergreen *Ceanothus dentatus*, whose small leaves are so attractive in themselves that they need no extra help.

It is the delicate twiners – those which must have supports – that look much happier when given firm branches, rather than a grid of netting, through which to explore. *Eccremocarpus scaber* and the annual morning glory (ipomoea) are examples which can be used together with flowering quince or *Hydrangea petiolaris*.

Whether standing alone or with an associate, climbers and wall shrubs form the backdrop for planting in layers where there is space at their feet for lower-growing plants. Where ground space is inadequate for other planting, such as on a house wall, climbers can make the entire picture. Height is often a crucial element in planting schemes. In a large mixed border it is essential and can be used to great effect; in a small garden, where space is at a premium, walls, fences and trellis screens offer numerous opportunities, and an archway or pillar can add a vital vertical element. Remember that an arch can do double duty and can also frame a focal point at the end of a pathway.

Choosing climbing plants is exciting, but first you must have supports for them. Lucky are those who have attractive house or garden walls, and even more fortunate those with an old wall already stocked with vine-eyes through which to thread stout wires for the climbers to twist and twine and make their way to the top, effectively displaying themselves. But never despair: even the smallest garden without a wall can have climbers, although you may have to use your imagination.

You can make a 'wigwam' of 2.5m/8ft bamboos (50cm/24in in the ground and 2m/6ft for the climbers), and put one or a series of these through the centre of a border. Arches have an architectural element, and they act as a frame through which you see a focal point or a special feature. They can become the ever-open doorway through which you pass from one 'room' of the garden to another. Wigwams and archways add immediate height, but unlike trees they do not create an appreciable amount of shade, and they provide an ideal opportunity for growing climbing plants.

A series of connected arches along and over a pathway becomes an arcade creating shade and an even greater opportunity for climbers. Arcades and pergolas give the space for vigorous climbers to spread luxuriantly along the top and from one pillar to the next, but for archways it is wise to choose plants that will only take over their allotted space.

A wigwam, ideal for summer sweet peas, could go in a different place each year. Scarlet runner beans are both decorative and productive (runner, or climbing French beans give the best value for space of any vegetable), and in a small garden where space is at a premium and home-grown vegetables are appreciated, I would consider planting them with the sweet peas. If you decide to make a more permanent frame of metal or treated wood, spring-flowering clematis – *Clematis macropetala* or

*Clematis* 'Etoile Violette' dominates – both in height and colour – Peter Healing's long, narrow early summer–autumn border. It is supported on 2.5m/8ft angle irons (once used to surround a tennis court) wound round with string. When the clematis is pruned to the ground in February, the string is renewed. To the right are the fine stems of *Verbena bonariensis*, a good plant to grow in paving, where it will re-seed. In the foreground annual *Brachyscome* 'Purple Splendour' grows in front of the perennial *Salvia nemorosa*.

*C. alpina* – would give April-June colour and then the sweet peas, beans or the annual *Tropaeoleum peregrinum* could take over later.

At Powis Castle, there is a long border, planned to reach its peak of colour in late summer; which has balloon-shaped frames supporting autumn-flowering clematis constructed at intervals along the centre. Peter Healing at The Priory, Kemerton, has the same idea. In both borders the clematis blend in well with the herbaceous flowers, giving extra height and also an element of structure and firmness.

A large trunk, with its side branches cut off to leave side stumps of 30cm/12in, or a post clad with a surround of netting can make good supports for clematis or *Jasminum nudiflorum*. The jasmine will brighten a border in winter and will be integrated into tall herbaceous plants in summer. Ivy is, of course, the obvious climber for a sunless wall, and will just as happily transform an ugly post. It has two advantages: the evergreen leaves which continue to look wonderful in winter, and the ease with which it can be clipped into shape.

Where a flowering climber is needed, roses at once spring to mind. Some are best trained carefully against a wall; others like the sun all around them so they are better suited to spiral up a pillar. For walls, you could choose the deep red Hybrid Tea *R.* 'Climbing Etoile de Hollande' and *R.* 'Guinée'. *R.* 'Climbing Lady Hillingdon' is a rich apricot yellow. *R.* 'Paul's Lemon Pillar', another climbing Hybrid Tea, has large creamy-yellow flowers tinged with green at their centre – it is not repeat-flowering but a clematis such as 'Jackmanii Superba' could take over in July and August. For a deeper, stronger yellow, choose *R.* 'Golden Showers', a continuous flowerer through summer and into autumn with semi-double blooms.

Climbing Bourbon roses are good for pillars. *R.* 'Blairii Number 2' is pale pink, *R.* 'Gloire de Dijon', a combination of rose, salmon and yellow. Then there is the deep rose-pink *R.* 'Zéphirine Drouhin', the thornless rose which often starts to flower in May and will carry blooms through the summer.

Most of the old rose climbers – Noisettes, Bourbons and climbing Teas – are especially suited for arches and arbours. The pure white 'Aimée Vibert' (a Noisette) has clusters of semi-double flowers, produced regularly throughout the summer. 'Blush Noisette', another which flowers in clusters through the summer, has a delicious scent, so is most suitable for an arch by a pathway. Another old Noisette favourite is white 'Madame Alfred Carrière', but this is perhaps better used to take advantage of the long stems (up to 6m/20ft), planting it to grow through a fence or along the top of a low wall.

You have a much wider choice of climbing roses for a pergola. The Ramblers, sending up their long stems – often up to 8m/25ft

The climbing rose 'Blairii Number 2' has highly fragrant flowers with pale pink outer petals and deeper pink centres which open in a wonderful display in June followed by occasional blooms later. It will climb to about 4m/14ft. It is a good blend with *Clematis* 'Lasurstern', which also has a burst of flowers in mid-summer and then flowers again in autumn. I like the way the foxglove imitates the rose with pale buds and darker petals.

– will make a complete canopy, so need a strong support. They would also do well climbing up an old apple tree. The beauty of these Ramblers is the flexibility of their stems. You can train them to your will; but try to do this when there is sap in them; in winter when the sap is down they are more apt to snap at a joint when you are training them. My choice of Ramblers are those whose flower trusses seem to bow down as though wanting to be admired. They include 'Bobbie James', a very fragrant musk Rambler with trusses of semi-double creamy-white flowers, 'Félicité Perpétue', which has buds speckled with pink that open to white, 'Francis E. Lester', with its blooms of white flushed with pink, white 'Rambling Rector', and 'Wedding Day', with its yellow pointed buds which open to white.

I have not chosen 'The Garland', as the clusters of small blooms are carried on stiff, erect stems, so that the flowers, often far out of range, are facing upwards into the sky. The other general favourite I have not used is *R. filipes* 'Kiftsgate', which is so vigorous that it is more suited to grow up a tall tree where it can expand and express itself without hindrance or pruning.

If you want more colour (and you have a sheltered garden), then choose the Noisette *R.* 'Maréchal Niel', a famous rose dating back to 1864 with soft yellow blooms and a strong scent. (But today, with so many conservatories being built, I would especially recommend this rose for a cool house.) If you are including yellow in your scheme, 'Mermaid' is a must: it is constantly in flower, has large and luscious single yellow blooms and almost evergreen foliage.

The Rambler 'François Juranville' has rich salmon-rose flowers scented of apples, and if you want to be given a slight surprise among the whites, pinks and yellows, use *R.* 'Veilchenblau' – it is called the blue rambler, but I think of it as a dark magenta with a suspicion of white in the petals.

Roses and clematis are traditional companions. They combine well growing up the same post or pillar. You will be pruning the roses in February and March, so it is best to choose clematis which need to be cut back hard at the same time as the rose is pruned. (This will save a great deal of disentangling of clematis stems from the rose thorns – and much tearing of your hands.) In

LEFT *Clematis* 'Niobe', which requires hard pruning each spring, climbs through the thornless rose 'Zéphirine Drouhin', a wonderfully free-flowering, sweetly scented rose, good to plant by your doorway.

RIGHT Rugosa rose 'Fru Dagmar Hastrup' – not a climber but a rose of great virtue – makes a striking display of hips. Climbing through it is the wild clematis, old man's beard. This has seeded itself, and each autumn and early winter the seed heads are wonderful, especially with the slanting rays of the evening sun shining through them.

OPPOSITE In the late Humphrey Brooke's remarkable rosarium at Claydon in Suffolk this deep pink rose climbed by his front door and into his bedroom window, together with *Lonicera periclymenum* 'Serotina'.

fact, this means those which flower in the late summer and autumn on the current year's growth – the small-flowered varieties which include the lovely Viticellas, all with enticing names like 'Etoile Violette', 'Royal Velours' and 'Alba Luxurians'. I particularly like these positioned so that you can see the sun shining through their sepals because it makes the colours vivid and exciting. The Texensis group all have bell-shaped flowers; the best known, *C.* 'Gravetye Beauty', has rich ruby-red flowers which slowly change from bells to stars. Some of the large-flowered clematis also bloom late in the summer and on into autumn and need the same hard pruning in February or March. There is a wide choice of colours to mix or match with your roses, including the mauvy-pink of 'Comtesse de Bouchaud', the purple of 'Jackmanii Superba', the sky-blue of 'Perle d'Azur'.

Climbers, like other plants, can be chosen to flower in succession. A combination of honeysuckles could be alternated with the rose and clematis combinations: for example, *Lonicera periclymenum* 'Belgica' to flower in May and June combined with *L.p.* 'Serotina', the late Dutch honeysuckle, for July to September flowers – both with a strong scent; or try *L. japonica repens*

(*L.j. flexuosa*) combined with *L.j.* 'Halliana', flowering together through from June until October. The lower stems of honeysuckle become leggy and unattractive as they get older, so you could hide these either with old-fashioned annual sweet peas which do not grow too tall, or with perennial *Hosta* 'Honeybells', its fresh green leaves topped in late summer with scented lilac flowers. A different idea to give spring interest to the base of your climbers is to plant bold clumps of *Helleborus orientalis*, mixed with grey *Helichrysum italicum (H. angustifolium)* and *Ruta graveolens* 'Jackman's Blue', to give an evergreen ground cover.

Among other interesting climbers to incorporate is wisteria, but this must be planted on a wall or pergola on its own or with climbing annuals, for its strong twining branches will throttle any plant it twines round. *Actinidia deliciosa (A. chinensis)*, the Chinese gooseberry or kiwi fruit, has huge leaves and scented creamy-white flowers followed by fruits the size and shape of an egg. It is perfectly hardy, and although it requires a good long summer for the fruit to ripen, it is well worth growing for its leaves and flowers. Remember you need a male for every four or five females.

The ornamental vines, *Vitis* 'Brant' and *V. vinifera* 'Purpurea', are ideal planted alternately along a pergola, where they can clamber about and hang down their bunches of grapes. Both have attractive leaves and look good with grey or golden foliage plants at their feet and the yellow-flowered *Clematis tangutica* clambering through them. I am often surprised how hardy the passion flower, *Passiflora caerulea*, is. Try it on your pergola, planting it in spring. It prefers an acid soil to chalk or lime, blooms from June to September, and the flowers are followed by deep yellow edible fruits. For safety, protect the base of the plant in winter – bracken is often recommended but my philosophy is to protect it with an evergreen plant with dense foliage – *Hebe rakaiensis* or santolina, *Senecio* 'Sunshine' or a clipped box shaped to look as though it is draped round the lower stem.

The silk vine, *Periploca graeca*, is a climber more suited to a pergola than a wall because of this vigorous habit; like wisteria, it is best growing alone. The flowers open in July and August in loose clusters and are yellowy-green outside and reddish-brown inside. They are rich and velvety – perhaps more interesting than beautiful, especially for their seed follicles at the end of which is a tuft of silky hairs.

For the first summer or two after you have planted your climbers, you can add annual climbers – sweet peas, *Cobaea scandens, Tropaeolum peregrinum* (the canary creeper) or *Eccremocarpus scaber*, or ipomoea (morning glory), which will clothe the pillars for you while the permanent climbers are establishing themselves.

The planting principles are the same, whether for an archway, arbour, pillar or pergola. Be sure to prepare the ground deeply and well before planting, digging in plenty of well rotted manure and then mulching or fertilizing in spring. You should also think what will go well around their bases. It could be a ground cover – London pride, lamium, nepeta, violas, *Veronica cinerea* – but, whatever you choose, it should be an addition, not a distraction, and must be tidy as well as reliable. If you prefer a formal look, you could use box, either as a geometric-shaped edging around the base of your climbers or neatly and horizontally trimmed to make a platform.

## Plants for walls in shade or partial shade

The question of aspect does not arise when you are choosing plants for pillars or pergolas, but when you think about clothing walls you obviously have to consider this. Always remember that the rain will not get too readily to the base of the wall, so the ground will tend to be dry. Many of the shrubs which thrive in a shady place can be used for north- and east-facing walls.

There are self-clinging climbers like *Parthenocissus henryana*

which turns a wonderful rich red in autumn but must be kept in check by hard pruning every other year. Ivies, especially those with golden markings on their leaves, are good. *Hedera helix* 'Goldheart' and *H.h.* 'Buttercup' will brighten a dark corner; for added interest golden feverfew or Bowles' golden grass may be planted at their feet. The two large-leaved ivies that are especially effective are *H. colchica* 'Dentata Variegata' and *H.c.* 'Sulphur Heart' (*H.c.* 'Paddy's Pride'). Both look best when allowed plenty of space. The former is extremely useful for picking, especially when in flower in autumn and early winter, but it is particularly heavy and really needs some extra help to keep it clinging to the wall. 'Paddy's Pride' keeps tidily to the wall and can have companions with it – a deep purple *Clematis* × *jackmanii* and the yellow rose 'Golden Showers'. To complete the picture, plant *Phygelius aequalis* 'Yellow Trumpet', with pale yellow trumpet flowers, and the low saxifrage London pride at its feet.

A north-facing wall that I was in despair of ever giving an interesting look – the soil was poor and there were trees taking what poor natural light there was – has been transformed by planting a line of different variegated ivies 30cm/12in from the wall and 50cm/18in apart and training them up wires set diagonally at 45° to the ground level, so creating a diamond-shaped trellis of ivy.

Many clematis will flower well on a north wall, as long as they are not shaded by overhanging trees or too exposed to the elements. In spring the *alpina* and *macropetala* varieties will do well, especially if they have a twiggy shrub as a host. Of the large-flowered summer varieties, 'Nelly Moser', 'William Kennett' and × *jackmanii* keep their colours well and flower freely. I have tried 'Perle d'Azur' but this has not done well for me. It is always upsetting when you see a clematis flowering profusely in a neighbour's garden and come home to your own disappointing specimen. You should write a note in your diary in a winter month, to move it or plant another in a sunny position. The mauvy-pink *Clematis* 'Comtesse de Bouchaud' would look well climbing through a white buddleja – they both require hard pruning in late winter. The shell-pink 'Hagley Hybrid', another to prune hard, would combine well with *Buddleja* 'Lochinch'. I have suggested only a small selection of clematis; the catalogue of a good clematis nursery will list many more.

There are other genuine 'climbers' which are suitable for north- or east-facing positions, from which you can select: the self-clinging *Hydrangea petiolaris* is a slow starter, so don't expect great things of it for a couple of years; once well established it can be kept trimmed by shortening the spurs immediately after it flowers in June and July. However, it is not a shrub to discipline too strictly – it is not in its character. In the same way, it would be impossible to train the Russian vine *Polygonum baldschuanicum*. Quite different in other respects, the hydrangea has a large leaf and flowers in flat panicles; the vine has a smaller leaf and in September and October is covered with a veritable froth of white panicles tinged with pink. The hydrangea has stiff, rather woody stems but the vine is a pliable twiner. We prune our vine hard back to the main stem each winter and it always lives up to its mile-a-minute reputation and shrouds the drainpipe by June.

Another equally vigorous climber which is wonderful in the right place, where it can wander and twine at will, is *Celastrus scandens*. The inconspicuous flowers transform themselves into dramatic fruits, starting orange and opening to show off scarlet seeds. When I planted mine, I made two mistakes: the first was to put it growing up a small tree which eventually it would have strangled with its strong twining arms and the other was to have only a single sex, so we had no fruits. As a result the celastrus has gone in favour of *Clematis tangutica* 'Bill Mackenzie'.

There are many shrubs which, although they will grow free-standing, do equally well and often even better given wall protection. They can be trained against a wall or allowed freedom to billow out. The flowering quinces, especially the *Chaenomeles speciosa* varieties, train beautifully, and with the right summer pruning – in fact spurring back the current year's growth to promising flower buds in June or July – they look wonderful in late winter and often through to May. Consider what you would give them as neighbours at their feet. Snowdrops or any polyanthus or narcissus would complement white *C.s.* 'Nivalis'. *C.s.* 'Umbilicata', with salmon-pink flowers, could have epimedium, tellima, *Helleborus foetidus* or *H. argutifolius* (*H. corsicus*) at its base, or some strong leaves – hosta or tall ferns, brunnera, bergenia – to give green interest in later months.

Thinking of spring, it is impossible not to mention forsythia. If this were a rarity we would appreciate it more, but I would prefer it if the yellow flowers were a softer, paler, primrose yellow, not quite so strident and demanding of attention. But I have seen it in one situation in which I think it looks stunning, in the conservatory garden in Central Park, New York City. Here *F. suspensa* is planted at the top of a high sunless retaining wall and allowed to cascade down in profusion – a very clever planting, making a dark, passage-like place look alive and glowing. Ferns at the base of the wall look perfect.

Less exotic but sweetly scented are the early and late Dutch honeysuckles, and the old stand-by *Cotoneaster horizontalis*. This latter it is possible to train, fanning out its branches up a wall – any companion would spoil the latticed effect of its tracery. It has two moments of glory, the first in May when the bees in their hundreds are busy collecting honey from the white flowers, and again in autumn when the house sparrows and finches are devouring the red berries. It is extremely rampant in all directions, so must be kept under control. I have *C.h.* 'Variegatus' growing against my north-west-facing wall, where it is quite decorous, but seldom noticed. It would be better grown as a mound, perhaps over a large stone marking the corner of a shrub border.

Other stalwarts which are best grown alone are the pyracanthas. They are evergreen and are the answer for a difficult situation, in shade and on poor soil. Among the most striking are *P. rogersiana* with red berries, and *P.r. flava* with brilliant yellow. They are good on a wall, free-standing or as a hedge. *P.* 'Mohave', with orange-red fruit, is more spreading, so adapts well to a lowish wall where it can drape itself, displaying its berries over a front gate. *P. atalantioides* is very reliable – a vigorous grower which on a house will reach the first-floor windows unless given a free hand – but you must be prepared to support it well and tie it back securely, as the branches become surprisingly heavy with berries. The birds usually leave these until well after Christmas.

ABOVE LEFT A shady wall supports *Hydrangea petiolaris*, the self-clinging climbing hydrangea with vivid dark green leaves, which is smothered in June and July with flat heads of white flowers. Prune back any branches if necessary, in spring, to keep this shrub growing tidily against the wall. Hostas and ferns are an ideal choice for the same conditions at the foot of the wall.

ABOVE RIGHT Shade-tolerant *Chaenomeles speciosa* is resplendent in full blossom with matching pink and white hyacinths to add scent.

RIGHT For winter interest one of the best climbers for a north- or east-facing wall is the male form of *Garrya elliptica*. The silky catkins grow longer in winter and each flower has prominent anthers which ultimately are yellow with pollen. Free-standing garrya makes a rounded bush, but against a wall it should be pruned and tied back to make a green curtain.

# A shady wall in early summer

1 *Chaenomeles speciosa*
2 *Clematis* 'Nelly Moser'
3 *Pyracantha atalantioides*
4 *Jasminum nudiflorum*
5 *Hydrangea petiolaris*
6 *Hedera colchica* 'Sulphur Heart'
7 *Rosa* 'Golden Showers'
8 *Lonicera × americana*
9 *Pileostegia viburnoides*
10 *Parthenocissus henryana*
11 *Helleborus argutifolius*
12 *Phyllitus scolopendrium*
13 *Helleborus orientalis*
14 *Clematis* 'Jackmanii Superba'
15 *Phygelius aequalis* 'Yellow Trumpet'
16 *Helleborus foetidus*
17 *Asplenium nidus*
18 *Adiantum pedatum*
19 *Euphorbia amygdaloides robbiae*

It is surprising how many good plants will do well on and under a shady wall. Along this north-facing wall of about 20 metres (25 feet) long, I have used a mixture of evergreen and flowering shrubs and climbers, with mostly evergreen plants at their feet. The ferns, ivies, hellebores are almost automatic choices – but even among these, there is a wide variety of shapes and colours to choose from; and it is well worth while thinking about those clematis and roses which are recommended for north walls in the catalogues of the specialist nurseries. As in a mixed border, it is important to think about winter colour: *Jasminum nudiflorum* gives a splash of yellow, as do forms of ivy and *Euonymus fortunei*. Autumn interest will be provided by the vine as its leaves turn red. (*Vitis* 'Brandt' also excels in the sun). If you want berries, choose a pyracantha and prune this neatly back on to the wall – it flowers and berries on old wood.

All these pyracanthas live up to their common name, fire-thorn, so beware when pruning, which is best done in late summer; cut back the current year's growth to reveal the ripening berries, which are carried on the older wood.

Camellias are undoubtedly among the garden aristocrats and every garden should have one, somehow, but not on an east-facing exposure. They are evergreen and their oval shiny leaves are a joy at all times of the year, but they come into their full glory when covered in flowers. The sheer number of their varieties and cultivars is bewildering. For years I only admired them from afar, put off from growing them, by my very limey soil and by the successful growers who made me feel too ignorant to own them. Now my only existing camellia – given to me nine months ago – is in a half-barrel filled with an acid soil, standing where the sun never shines on it. It stands 2m/6ft tall and in January is completely covered in swelling buds full of promise. I live in the hope that an horrendous frost will not come and ruin the flower petals as they open. My resolve is never to write about a plant unless I have grown it or am planning to do so – now my ambition is to have many camellias in pots in my shady corners.

*Garrya elliptica* is wonderful in winter and remarkably tolerant of aspect and soil. The long grey-green hanging catkins (on male plants they are longer and better) start to show in late autumn and then extend until by February they will be 15-25cm/6-10in long. I have found from personal experience with a free-standing specimen that the leaves and tassels become badly scorched both by hard frost and cold east wind, an inevitable event at some moment each winter. Another specimen I know is in a nearby garden on a wall and quite protected from the wind, and I have never seen it scorched.

Wherever garrya is planted, it should have clematis to brighten its dull green leaves in summer. I have chosen *Clematis* 'Minuet' for its small white and pale mauve flowers.

Choose the double form of *Kerria japonica*, the Jew's mallow, and it will brighten a north-facing wall with its rich yellow flowers in May. Its green stems are striking all through the year, especially in winter. I prefer to allow it freedom from pruning or shaping, just cutting out any stems which are old to allow space for new growth. The flowers are such a strong yellow that its companions, if they flower at the same time, should be in contrast not competition: white tulips rather than yellow, or blue grape hyacinths. Late in summer you can put the annual *Tropaeolum peregrinum* to climb through its stems. For a permanent underplanting, try a deep purple *Helleborus orientalis* or polyanthus 'Guinevere'.

*Leycesteria formosa*, the pheasant berry, is a shrub with a strong hollow green stem. The flowers are white, but it is the wine-red bracts and later the reddish-purple berries which attract attention as they hang in panicles. The birds love the berries and will deposit the seeds, when digested, as they sit on a wall or fence; you will find seedlings in unusual places, often springing from the base of a north wall. It makes a handsome specimen shrub on its own.

I suppose we are all allowed to have our hates as well as our loves in the garden. I have banished escallonias – they seem to me to have a gawky growth habit, unexciting leaves and small flowers, and I wonder why I ever planted them. However strong these feelings, there will always be exceptions. For me, they are *Escallonia macrantha*, for its lovely gummy aromatic leaves, and *E.* 'Iveyi', the only truly handsome member of this family. I was bowled over by its beauty one September evening in Keith Steadman's garden in Wickwar where it was growing in a bed with tall shrub roses. Never mind that it may not be utterly hardy – we are now entering the epoch of greenhouse effect. *E.* 'Iveyi' has wonderful waxy white flowers set against glossy foliage, an undoubted aristocrat, and to meet it once is an experience. Against a wall it will have the extra protection it needs, and needs no associates.

Two rather more exotic shrubs which will cope with a north-facing wall but need the extra protection of a sheltered garden or cool conservatory or verandah both come from Chile. *Berberidopsis corallina* has flowers of blood-red that hang in clusters. It must have a lime-free soil and is not self-supporting, so if possible give it a trellis or wire backing. The Chilean bell-flower, *Lapageria rosea*, has stiff, leathery leaves and long bell-shaped flowers, either crimson or white. It likes a light loamy soil, again lime-free. I fell in love with this plant in a small garden in Berkeley, California, and am planning to grow it in my unheated conservatory.

*Lonicera fragrantissima* needs to be in a shady place in order to flower well, and ours is at the back of a due-north-facing wall where it flowers profusely every winter.

Do not be afraid of trying to grow shrubs that are usually grown free-standing, against a north-facing wall as long as they tolerate shade and being clipped back. In a recent experiment I have planted *Viburnum plicatum* 'Mariesii' and *Viburnum tinus* alternately along a north wall, espaliering 'Mariesii' and allowing *V. tinus* to form a rounded bush.

At Barnsley, my north-west-facing wall has given me enormous pleasure. Built of mortared Cotswold stone, it is 60m/70yd long and 3m/10ft high, and is planted with a range of climbers and shrubs. Starting at the end by the temple garden, there is a fig, *Rosa* Climbing 'Lady Hillingdon', winter jasmine, buddlejas, *Kerria japonica,* Seven Sisters rose, *Clematis* 'Huldine',

*Ceanothus* 'Gloire de Versailles', *Clematis* 'Duchess of Edinburgh' and *C.* 'Blue Moth', *Itea ilicifolia, Leycesteria formosa, Kolkwitzia amabilis, Deutzia* 'Mont Rose' and *D. scabra* 'Pride of Rochester', *Rosa gentiliana,* the Sweetheart rose and *R.* 'Dearest', *Clematis* 'Perle d'Azur', euonymus, *Hedera colchica* 'Sulphur Heart' (*H.c.* 'Paddy's Pride'), *H. helix* 'Goldheart', *Rosa* 'Veilchenblau', *Lonicera* 'Dropmore Scarlet', *Rosa* 'Golden Showers' and *Mahonia* 'Charity'. Along the base of the whole wall is a mass of *Helleborus orientalis.*

### Plants for sunny walls

A south-facing wall is both an excitement and a challenge. Plants which are marginally hardy can be given a chance – it is in the luck of the draw (the weather) how long they will survive. As we have discovered during the last few years, winter and early spring weather is very fickle. Hard frost and searing wind in November and December can play havoc with shrubs when their stems are still full of sap. The moisture will act like water in a pipe, expanding as it freezes, so bursting the bark and cambium of the stems. After a hot summer when the wood has had the opportunity to ripen fully, this is less likely to happen. Hence some shrubs like the crape myrtle, *Lagerstroemia indica,* are perfectly hardy in America where the winter temperature drops many more degrees below freezing than it does in England, but will not survive here, as the wood has not had enough heat to ripen it.

Abutilons are among the most beautiful shrubs in flower and leaf. They definitely need a sheltered wall, preferably south-facing. We had a good specimen of the white *Abutilon vitifolium* 'Veronica Tennant' for several years, and eventually it reached 3.5-4m/12-15ft before it was beaten by the exceptionally hard winter of 1976. The large, maple-shaped leaves are soft and downy. *A.* × *suntense* is lovely; it has violet-blue flowers and grey felted leaves and stems. As a ground cover under these, dianthus, *Verbena* 'Sissinghurst', *Sisyrinchium striatum* and *Salvia involucrata* 'Bethellii' would all suit a sunny border and flower either with, or after, the abutilon. *Diascia vigilis* has a long flowering time, and the abutilon branches would support its lax and wandering stems. The closely allied *Abutilon* × *hybridum* varieties 'Ashford Red', 'Canary Bird' and 'Kentish Belle' are more suited to cool house treatment. They will flower for longer than the vitifoliums, which have one glorious burst.

There are several genuine climbers to grow on your sunny wall. Solanums are among my favourites; as they have no tendrils, aerial roots or twining shoots, they need support or else tying on to wires or trellis. *Solanum crispum* 'Glasnevin' is a

OPPOSITE FAR LEFT As long as you feed your climbers, you can have several growing almost from the same place, twining through each other. Here *Clematis* 'Lasurstern' is used with *Solanum crispum* 'Glasnevin', a fine form of the Chilean potato tree.

OPPOSITE CENTRE Spring-flowering clematis can be a boost to one's gardening morale in April, and evergreen shrubs often require a partner to brighten and give them more life. Here *Clematis macropetala* scrambles through *Elaeagnus pungens* 'Maculata'.

OPPOSITE RIGHT *Vitis vinifera* 'Purpurea' act as a support for *Clematis* 'Perle d'Azur' and *C. viticella*.

RIGHT Crossing paths in the kitchen garden at Tintinhull are marked by four specimen *Lonicera japonica* 'Halliana', growing up and through metal tree protectors. The paths are lined with *Nepeta* 'Six Hills Giant'.

vigorous scrambler with rich violet-blue, yellow-centred potato flowers which bloom from June until October. Choose a yellow rose, *Cytisus battandieri, Coronilla glauca* or *Fremontodendron californicum* as neighbours – their golden flowers will echo the yellow centres of the solanum.

Unlike the solanum, which must be tied in, trachelospermum is a beautiful self-clinging climber which will attach itself to a wall – its young green stems will also twine. The small tubular, jasmine-like flowers are very fragrant and come in July and August on the short laterals from old wood, so pruning consists of shortening long thin ends in spring when growth shows signs of starting. *Trachelospermum asiaticum* has creamy white flowers with a buff yellow centre turning yellow. The white *T. jasminoides* – not quite so hardy – needs a warm wall or conservatory, and *T.j.* 'Variegatum' is a lovely climber for the conservatory.

*Lonicera* 'Dropmore Scarlet' does well in full sun and must have a plant with an equal strength of colour as a companion, and one which will keep the straggly lower stems of the honeysuckle well covered. For a scarlet as intense as the honeysuckle's choose the Cape figwort, *Phygelius capensis coccineus*, with nodding flowers on 1m/3ft stems in late summer. For a contrast, the purple-leaved form of *Pittosporum tenuifolium* would hold its own well. I would also like the contrast of growth habit of *Phormium*

'Dazzler', with narrow, shining, deep red leaves which droop elegantly at the tips. *Cotinus coggygria* 'Notcutt's Purple' is another shrub with rich purple foliage, and you can keep this clipped to size by pruning it hard, down to the old wood, in early spring. Then of course yellow foliage could be used, so why not the golden form of privet, *Ligustrum ovalifolium* 'Aureum'. Again this responds to hard pruning and the foliage will keep a good colour in the summer, remaining on through most of the winter.

I have looked with envy at the luxuriant growth and flowers on the trumpet vine growing on sunny walls in Mediterranean lands. With a succession of not too hard winters, *Campsis radicans* will become established here in full sun and out of the wind – well worth a try. It is a vigorous climber, making several feet of growth each summer, and as it flowers (in August and September) on the current season's growth, you can prune it hard in early spring.

One of my favourite evergreen shrubs, which is best given the protection of a south wall, is *Itea ilicifolia*. It has soft, shiny, holly-shaped leaves, and in August and September a display of greeny-white tassels, 25cm/10in long, elegant, slender and drooping. Rather surprisingly, they have a definite evening scent, especially when brought indoors.

There are many more from which to choose – I hope your wall

is long, so that you can enjoy them. Both the evergreen *Carpenteria californica*, with large white flowers, and the yellow *Fremontodendron* 'California Glory' (and *F. californicum*) can be allowed to billow out from the wall, as they make rounded bushy shapes. The last is fast-growing, and will probably thrive and flower better and be longer-lived on poor soil, where it will grow less vigorously.

If, as I do, you love the scent of *Aloysia triphylla* (*Lippia citriodora*) leaves, then you must plant this in full sun, perhaps given a covering of bracken at its base and protected by another shrub in front – *Choisya ternata*, the evergreen Mexican orange blossom, would help give it cover.

Every garden should have a ceanothus if the soil is right. They will not thrive on shallow chalk, but are tolerant of an acid or alkaline soil. The evergreen *Ceanothus* 'Cascade' has masses of bright blue flowers on long arching sprays, and looks lovely against a stone or brick wall. *C. dentatus*, flowering in May, is more erect and has smaller leaves. *C.* 'Puget Blue' has especially glossy leaves and outstanding bright blue flowers. Plant this to coincide with wisteria flowers and the two will cover the front of your house.

For a spectacle of leaves in spring and summer, *Actinidia kolomikta* is hard to better. The young leaves open pale green, then slowly become transfused with pink and white. They are unusual, attractive and the leaves remain beautiful right through until September, when the pink fades and the white becomes green. I believe that the leaves of male plants are more attractively variegated.

Finally, the south side of a tall house is the ideal place for *Magnolia grandiflora* – the flowers are scented and beautiful, the leaves large and shining. You must be patient for the flowers, but the variety *M.g.* 'Exmouth' is reputed to flower at an early age.

LEFT On a sunny wall in the Oxford Botanic Garden is *Wisteria sinensis*, with yellow *Azara serrata* between them, and *Abutilon vitifolium* beyond. At their feet is the white *Olearia phloggopappa* (*O. gunniana*) and *Cistus* 'Silver Pink'. This makes a symphony of lilac tones with the azara giving a touch of the complementary colour, yellow, and also a strong waft of scent.

OPPOSITE The bright yellow flowers of Moroccan broom, *Cytisus battandieri*, smell strongly of pineapple. This shrub, with its evergreen leaves, is a fast grower and suitable for a high wall. At its feet, at Brook Cottage, Alkerton, are *Campanula portenschlagiana* (*C. muralis*) and the large globes of *Allium christophii*. On the right *Carpenteria californica*, a bushy evergreen with white flowers, enjoys the sunny, well-drained situation with sea thrift, *Armeria maritima*, lining the pathway. The yellow and the mauve are another good example of a planting of complementary colours.

# Mixed Borders

The golden and mauve end of the garden near the fountain at Barnsley House in late May. The border has a background of golden-leaved trees – an elm, *Gleditsia triacanthos* 'Sunburst' just coming into leaf and *Chamaecyparis lawsoniana* 'Lane' – with pale mauve lilac and an old cooking apple tree through which *Viburnum opulus* 'Roseum' (*V.o.* 'Sterile') emerges. *Angelica archangelica*, polemoniums, *Spiraea* 'Arguta', and a golden privet with hostas, create a carpet in front. In the foreground the round heads of *Allium aflatunense* contrast in shape but blend in colour with the spikes of *Polygonum bistorta* 'Superbum'.

Today more people have borders planted with a mixture of shrubs, herbaceous plants, ground cover, bulbs and climbers than with a purely herbaceous display or with a Victorian shrubbery. Herbaceous beds are glorious for only three months out of twelve, and a shrubbery, although peaceful and lovely to wander in at all times of the year, is unspectacular in its own right – in a large garden it is better as one among several features. The joy of mixed planting is the extension of beauty from one season to the next: winter and early spring can be almost as satisfying as high summer.

Mixed borders tend to enlist the most energy and command the most attention of any area in the garden. Throughout this book I have tried to emphasize the importance of planting in layers – encouraging bulbs and annuals to occupy ground beneath and between shrubs, and allowing climbers to twine themselves up supporting hosts of all kinds. I have also tried to show how one plant can be made to take over from another, creating varying interest in the same spot throughout the year to reflect the changing seasons. It is in the mixed border that these twin concepts find their best expression.

Planting in layers may not be something you have thought about a great deal, other than to fill an obviously bare spot under a deciduous shrub or tree. It can become a most rewarding game, however, and transform your mixed border from an obvious statement, with shrubs punctuating herbaceous infill in the usual manner, into a subtle picture full of small incidents that it is a pleasure to walk along and absorb. In mixed planting there is so much to choose from – ground-hugging alpines, annuals and biennials, climbers and small trees, as well as the more usual ingredients of shrubs and herbaceous plants – that lasting and satisfying combinations are easy to create.

Planning this type of border needs a thoughtful approach. You must consider carefully all the different types of plants you want to use, making a list and deciding how you will integrate them. Never think of plants in isolation – have a picture in your mind of good neighbours, co-ordinating colours and sympathetic textures. Think of a plant at all moments of its life and you begin to assess its value both to you and your garden through the whole year. At the same time you must think about a succession of interest – either from flowers or foliage – through the changing seasons. In a mixed border the middle-height and taller shrubs will be the backbone which, to give interest in the early months of the year, you can surround with bulbs, hellebores, polyanthus and other winter and spring flowers and, for a succession of colour through from April until autumn, with herbaceous perennials and summer- and autumn-flowering bulbs.

Each plant will have its own strength of colour, texture or mass, and flower at different times. One part of the back of the border may predominate during the spring and autumn, one part of the front during the height of summer. In any successful scheme there will be a balance and harmony of all these interests. Although this sounds very demanding, it is possible to achieve by careful planning, always thinking about successive planting, so that one plant comes through or is very close to another – for example, crocuses through ajuga, hostas taking over from tulips, fennel covering the dying leaves of eremurus, shrubs acting as supports for clematis, roses closely underplanted with violas. Remember that low plants – bulbs and polyanthus – which flower before the deciduous shrubs, can be seen just as easily if they have a position farther back in the border than you might naturally plant them.

Just as the middle and taller shrubs are the permanent elements from which you can plan the seasonal interest of a border, so they are also the central backbone around which you can plan successive heights, or layers of plants. As well as thinking about the perennials and bulbs which come up beside and through the shrubs, the picture must include the tall shrubs and trees, climbers behind and above, and the evergreen low-growing shrubs and plants which give shape and substance to the front of the border. Always keep in mind that ingredients may be added at any time to finish off the picture – or perhaps to create an element of surprise. In this respect gardening is like cooking: you can always follow the recipe devised by an expert and create a perfect dish, but if you add a special element of your own it is transformed into something unique – unexpected to your guests and supremely satisfying to you.

As in a true herbaceous border the use of heights is important, and in a mixed border it is easier to achieve a good effect: you already have inlets between the shrubs, giving you the opportunity to frame some of the choicer perennials. There is no need to adhere closely to keeping your heights too regimented; in fact, a taller shrub or two used in the middle of the border can help create this all-important rhythm to your design. So a weigela, deutzia, kolkwitzia or even a buddleja will not look out of place, especially if they have ascending branches and foliage which does not give too heavy or dense an effect. To make my point, *Elaeagnus pungens* 'Maculata' and *Ilex × altaclerensis* 'Lawsoniana' give a light effect through the brightness of the golden markings of their leaves, whereas I prefer to use the more solid-looking evergreen *Choisya ternata* as a full stop at the end of a border or at the back to give substance.

Other taller shrubs which can well have a more forward place are those with an open look created by their small leaves and graceful habit. Good examples are the common tamarisk and the Spanish broom, the yellow-flowered *Spartium junceum*, and possibly *Spiraea* 'Arguta' with white flowers. (This latter you must prune carefully, thinning out some of its branches to enhance its delicate lines.)

Think, too, about the density of a shrub. Cryptomeria is obviously completely dense – you cannot see through it – but it has a light quality because of its feathery leaves. Osmanthus, though the leaves are uniformly dark green, also has a not-too-heavy feeling because of the way in which the branches grow, letting light through them and between the leaves. In summer *Cornus alba* 'Elegantissima' and *C.a* 'Spaethii' create a light of their own

These photographs, taken from the same spot, show the effects of the changing season from spring to summer. They illustrate the principle of planting for successive interest. The idea is that when one group of plants is going over, another is already growing up through them to take their place.

OPPOSITE ABOVE The ground is thickly planted with early bulbs. *Narcissus* 'February Gold' turn their faces to the sun. Scillas are naturalized under the deciduous shrubs.

OPPOSITE CENTRE By early May the picture has changed dramatically. The centre stage is now held by the violet-pink tulip 'Dreaming Maid' growing through blue forget-me-nots. The yellow of the daffodils has been replaced by *Euphorbia polychroma*. Behind on the right a mound of *Aruncus dioicus* will be flowering in July while the leaves of *Iris foetidissima* 'Variegata' are evergreen. In the foreground the semi-evergreen snowberry, *Symphoricarpas orbiculatus* 'Foliis Variegatis', is making new leaves. The foliage of *Stachys byzantina (S. lanata)*, hardy geraniums and the saxifrage, Irish pride, are taking on a fresh summer look.

OPPOSITE BELOW At the height of summer, this bed is a glowing tapestry of colour, the key notes being pink, mauve, purple, grey and white, offset with different greens. In front, *Asphodeline lutea* and *Campanula persicifolia* mingle with the grey foliage of *Stachys byzantina* and *Artemisia pedemontana*. The pink *Spiraea japonica* 'Little Princess' has a lavender and pink alliums as companions. Behind, the bold spikes of *Salvia × superba* 'East Friesland' and *Penstemon* 'Purple Bedder' break the line in front of the group of white *Lychnis coronaria* and the half-hardy *Argyranthemum frutescens*.

ABOVE Just two weeks later, in late July, the scene is subtly but noticeably different. The spiraea is fading and *Erigeron* 'Four Winds' is in full bloom in front. A creamy white campanula, penstemon, astrantia and the lychnis are merged together so no soil is visible, but a self-sown poppy has struggled through. *Lavatera olbia* 'Barnsley' will remain in flower until the frost comes – this shrub is also ideal for picking, the buds opening in succession in water. This is the moment in the year when dead-heading is all-important to keep the borders looking well groomed.

The change from winter to spring in two different parts of the garden at Barnsley House.

LEFT ABOVE At the end of a border in January, the evergreen *Juniperus × media* 'Pfitzeriana', covered with frost, is surrounded by grey *Santolina chamaecyparissus* and *Stachys byzantina*, while the evergreen leaves of *Iris foetidissima* 'Variegata' give extra winter interest.

LEFT BELOW By May the flower stems of the stachys are almost hiding the santolina which we always clip hard back in spring in order to keep this grey shrub compact and shapely. The bright orange-red flowers of *Euphorbia griffithii* 'Fireglow' echo the red of the tulips.

OPPOSITE LEFT Between November, when the beds are tidied, and early spring the clipped box balls (*Buxus sempervirens* 'Suffruticosa') are important and act as an invitation to walk along the patterned brick path beside the laburnum tunnel to watch for the first bulbs to come through and the hellebores to open. The ground cover on the right is *Waldsteinia ternata* which has small yellow flowers in spring.

OPPOSITE RIGHT By spring the box takes second place to the summer snowflake, *Leucojum aestivum*, the white form of honesty, *Lunaria annua*, with variegated leaves, primroses and primulas which are allowed to self-sow, a few ferns and *Smilacina racemosa*.

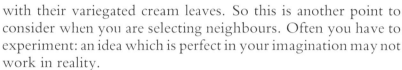

with their variegated cream leaves. So this is another point to consider when you are selecting neighbours. Often you have to experiment: an idea which is perfect in your imagination may not work in reality.

### Evergreen shrubs

When you are designing your mixed border, it is a good idea to begin by marking the evergreen shrubs on to your plan – those which will be strong points all through the year. There is a huge choice of evergreen shrubs, so start by making a list, analyzing each shrub for its own special quality of shape, colour and texture. This will help you fit them into your plan. For instance, some shrubs can be clipped, others make a natural shape; some, especially the broad-leaved evergreens, can be pruned to the size you want, others dislike being restrained.

Evergreens provide colour all through the year; in winter they become a background for herbaceous seed heads, and for red, yellow or tawny stems, and they are often useful for picking. The height and distinctive shapes they give are important throughout the seasons; but remember that there will be a difference in effect between the presence of, for example, the spikes of a phormium and the dense columns of a fastigiate conifer.

Conifers such as *Juniperus communis* 'Compressa' make dwarf columns. I like these planted in a low pool of contrasting or complementary foliage, with flower spikes which echo the vertical shape of the junipers. *Polygonum affine* 'Dimity' is a wonderful carpeter, only 15cm/6in tall, with pink and red poker flower spikes in late summer. You could add *Allium cernuum*, a rich lilac-purple, or *A. carinatum pulchellum*, a darker, duskier purple, to push through the polygonum in June and July. The round allium flowers would make a strong contrast to the upright junipers.

This combination is right for a low effect, but where you want a taller look, use *Juniperus communis* 'Hibernica' (reaching 3m/10ft), surrounded by *Polygonum bistorta* 'Superbum' (often 90cm/36in tall), with *Allium aflatunense*, again with round heads of deep lilac. *A. siculum* (correctly *Nectaroscordum s.*) has a different look: each individual flower hangs like a bell, and then when they ripen they spring upright and become straw-coloured. The lesson here is to remember that bulbs can grow through the foliage of other plants, giving two or more elements of interest to one space.

A similar vertical look can be achieved with several conifers – *Chamaecyparis lawsoniana* 'Pembury Blue' for silver-blue effect, *C.l.* 'Howarths Gold', a golden-yellow with soft foliage, and *C.l.* 'Green Pillar', a rich green. My preference is to group these in one colour rather than make a medley of blue, grey and green. You can create an interesting picture using vertical, horizontal and rounded conifers which will stand out in winter and in summer will act as a foil to herbaceous plants with larger leaves.

A different effect of height is achieved by using the sword-like leaves of *Phormium tenax*, the New Zealand flax, or the spiky leaves of the yucca. The strong rigid foliage of phormium is a perfect foil to the rounded leaves of bergenia: together they can take on interest for the whole year. Phormium also makes a good contrast to euphorbia's rather gentle, individual leaves. You may be more selective and grow *P.t. purpureum,* associating this

OPPOSITE In Anne Dexter's tiny Oxford garden, which makes superb use of every inch of space, the shrubs down the borders have a yellow and purple theme, with golden privet, golden elm, *Berberis thunbergii* 'Somerset' and *B.* × *ottawensis*. The blue *Clematis* × *durandii* climbs over the golden

*Lonicera nitida* and *Clematis* 'Perle d'Azur' scrambles above. The purple cotinus has the rose 'New Dawn', white *Clematis* 'Huldine' and pink *C.* 'Comtesse de Bouchaud'. The sunken path cleverly increases the dry wall area over which plants can drape. There are campanulas, erodiums, *Geranium flanaganii*, small

grasses and *Hosta venusta*. Among the shrubs are monkshoods, libertia, phygelius and *Lysimachia ephemerum*.

ABOVE In Mr and Mrs Paice's garden in Gloucestershire, the plants are allowed to spill out on to the gravel paths, blurring the geometric lines of the design. The spears of

phormium give a firm structure to the planting, and the colour scheme of pale yellows and white is composed of *Abutilon* 'Canary Bird' with a white buddleja in the background, and *A.* × *milleri* 'Variegatum' with *Argyranthemum* 'Jamaica Primrose' in the foreground.

with grey-leaved *Senecio* 'Sunshine', but I play for safety in my Cotswold garden and go for the hardier green-leaved species.

Gertrude Jekyll had the idea of using spikes as the main 'full stop'. To quote from *Wood and Garden*: 'a path cuts through the border, and passes by an arched gateway in the wall to the Paeony garden and the working garden beyond. Just here I thought it would be well to mound up the border a little, and plant with groups of Yuccas, so that at all times of the year there should be something to make a handsome full-stop to the sections of the border, and to glorify the doorway. The two extreme ends of the border are treated in the same way with Yuccas on rather lesser mounds.'

William Robinson found these plants equally useful. In *The English Flower Garden* he wrote: 'In its own peculiar habit and style of growth the Yucca has no rival among hardy plants. Though the stiffest of all garden plants, it has grace and elegance, under all conditions, if the plant is not cramped for room . . . The

effect of well-developed Yuccas is equal to that of any hot-house plant that we can venture to place in the open air for summer, while they are green and ornamental at all seasons. The free-flowering kinds, *Y. filamentosa* and *Y. flaccida*, may be associated with any of our nobler autumn-flowering plants, from Gladiolus to the great *Statice latifolia*.'

A coniferous evergreen I enjoy using is *Cryptomeria japonica* 'Elegans', but you must allow it space to spread – up to 1.5m/5ft tall – for it has a bushy habit and by clipping it you lose much of its airy quality. The foliage is soft and feathery, a browny-green in summer turning a fine coppery-bronze in winter; this colour persists until the days warm up in spring. As neighbours I would choose any of the warm reds through to orange and deep yellow. (A clear yellow such as *Oenothera biennis* would be just wrong.)

Against the cryptomeria's bronze foliage, the scarlet stems of *Salix alba* 'Britzensis' (*S.a.* 'Chermesina'), or those of *Cornus alba* 'Elegantissima', look rich and glowing in winter. This dogwood

has leaves with white margins and mottling to stand out boldly against the cryptomeria. In a broad border where there is enough depth, then *C. controversa* 'Variegata' should be used. Its skeleton with horizontal branches is distinct in winter, and in summer its variegated leaves show up against the cryptomeria. Sunlight is essential to appreciate form, shape and variegated foliage, and in a south-facing border the sun will fall on and lighten the cornus or other variegated foliage throughout the day.

A few broadleaf evergreen shrubs are important in the mixed border for structure and for year-round shape.

Holly and ivy are plants which perhaps come top of the list. Holly is what you make of it. It can be a part of the background scene, a foil to set off other shrubs and woodlanders, or it can become an outstanding feature in its own right. Clip it and it will take on a new character, combining shape, mass, texture and foliage colour. If you have an elderly specimen in your garden, then start working on it at once; in a new garden never be

OPPOSITE A yucca can be very useful as punctuation in a border – either as a full-stop at a corner, or as an exclamation mark in the centre. Here *Yucca flaccida* 'Ivory' makes a fine display in the long borders in the Royal Horticultural Society's gardens at Wisley. Yuccas like sun and a well-drained soil. As a crown produces a flower spike it dies, but side shoots are always present to carry on. They can be raised from seed and will take at least four years to flower; they can also be increased from root cuttings using the root-knobs. This clone, which was raised by Rowland Jackman of Woking, is free-flowering and reliably hardy. The flower spikes stand well above the leaves, each individual bloom carried horizontally from the stem.

ABOVE A spring view looking across a mixed border towards the herb garden at Barnsley House. In the foreground oriental poppy and delphinium leaves are emerging. A dark form of *Lunaria annua* does well in the shade and so does the evergreen *Daphne laureola*, which seeds itself around. The long bare stems are of *Paeonia delavayi*, which we propagate from seed. Up the tree trunk is *Euonymus fortunei* 'Variegatus', which will climb when it is given a support; otherwise it will remain as a rounded shrub. This gives the border a strange shape at the corner and also provides an interesting evergreen backdrop.

it, use it as ground cover or in pots on the patio, trail it down a difficult wall or have it as an arborescent shrub or as a mound, clinging to a stone at the front of your border. The leaves are crinkled or lacy, golden or spotted, pointed or spear-shaped. It is hard to believe that there are so many varieties, and all available for you to buy and grow in your garden.

My first inspired encounter with ivy was in a garden where the small-leaved variegated forms were planted to grow over and encouraged to envelop 50×30cm/20×12in stones put at the corners and edges of pathways, so that they became interesting cushions.

Variegation in foliage often adds glamour to an otherwise un-noteworthy shrub and makes it desirable. For instance, the ever-green *Rhamnus alaternus* with dark green leaves will succeed in any soil in any situation – in fact it is the ideal shrub for industrial or seaside plantings – but lacks the lustre and speciality of *R.a.* 'Argenteovariegata', the buckthorn with green leaves marbled and margined with cream. This is one of my star plants for winter: it is tough, evergreen, will clip without complaining, and is not so dense or heavy as holly or ivy. I have recently planted it in front of a berberis where the afternoon sun catches it to perfection. I know I would like it as a shrub growing in front of a large house, in contrast to *Magnolia grandiflora* which has huge, shiny, leathery leaves.

The whole mass and texture of *Viburnum tinus*, good as it is in the shrubbery, is too pedestrian for your mixed border. (Do use it elsewhere in the garden, for it has moments of real excellence in January and February when it is covered in white flowers.) The variegated form, *V.t.* 'Variegatum', with creamy-yellow edges to its leaves, is good for a north-facing corner, but much better, I believe, is a form of the Portugal laurel, *Prunus lusitanica* 'Varie-gata'; the leaves, irregularly margined with white, take on a pink flush to match its young red stems.

Some shrubs are beautiful in both their green and their varie-gated forms: euonymus, *Daphne odora* and *Elaeagnus pungens*, for instance. Euonymus has recently become widely available at gar-den centres, especially in its forms *fortunei* and *japonicus*. They are both best-sellers, presumably because of their well-marked, eye-catching leaves. They are evergreen shrubs and look at their best in spring as the young leaves shine out with their variegations of silver or gold. My *E.f.* 'Silver Queen' has become – over the years – quite a sensation in the way it has taken off, or rather up, a pear tree trunk and also up the wall of the house. You can learn from a fortunate accident, and next time you do it, it will be a purposeful plan. My euonymus started climbing the pear tree, so we put a young plant up the face of the house.

Here are some of my favourite evergreen shrubs which have

daunted – you will be surprised at just how quickly a young holly will grow.

The holly genus comes in many different colours and forms, with leaves of varying size, shape and degree of prickliness. *Ilex × altaclerensis* 'Lawsoniana', one of my favourite hollies, has few prickles and a beautiful leaf with three distinct colours – dark green, lime green and yellow. In winter it becomes even more important. I have it growing at the golden end of our long border, near a gleditsia and an old and well clipped golden privet, *Ligustrum ovalifolium* 'Aureum', now almost completely mantled by a spring-flowering *Clematis macropetala*. Yellow tulips may be used between golden shrubs such as these, and later their places can be infilled with white honesty (*Lunaria annua alba*) and sum-mer snowflakes (*Leucojum aestivum*).

Ivy, used with imagination, is one of the best plants in any gar-den. A north-facing wall can be transformed, as I have described in the chapter on climbers. You can cover pillars and arches with

the qualities of good individual foliage, different textures, and varying shapes and density.

My mixed border would be incomplete without the evergreen *Hebe* 'Mrs Winder' and *H. rakaiensis*. The former has attractive leaves, showing purple especially on their undersides. It comes late into flower, so is ideal for autumn and even winter interest, but it is for its foliage and mushroom shape that I like it – not too solid and with a slightly jagged outline, but a useful patch of greenery throughout the year. *H. rakaiensis* is an even more useful evergreen shape with a perfect rounded habit and the ideal choice to act as a full stop at a corner or the end of your border, as Lanning Roper taught me many years ago. Like him, I don't like borders which die away at the edges. You can fill the space between the hebe and the edge of the border with spring bulbs – lots of *Iris reticulata* to flower in February and March, and primulas for April. Let the iris remain, but the primulas can be dug and divided after flowering and may be lined out in a shady part of the garden, ready to take up their positions in autumn. Low summer bedding plants can replace them. You could also associate the hebe with low-growing evergreen plants such as *Saxifraga × urbium* 'Variegata' to make a surrounding carpet.

I like grey foliage as a contrast to the dark hebe leaves – *Senecio bicolor cineraria (Cineraria maritima)* which incidentally is very easily grown from seed sown in April, or the glaucous-leaved *Echeveria glauca*, if you have space to overwinter the plants indoors. Another idea is to surround the hebe with permanent grey leaves pierced by bulbs. The grey could be *Cerastium tomentosum*, snow in summer, *Veronica cinerea, Stachys byzantina (S. lanata), Artemisia splendens, A. canescens*, or your own favourite low-growing, grey-foliage plant. For a change I have planted yellow Dutch iris, so good for picking, among the stachys. As soon as the iris finish flowering you can cut the foliage to ground level so that it does not interfere with the grey look. You can make a special picture by growing *Senecio* 'Sunshine' or *Phlomis fruticosa*

with the *Hebe rakaiensis*, grouping double white *Tulipa* 'Mount Tacoma' round the shrubs. Interplant the tulips with white *Penstemon* 'Snow Storm' to flower through the summer.

A shrub which I believe should be in every garden and which can make a superb impact in the mixed border is *Osmanthus × burkwoodii*. It has a splendid shiny leaf and small white tubular flowers useful for picking in April; they have an incredibly strong, sweet scent – never cloying. It is a bold shrub with a small leaf and can be used in association with paler foliage. I have it with a sweet cicely, *Myrrhis odorata*, on one side; this flowers in June and we cut it right to the ground very soon afterwards. New growth appears miraculously almost the next day. On the other side is the September-flowering *Physostegia* 'Rose Bouquet' and one of the hardy autumn-flowering chrysanthemums. If you have limited space then *O. delavayi* is a smaller substitute, but less hardy. There is not a moment in the year when it does not look good, and you have the extra bonuses of strongly scented flowers and a shrub you can pick and keep clipped into the size and shape you need. To allow you to see its full shape I would put herbaceous plants that die down in winter round it – acanthus for size of leaf and contrast of texture, and *Cynara cardunculus*, the cardoon, to stand out boldly with its silver-grey leaves in front of the osmanthus. In both examples the deeply cut leaves make a fine contrast of shape. Put white narcissus or white tulips round it to coincide in flowering time. With these combinations you can then add herbaceous flowers of any colour.

*Choisya ternata*, Mexican orange blossom, has dark green shining leaves which are aromatic when you crush them. Allow it enough space to develop to its full potential – a rounded shape 2m/6-7ft wide and high. It may be tender during its first winter, but only because it grows fast and the young soft stems may get frosted. My advice is to buy a plant which is mature enough to have old as well as new wood and then, in its first year, to give it slight protection with a surround of netting or sacking to prevent

LEFT ABOVE AND BELOW A border at Barnsley House in April, and later in June.

The colours are predominantly yellow, mauve and, inevitably, green. The *Helleborus foetidus*, in flower since January, will soon have to be cut. In the left foreground *Euphorbia polychroma* is trouble-free and contained. The groups of cowslips will be taken up and kept in a shady spot for the summer, in order to make space for annuals. Beyond them are blue grape hyacinths and the tulip 'Prinses Irene' is the end feature. Down the centre of the border, the perennial wallflower, *Erysimum* 'Bowles' Mauve', are tucked in close to the *Potentilla* 'Elizabeth' for protection. This wallflower contrasts well with the various yellows and lime greens. By June the colours have changed to pinks and more mauves. Aquilegias and violas are allowed to seed themselves. *Geranium endressii* covers any dying daffodil leaves and protects the hardy agapanthus which are planted close by and through the grey *Artemisia ludoviciana*. This artemisia becomes untidy as the flower stems grow, and we cut these right down when they start to flop; fresh new growth soon develops. The taller central features are *Phlomis russeliana*, with bold leaves and strong stems carrying whorls of yellow flowers, and *Aconitum* 'Ivorine'. This monkshood has soft, attractive leaves and hooded ivory-white flowers. On the right can be seen the heads of the tree onion, *Allium fistulosum* 'Viviparum', leaning over from the herb garden.

OPPOSITE One of the well-filled borders on the terraces at Powis Castle. The generous informal groups of plants are contained in an immaculately clipped box hedge. The planting was originally by Graham Thomas; now it is in the able hands of Jimmy Hancock. Many tender plants are wintered indoors, but the high walls give wonderful protection. A visit to this garden at any time is an inspiration but it reaches its peak in late summer.

scorching by the wind and to reduce the frost. The white flowers open chiefly in May and June but you will get extra blooms later in the year. I like to surround it with companions flowering at the same time – *Dicentra spectabilis alba, Iberis* 'Snowflake', or perhaps *Tiarella cordifolia*, which has a sea of fluffy foam flowers over a solid mass of heart-shaped evergreen leaves. These leaves become bronzed in winter and would contrast well with the choisya's shining dark green foliage. Another idea is to give the choisya a surrounding carpet of white narcissus or tulips to come through *Anthemis punctata cupaniana*.

Plants with spiky leaves contrast well with the round shape of the choisya, but select those which will not hide or dwarf it: try *Iris foetidissima* 'Variegata' or *Sisyrinchium striatum*, both 50 cm/20 in tall, or a skirt of a low grass such as *Festuca glauca* (25cm/10in), *Milium effusum, Molinia caerulea* 'Variegata' (45cm/18in) or the grey *Helictotrichon sempervirens* (75cm/30in) – the height refers to the leaves, not the flower spikes.

Other plants which have a grass-like quality include dierama, gladiolus, hemerocallis (day-lilies), crocosmia, low phormiums and, of course, liriope, more often seen in America where the climate is too dry and hot in summer for grass to succeed. When you are considering these plants, you must remember their flower colour as well as their shape and height.

Another evergreen family useful to incorporate into the border are the daphnes, which, being scented, should have a front place. I prefer the white form of *Daphne mezereum* to the purple-red one and, since it flowers in February and March, the white should be reflected by using drifts of the large-flowered white Dutch crocus or a species such as *Crocus chrysanthus* 'Snowbunting' around it.

If this is a place you wish to keep to white flowers, you can either drop in white annuals – petunias, *Lavatera* 'Mont Blanc', tobacco plants (*Nicotiana affinis*) – or you can have perennials which will not swamp the daphne. My suggestions are *Gypsophila paniculata* 'Bristol Fairy' or *Aster divaricatus* (syn. *A. corymbosus*), which will succeed in half-shade. Allow this to flop rather than be staked, as the wise counsellor Gertrude Jekyll recommended; she describes it as a filling plant for edge spaces that want a pretty trimming. These trimmings are the touch which makes a garden special rather than just pretty. *Daphne × burkwoodii* 'Somerset' is a dome-shaped shrub, usually less than 1m/3.3ft high. Its soft mauve-pink flowers open in May and June and I would choose dianthus, *Nepeta mussinii, Phlox* 'Chattahoochee' or the double form of *Cardamine pratensis* to surround it.

In early spring the chartreuse green flowers of *Helleborus foetidus* look striking growing with the pale yellow-flowered *Mahonia × media* 'Charity' and round the dark evergreen *Osmanthus*

*delavayi*. Both of these shrubs flower early in the year and are highly scented – two great qualities which to my mind make them indispensable in the garden.

There is a wide choice of evergreen shrubs which do not grow taller than 1m/40in and really earn their space in the border. Many of the cistus, for example, make good border plants. The sage-green leaves of *C. × corbariensis* harmonize well with darker green or grey foliage. Its flower petals have an attractive crumpled look as they first open. I like *C.* 'Silver Pink' for its grey-green leaves and pink flowers with yellow stamens. Planted beside *Heuchera* 'Palace Purple' with an *Acer palmatum dissectum*, the three sets of leaves contrast well in the autumn when the acer's leaves take on a bronze-to-crimson look.

Many smaller evergreens are also good value in the border. *H. × franciscana* 'Blue Gem' has bright blue flowers all the summer, and *H.* 'Midsummer Beauty' lavender-purple flowers and especially attractive shiny green leaves with reddish undersides. *Rhododendron impeditum*, one of the lowest growing of the genus, has grey-green fragrant leaves, which turn bronze in winter, and blue flowers; it makes a front of the border shrub on acid soil. *Sarcococca humilis* makes a dense evergreen bush up to 60cm/24in tall – its joy also lies in the astonishingly strongly scented February flowers. Combine this with *Helleborus orientalis*.

Three deciduous shrubs which are useful in the mixed border.

FAR LEFT *Viburnum farreri (V. fragrans)* is an old favourite which blooms from November through winter on leafless stems. The pale pink buds open to highly scented white flowers. Left unpruned it will reach 2.5m/8ft. The young leaves are bronze at first.

LEFT *Viburnum carlesii* 'Diana', one of the most fragrant viburnums, makes a more compact and rounded bush than *V. farreri*. The flowers and leaves emerge together in April and May; the clusters of buds are red and, when open, show that the inside of each petal is pink.

OPPOSITE *Philadelphus* 'Belle Etoile' makes a firm host for the mauve-flowered *Clematis* 'Prince Charles', both of which bloom at the end of June. Our borders need colour then, while waiting for the flush of herbaceous flowers in July. This philadelphus becomes 1.75m/5½ft high and just as broad. The highly-scented flowers are single and white, with a blush of pink at the base of each fringed petal.

## Deciduous shrubs

Deciduous shrubs will be bare of their leaves for probably six months of the year, so you must assess your chosen shrubs for their stems and their overall winter shapes as well as for their summer flowers and perhaps also their autumn berries. The ground under deciduous shrubs, even in the back of the border, will be visible until the leaves start to appear, so this is the ideal place for the earliest bulbs – I have talked about this in the chapter on bulbs and will return to it later.

Be selective in your choice, considering first shrubs with attractive stems such as *Spiraea* × *vanhouttei*, which takes on a lovely, almost mahogany colour and shines in the sunlight. This is an excellent back-of-the-border shrub, growing up to 2m/6-7ft, its sprays arching forward with the weight of the foliage and glistening white spring flowers. Winter aconites, *Eranthis hyemalis*, can be planted round its base.

There are many tall or middle-height shrubs which can serve the same purpose. If your soil is acid, the Japanese maples are ideal. *Acer palmatum* 'Senkaki', with bright coral-red stems, is often used as a specimen shrub in the lawn or wild area, but it also looks striking at the back of a deep border where it could be underplanted with scillas or snowdrops to contrast with its coral stems. To get the best bark effect with single-stem trees, you must take off the lower branches at an early age so that the trunk is revealed in its full beauty.

Dogwoods are grown for the colour of their winter stems, ranging from the bright scarlet of *Cornus alba* 'Sibirica' to the butter yellow of *C. stolonifera* 'Flaviramea'. They are often planted in groups and beside water, but in a small garden, used in the back, middle or front of the border, they can associate per-fectly with early bulbs and herbaceous plants, which will pick up the red or yellow of their stems. Try golden-yellow crocus, early narcissus, red windflowers (*Anemone* × *fulgens*) or early red or yellow tulips, which should all flower before the dogwoods de-velop their leaves. A carpet of winter aconites, *Eranthis hyemalis*, will flower in February and the leaves disappear in May. Among complementary herbaceous plants, doronicums can be used for early spring yellow, *Euphorbia griffithii* 'Fireglow' for April effect, crocosmias, or annual *Oenothera biennis* for later summer; these seed themselves readily and will push their stems through the cornus branches. Shrubs, too, can associate well with dog-woods – *Ilex* × *altaclerensis* 'Golden King' beside the yellow-stemmed cornus and, beside the red-stemmed variety, one of the few deciduous hollies, *I. verticillata* 'Winter Red' (more often seen in east-coast American gardens than in England).

With the cornus you could also use ferns which like shade in summer. The royal fern, *Osmunda regalis* (1.2m/4ft high), whose fronds turn a rich autumn colour, would make a striking com-bination. The ostrich feather fern, *Matteuccia struthiopteris*, also likes a place that is shady but not too dry, and is lovely in spring as its pale green fronds uncurl – in slanting sunshine they look transparent gold. One of my favourite ferns, *Polystichum setife-rum divisilobum*, keeps its fronds through the winter; these need only be cut back as the new ones develop.

At every week of the year, some shrub should be flowering in your garden. Some winter- and early spring-flowering shrubs bring more than a touch of pleasure for the way their beauty is enhanced by fragrance. Winter sweet, *Chimonanthus praecox*, earns its place in the border – and its name – because of the highly scented flowers which cover its twiggy branches before the leaves come out. Unfortunately it has an uninteresting summer look; but you can soften or enhance it with an annual climber or, better still, a perennial climber which will be cut back hard each winter, thus liberating its host. The *jackmanii* clematis are perfect for this.

Deciduous magnolias can be made even more beautiful in early spring when associated with bulbs. *Magnolia × soulangeana* and the smaller, slower growing *M. stellata*, both lime-tolerant, can have snowdrops, grape hyacinths, chionodoxas or the delicate *Erythronium* 'Pagoda' and *E.* 'White Beauty'.

Another deciduous shrub I treasure is *Ribes sanguineum* 'Brocklebankii', with yellow leaves and pale pink flowers. You can plant a clematis to grow through it, and underplant it with early spring bulbs – *Iris reticulata*, chionodoxas and scillas or muscari. These can all be left to fend for themselves and by May their foliage will have died down.

There is a viburnum worth having for almost every month of the year, and many can be integrated successfully into the border. Ranging in height from 1.5-2m/5-6ft, they are all quite different in character; as well as the evergreen varieties, you are bound to find at least one or two deciduous varieties to fit into your mixed border scheme. *Viburnum farreri (V. fragrans)*, an old favourite, will give you a few flowers for your Christmas bunch and will continue flowering through until March, and so will *V. × bodnantense*. For spring I would choose *V.* 'Anne Russell', with pink buds opening to highly scented white flowers. *V. carlesii* and *V. × carlcephalum* are equally white and fragrant. I love to see them underplanted with white narcissus, which flower at the same time, or with blue scillas.

I associate viburnums with fragrance, but the varieties of *V. opulus*, the British native guelder rose, have another attribute – bunches of translucent autumn berries which follow the white June flowers. To digress: this shrub is now available grown as a standard, and a small walk of them either side of a path would become quite a dramatic feature, both in flower and in berry. For a small garden, *V.o.* 'Compactum' only grows to 90cm/36in and has an attractive dense habit and red fruits (I have seen it used very successfully as a low hedge). For its yellow fruits, choose *V.o.* 'Fructu-Luteo', a taller and more massive shrub.

Philadelphus generally do not have particularly graceful figures at any time of the year – their real strength lies in the flowers. For June flowering, choose *Philadelphus* 'Manteau d'Hermine', which has double white flowers but is not as fragrant as the taller varieties. Surround this with white honesty or low-growing *Erysimum* 'Bowles' Mauve', tradescantia or the snow-white double rose 'Snow Carpet' which grows to only 50cm/18in. With *Philadelphus coronarius* 'Aureus' the bright

yellow leaves are the attraction; I have it growing on the corner of a path, matched on the other side with *Weigela* 'Looymansii Aurea'. Under each are cowslips in profusion each spring, followed by bedding plants which change annually. This year we have *Verbena peruviana* 'Alba'.

The large-flowered lilacs have leaves which are too uninteresting to occupy space in the border – they should be in the shrubbery, where foxgloves and *Hesperis matronalis* could surround them. The syringa species are different. Their leaves are smaller, they are not so tall, and they flower twice in the season, in May and again in September. My choice is *Syringa microphylla* 'Superba', underplanted with dog tooth violets or the Pasque flower, *Pulsatilla vulgaris*.

Luscious herbaceous peonies are among the aristocrats of the June and July border, but their glory is short-lived and in my opinion they should share a special border and special companions – as I describe in the chapter on ground cover and low-maintenance plants. However, the tree peony (*Paeonia delavayi*) hybrids are quite a different matter. The crimson-to-marmalade flowers are small but well scented; they only last for a week or two, but the leaves are dramatic and deeply cut. Do not take off the seed heads, for they will open to reveal wonderful ebony-black and shining seeds. The leaves are best pulled off when they become brown and the tawny brown stems will stand up erect and strong, forming their own vertical pattern all winter. Tree peonies can be companions for any 1-1.2m/3-4ft later-flowering herbaceous plant; their leaves will give the bulk and background green to delphiniums, lupins, phlox and Oriental poppies. The spaces between these different plants can be infilled with even later-flowering penstemons and nicotianas.

Progress and change in one of the mixed borders at Barnsley House from April until July. (A winter and a May view of this border, but viewed from the other end, can be seen on page 92.)

OPPOSITE ABOVE The permanent and dominant feature is the *Juniperus × media* 'Pfitzeriana', its lower side shoots all clipped off to give the effect of a multi-legged table. This gives the opportunity to tuck shade-loving plants underneath.

Effect is achieved with foliage plants which also flower. In the right foreground the chartreuse flowers of *Euphorbia amygdaloides* 'Superba' are neighbours to an interesting assortment of leaves; the large, shiny, leathery bergenia is surrounded by the emerging leaves of *Geranium pratense*, delphiniums and slightly taller oriental poppies. Beyond, the variety of different shapes is made up from spikes of iris leaves, soft, feathery fennel and a few (not enough) tulips. Another strong feature in this border is the

group of tree peonies, *Paeonia delavayi*, on the right; they flower in May but the pretty foliage makes a contribution until October.

OPPOSITE BELOW By the end of May the oriental poppies are coming into full flower, with more buds waiting to unfurl their creased red and black petals. Their glory is short-lived – only two to three weeks – but we must have them, and then they are ruthlessly cut down to the ground to make room for hardy annuals.

BELOW The geraniums are cut down, too, and their new leaves help to support *Penstemon* 'Alice Hindley'. Self-seeded plants of *Campanula persicifolia* are kept near the edge of the border to allow us to dead-head them often and so keep a succession of blooms. By August the stately flower stems of *Acanthus spinosus* will become a central feature; and the progress of the *Sedum* 'Autumn Joy' will culminate in their lovely flat flower heads, so attractive to butterflies.

If you can live with the sharp spines of the berberis – there are, I know, some people who cannot – then this family has several species, evergreen and deciduous, which are a valuable asset in the garden. The flowers and often the berries are another attraction. *Berberis thunbergii atropurpurea* makes an excellent hedging plant, and *B.t.* 'Atropurpurea Nana' can be used either as a carpet surrounding a golden foliage shrub or, maybe better still, round grey *Artemisia* 'Powis Castle' or *Senecio monroi*. I use *B.t.* 'Rose Glow' for its variegated foliage – the young leaves are mottled with silver, pink and bright rose. *Berberis × ottawensis purpurea* has deep maroon-red leaves; as they open in the spring they look wonderful surrounded by pink tulips, the early double *Tulipa* 'Peach Blossom' or the lily-flowered *T.* 'China Pink'. This berberis and the other tall forms make perfect supports for autumn-flowering clematis, such as Texensis clematis 'Duchess of Albany' or Viticella clematis 'Alba Luxurians', and everlasting peas.

Near the berberis we have *Lavatera olbia* 'Barnsley', which flowers continuously from June until frost, together with a dark blue 1.2m/4ft monkshood, *Aconitum carmichaelii* 'Arendsii', flowering in late summer. For continuing interest you could add the equally tall, lavender-violet *A. carmichaelii* 'Kelmscott', which will carry on until October. (I think it is so important to

LEFT Anne Dexter has made the best use of space in her small Oxford garden. *Clematis* 'Madame Julia Correvon' and the mid-season *C.* 'Victoria' are grown behind shrubs and trained to come over them, showing off their flowers to advantage. In the front are *Rosa* × *chinensis* 'Mutabilis' and *Lavatera olbia* 'Barnsley'.

ABOVE At Westwell Manor in Oxfordshire, the superb rose 'Madame Hardy' is planted with the long-spurred *Aquilegia* McKana hybrids – one of the most elegant of the granny's bonnets – making a lovely contrast.

OPPOSITE In a border at Jenkyn Place, a solid mound of red-leaved berberis has a harmonious skirt of dancing spears of *Polygonum affine*.

include enough autumn flowers.) Using the 'Barnsley' lavatera like this so that its quantity of delicate pale pink cups show up among the stronger colours of the aconites and the dark leaves of the berberis helps to focus your attention on a particularly satisfying garden.

I first saw this lavatera in 1985, looking wonderful against the wall of an old Cotswold barn in a friend's garden. She kindly allowed me to take a few cuttings, and the following summer David Barker of Hopley Plants noticed it here and predicted that it would become a best seller – as indeed it has. In spite of its almost fragile appearance it is amazingly obliging and will grow free-standing or against a wall, on any aspect (I have not yet tried it on a north wall or in very acid soil). Pruned quite hard – say to 60cm/24in – in spring, it can reach 1.5-2m/5-6ft by autumn. In fact this is a good way to deal with it in a limited space, for it is a fast grower. If you allow it a free rein and only prune lightly, a

2-year-old bush will easily reach 3m/9ft. Like any quick developer you must make sure it is adequately staked, or after a storm or strong wind you may find branches snapped at the junctions. A word of warning: although it will withstand a certain degree of frost, it may get killed to the ground in extremely hard weather. If that happens, new shoots which appear from the root stock may well flower as *L.o.* 'Rosea', of which it is a sport. It is wise to keep an eye open for any shoots which come up from the root and cut them away if necessary. 'Barnsley' roots very readily, so make sure you take cuttings against a hard winter.

The green- and purple-leaved forms of *Cotinus coggygria* make splendid backing-up border shrubs. By judicious pruning you can use them in different positions, as tall (2.5m/8ft or more), middle-height or front-of-the-border plants. We have pruned our tall specimen with purple leaves so that the stems, which branch out from the ground, are bare to about 1.5m/5ft, and the leaves make a splendid canopy at that height. A dark purple, autumn-flowering clematis grows through the stems, and together they are a feature among David Austin's modern shrub roses, 'Pretty Jessica', 'Wife of Bath' and 'Saint Cecilia'. There will be plenty of space to put in two other autumn-flowering clematis, and I would choose those with paler flowers – Viticella clematis 'Alba Luxurians' or Texensis clematis 'Duchess of Albany', with pink bell-shaped flowers. These two, and the existing clematis, all need hard pruning in the spring. (Never mix spring- and autumn-flowering clematis close together, or you will get into grave difficulties when pruning.) Our middle-height cotinus has green leaves and we have pruned it so that the canopy is only 90cm/36 in high. This rhus smokes wonderfully each summer, and in autumn the leaves turn an attractive yellow. As companions it has a *Lavatera* 'Barnsley' each side, and hostas and *Allium siculum* (correctly *Nectaroscordum s.*) in the front; for spring interest there are scillas and primulas.

One spring, perhaps eight years ago, I put in a rooted cutting of the purple-leaved cotinus at the very front of the border. Each March we prune this to 30cm/12in; for a week or two I worry that I have been too drastic, but so far it has always responded with new leaves that are large, luscious and purple. Its neighbours are the evergreens *Hebe* 'Mrs Winder' and a cistus grown from seed collected in Corfu. This is very similar to *Cistus* 'Silver Pink' but has even greyer foliage, which matches the undersides of the cotinus leaves. Behind is a 1.2m/4ft Japanese maple; when it was given to me, I secretly believed it would turn up its toes, disliking our lime soil. However, it has survived well for seven years and in the autumn the combination of it and the purple rhus is lovely. Mrs Winder's rather deep red stems blend in well too. Another way to use the purple-leaved cotinus is to place it near the dwarf almond, *Prunus tenella* 'Fire Hill' or *P. glandulosa*, and to plant pink lily-flowered *Tulipa* 'Mariette' or the double pale pink *T.* 'Angélique' between them. The leaves of the cotinus will be young and luscious as the tulips and prunus are in flower. The pink *Malva alcea fastigiata* and mauve *Thalictrum aquilegiifolium* will take over from the tulips and be echoed by the very pale pink of *Lavatera* 'Barnsley'.

Two tallish deciduous shrubs which make a worthwhile contribution to the border are kolkwitzia and the deutzias, both of which flower in May and June. *Kolkwitzia amabilis*, the beauty bush, has graceful but quite twiggy branches, each of which becomes covered with a mass of pink, yellow-throated flowers, and by July it takes on a different look with airy seed heads. The pink can be complemented by a tall-growing pink shrub rose – 'Fantin-Latour' or 'Madame Isaac Pereire' – planted beside it, or by a not-too-vigorous climber such as *R.* 'Zéphirine Drouhin',

'Climbing Cécile Brunner' or 'Souvenir de la Malmaison' in its climbing form. The strong branches of the kolkwitzia will support the climbing rose.

Another pink theme for summer is a combination of *Kolkwitzia amabilis* with *Campanula lactiflora* 'Loddon Anna' and pale blue delphiniums. In front of this tallish group – all at their best in June and July – *Artemisia lactiflora* (1m/40in), with delicate cream flowers, would fill the role in August and September, adding the *Aster amellus* 'Pink Zenith' (60cm/24in) and the taller, sturdy *A. novae-angliae* 'Harrington's Pink' (1m/40in). A few white lilies planted between the kolkwitzia and the artemisia would complete the picture. Kolkwitzia flowers on new wood, so you must prune some of its branches each year after flowering to keep a continuity of new growth.

The two deutzias I like best are *Deutzia scabra* 'Pride of Rochester', with double white flowers, and *D.* × *hybrida* 'Magicien', whose pink petals have the added interest of a purple streak and a white edge. It pays to prune the deutzias as soon as they finish flowering, and this will give growing time for new shoots for next year's flowers. The kolkwitzia and both deutzias have attractive, peeling winter bark. For a change from spring bulbs, underplant the shrubs with a circle of *Helleborus foetidus* or *Euphorbia amygdaloides robbiae*. For summer, when these will be past their best, you can have July- and August-flowering perennials in front: astrantia, cimicifuga, eryngium, rudbeckia or *Salvia uliginosa*.

Mount Etna broom, *Genista aetnensis*, may be grown as a tall standard, reaching maybe 3m/10ft. Use it as an element of height in the mixed border, either at the back, or perhaps more dramatically, only 3m/10ft back in a deep border. The foliage is so light it casts very little shade, and the panicles of yellow flowers look like falling fireworks in July. Planted this way and provided you do not crowd in too many solid-looking shrubs round it, you can grow alstroemerias round its trunk, to flower after the broom, or Japanese anemones, or *Crocosmia* 'Solfaterre'. This latter has apricot-yellow flowers and attractive bronze-green leaves, which stand out, erect and important.

Dyer's greenweed, *Genista tinctoria*, makes less of an impact than Mount Etna broom. It is smaller (80-100cm/30-40in) and we have found it difficult to support tidily. It might be best grown through another shrub, perhaps *Garrya elliptica* or a golden privet. With its sprays of yellow flowers, it would look rather dramatic coming through the garrya or privet foliage.

Another successful yellow theme to use in a mixed planting is the variegated snowberry, *Symphoricarpos orbiculatus* 'Foliis Variegatis', together with *Potentilla* 'Elizabeth'. Keep spring bulbs to yellow and white narcissus and white crocus, with cowslips and *Euphorbia polychroma*. In summer the yellow theme may continue and include *Phlomis russeliana*, *Coreopsis verticillata* and *Aconitum lycoctonum*, a very pretty ivory-white flower. At Barnsley *Clematis* 'Madame Edouard André' is planted between the snowberry and the potentilla, and from June to September you will suddenly see dramatic deep red flowers coming through their foliage. The idea of using clematis like this in a border is a variation on John Treasure's theme of having clematis growing prostrate over his heathers. You must choose varieties which hold their faces up, or you will lose their beauty.

A useful small tree for the mixed border is *Gleditsia triacanthos* 'Sunburst'. The leaves are lacy and bright yellow when young. I much prefer it to *Robinia pseudoacacia* 'Frisia': it is more graceful, with a finer leaf, and is a soft instead of a rather aggressive colour. It is a tree which will shoot from the old wood, so you can cut back the branches each spring before the sap starts to rise and thus keep its head narrow so that it does not create too much shade. In a friend's garden I have used four of them in line in a border only 1.5m/5ft deep and they are clipped into spheres on 1.5m/5ft stems.

In my own garden – at the golden end of the long border – we have a gleditsia as a single specimen and have clipped it back so that it is narrow and the branches are in defined tiers. In spring its associates are golden tulips and daffodils and *Helleborus foetidus*. I have tried to keep the colours in harmony through the year, using different tones of yellow with those colours that are com-plementary or opposite in the spectrum – violet/blue to contrast with the yellows, and orange to contrast with the blue. *Spiraea japonica* 'Goldflame' is best in late spring as it is coming into leaf and it then looks lovely with chartreuse green, the colour of the young bracts on *Euphorbia cyparissias*. This spurge has a reputation for being invasive, but I have found it controllable and like it for its needle-fine leaves. There are yellow violas, and the white *Viola cornuta* manages to scramble up and through the spiraea. Wherever we can find a space between the shrubs, perennials and bulbs, we put in cowslips (grown from seed we have saved).

I like to integrate roses into the mixed border. The New English Roses, bred and introduced by David Austin Roses, are ideal, ranging in height from 1-2m/3-6ft. They combine the recurrent flowering qualities and the wide colour range of modern varieties with the characteristic formation of flower and charm of the old roses. With their naturally bushy habit and generosity of flowers, they like to have space round them to show themselves to best advantage, so are best planted round with relatively low or airy growers such as aquilegias, *Stachys byzantina (S. lanata)*, diascia, scabious or low hardy geraniums, lavender or *Helichrysum italicum (H. angustifolium)*. In a small border one rose would be lovely but two or three planted together and allowed to blend make a bolder statement. There is a colour for every situation.

When we were choosing shrubs for late summer, my husband and I re-read an article, dating from 24 July 1949, by Vita Sackville-West. Her lasting influence on our gardens first made itself felt at that time – maybe unconsciously – when she was writing regularly for the Sunday *Observer*. We were all slowly emerging from the effects of war and that down-dragging word 'utility'; vegetable growing and digging for victory were becoming shadows of the past. Vita made us sit up and put new life and new plants into our gardens. We cut out several of her articles (they have now been published as a book), including one which dealt with the 'awkward moment between June and September . . . when the garden is apt to go blank and colourless . . . So we turn to our faithful friends the flowering shrubs; to find very little. Still there are some.'

The three she wrote about that I have always remembered were the trio for 'a blue and silver corner'. *Perovskia atriplicifolia*, Russian sage, makes a soft, cloudy blue effect in August and September. It will be lost, overpowered, if it is too close to strong colours – orange and pillar-box red – but put it beside pale pink or nearing-white and its deeply cut grey leaves and blue flowers will attract your attention. It is a good choice to flank each side of stone steps, and may be mixed between an almost white hardy fuchsia. You could sow seeds of love-in-the-mist, nigella, in the autumn between the perovskia, and these will show through and

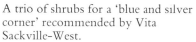

A trio of shrubs for a 'blue and silver corner' recommended by Vita Sackville-West.

ABOVE LEFT *Perovskia* 'Blue Spire' is a sun lover with grey-green, aromatic, deeply cut leaves. Given a well-drained place it will become a blue cloud in late summer. Here it is complemented by a pouffe of pale blue *Viola cornuta*, a good colour to echo the perovskia's pale grey stems.

ABOVE RIGHT The low arching branches of *Caryopteris* × *clandonensis* form a tidy rounded bush with scented grey-green leaves. I feel it is an essential low shrub for the border, especially as it flowers late in the year, in September and October. The form *C.* × *c.* 'Kew Blue' in this picture is a darker blue. *C.* × *c.* 'Heavenly Blue' has deeper blue flowers and a more compact habit.

RIGHT *Ceratostigma willmottianum* is a valuable, showy and reliable shrub for the autumn border. The rather wiry stems usually die to the ground except in very mild places. Use this in association with grey santolina, *Artemisia* 'Powis Castle', or if you have a special autumn border then it combines well with hardy fuchsias. The border could have massed bulbs for spring.

My own star turn for August and September is the combination of *Teucrium chamaedrys* echoing the deep purple of *Buddleja davidii* 'Dartmoor', with its huge complex panicles of flowers hanging gracefully in a real weeping habit right from the base. It is far more elegant than the usual *B.davidii*.

**Evergreen and grey plants for the front of the border**

It is just as important in both summer and winter to have an intermittent spine of evergreen or grey plants along the front as it is to have a good framework of trees and shrubs at the back and middle of a border. As well as the low-growing evergreen 'edging' shrubs like the hebes or helianthemums, I like plants with exciting leaves such as epimediums, euphorbias and bergenias.

Among my top favourites for spring are the various pulmonarias or lungworts, often in flower from very early in the year. They like summer shade and are at their best at the edge of woodland, but I love them in my borders. They can stand on their own and must be near the front so you can fully enjoy the flowers. Best of all is *Pulmonaria angustifolia azurea*, a lovely bright blue. There are several distinctive varieties: *P. vallarsae* 'Margery Fish' has mottled green and silver foliage and pink and blue flowers. *P. saccharata argentea* has outstanding silvery leaves.

The leaves of epimediums are important, too, and it is essential, in order to get the full beauty of leaf and flower, that you harden your heart and cut down the old leaves one February day before the flower stems push through. If you fail to do this, the flowers will be hidden and when the new young leaves come through they will be swamped by last year's rather elderly foliage. Each leaf is heart-shaped, prettily patterned with pale green veins between rust red. For flowers you have a choice of yellow, gentle orange, rose pink or even red, but in my experience the yellow-flowered *Epimedium perralderianum* establishes best, although it does need some shade and a rich soil.

Companions for the epimediums will vary according to the colour you choose: daffodils with two shades to reflect the yellow flowers of the epimediums and the bronze tints of their leaves, or blue muscari to contrast with the orange-flowered *E. × warleyense*. I have them beside *Hosta fortunei* 'Aureo marginata' and early narcissus. The hosta and epimedium leaves are an especially effective combination later in summer. Another thought is to surround epimediums with soft-coloured wallflowers in shades of cream, yellow and orange.

I have *Epimedium × versicolor* 'Sulphureum', which carries its green and bronze leaves on wiry stems, beside a dark green prostrate *Picea abies* 'Nidiformis' with *Dicentra formosa* 'Stuart Boothman' growing around them. There is not a day in the year when this completely trouble-free combination is not beautiful.

flower next May, in fact soon after you have given the perovskia its annual spring clip. The second shrub recommended by Vita is *Caryopteris × clandonensis*, a grey-leaved shrub with powdery blue flowers, which must be cut back severely in spring. Put this at a corner of your border and surround it with annual *Convolvulus minor* to flower through June and July. The third was *Ceratostigma willmottianum*, a beautiful plant giving a fine display of true Prussian blue flowers for several weeks in the autumn; later the leaves turn a brilliant crimson. We have tucked it in under *Berberis dictyophylla*, a 2m/6ft barberry with grey undersides to its leaves. These turn a deep red before they fall, so keep pace with the ceratostigma in autumn. By now the everlasting pea, *Lathyrus latifolius*, which we have growing through the berberis, will have finished flowering. A nearby clump of lilies-of-the-valley has spread itself and now shares the ground with the berberis, the pea and the ceratostigma, so from mid-spring right through until late autumn this patch has colour and interest.

After a mild winter *Euphorbia amygdaloides* 'Superba', an ever-green herbaceous plant which the great plantswoman Nancy Lindsay gave me twenty-five years ago, looks wonderful in a border with its lime-green flowers on strong 50cm/20in stems. It may become invasive when the winter weather favours it, but will get severely cut back by heavy and lasting frosts. I have it in association with a very fine form of *Lunaria annua*, which has an exceptionally dark purple flower. These two colours, chartreuse yellow and deep purple, are spectacular together – the flowers of the euphorbia also match to perfection the sharp pale green of the opening leaves on the lime trees.

Grey foliage goes well with most colours, and in the grey leaves of santolina, lavender and grey sage alone, you have a variety of leaf size, colour and texture as well as of form. In spring and all through the summer the grey *Santolina chamaecyparissus (S. incana)* and *S. pinnata neapolitana* and the green *S. rosmarinifolia (S. virens)* contrast well first with the bulbs and then with the spikes of herbaceous plants. They are best clipped hard back in spring, which gives you the advantage of their shape and leaves all winter.

Santolina has many uses. Three, five or nine planted in a phalanx, the number depending on the size of your border, make a bold statement, like a batch of buns. Or use them in a stream, alternating with a contrasting low shrub or with herbaceous plants; this will give the border a rhythm by the repetition of a theme. Colours will depend on your basic scheme, the greys either complementing pale yellows, golds, purples and blues, or alternatively keeping to white, pinks and shades which harmonize with pink. The important point is the repetition of basic plants.

There are some flowers which I think actually require an element of grey to quieten them and if necessary you must add the grey leaves yourself. For example, the very vivid *Aster novae-angliae* 'Andenken an Alma Pötschke' must have the right neighbour – her colour is so vibrant that a flower of equal impact blooming at the same time would be almost impossible to take. A hollyhock seeded itself among our asters, and when this flowered it turned out to be an extremely pale primrose yellow. To my surprise it looked wonderful with the magenta-red of 'Alma Pötschke'. (I have tried *Salvia patens*, with remarkable rich blue flowers, but unfortunately this combination does not work, as the salvia flowers open in succession and in insufficient quantity at any one moment to stand up to the aster.)

The solution I have decided on is that this very vivid colour should be surrounded by, or at least have a front skirt of, grey. This could be a shrub such as santolina or *Artemisia* 'Powis Castle'. Both require hard pruning in spring to maintain their

shape. If you want to keep to herbaceous plants, then my choice would be *Artemisia ludoviciana*: this has leaves of a very soft grey and insignificant flowers, best cut off while they are still in bud. Whatever your chosen plant, it must be at least 50cm/20in tall, in order to hide the aster's untidy legs. (One of my particular dislikes is seeing stems of tall perennials covered with withering leaves.)

There are several hebes with grey leaves. My favourite for emphasizing a curve or a corner is *Hebe topiaria*, which has a wonderful rounded habit, looking exactly as though it has been neatly clipped. The grey leaves are packed tightly together, making it into a fine sphere. It is a splendid, satisfactory low edging shrub, not more than 30cm/12in high. Use it in lines each side of a corner to frame it or make a circle of seven, putting one in the centre and six evenly spaced round it. We find it neater in habit than *H. pinguifolia* 'Pagei', with its laxer, more spreading habit, but this also has its special uses: planted three or five in a triangle it will make a low grey block at the edge of the border; or it may be used on its own in a narrow ribbon bed, creating a grey pool. With grey I like primrose and soft lemon yellow, for instance *Achillea* 'Moonshine' – this has silver foliage anyway – *Kniphofia* 'Sunningdale Yellow' and *Oenothera biennis*.

The rounded evergreen clumps formed by rock roses are also good for the front of the border. Some make much tighter clumps than others; our favourite is one we call *Helianthemum* 'Cherry Red' – not only are the flowers spectacular but when they are over the whole plant makes a firm pincushion. Helianthemums range in colour from white through cream, primrose and orange to red; there are no blues or mauves. The double flowers (too full to close) have the advantage of remaining open in the evening. We have the yellow and pink forms, and I do not think they need companions – they are best on their own. I learnt the lesson many years ago of growing them in profusion, especially as they come into flower at a time of year, just before the roses, when there is not much other colour in the border.

Mounded effects can also be achieved with low spiraeas. They are not evergreen but their dense wiry stems give a feeling of solidity. I grow *Spiraea japonica* 'Little Princess' (50cm/20in), with rose-crimson flowers at their best in June. It is surrounded by *Allium cernuum*, now increasing and always reliable. *Spiraea nipponica* 'Snowmound' is nearby and the pure white flowers have *Erigeron* 'Four Winds' as neighbours. The erigeron is very low – only 20cm/8in – and creates an almost unbroken carpet of starry mauve flowers in May.

Spiraeas are easy to find companions for. We have *Salvia nemorosa* 'East Friesland', with vivid violet-purple spikes in June and July; as the flowers drop, the paler, rather papery bracts remain. A mass planting of the dark-leaved *Penstemon* 'Rich Ruby' creates a good background for the spiraeas, flowering from July onwards. The dark colours could well be sombre, so to lighten the effect there is grey *Artemisia canescens*, astrantia with a pale flower, and white annuals.

For the yellow, orange, red border you should choose the popular *Spiraea japonica* 'Goldflame'. The leaves, gold and green and red and always striking, are freshest in spring; later in the year, although the shrub is not tired, it no longer makes quite such an impact. Maybe I should not be greedy, expecting a single plant to do too much for me for too many months, and should use my own imagination to bring out its quality later. This spiraea enjoys sunshine and is lovely in spring with cowslips, yellow and blue violas, the acid yellow of *Euphorbia cyparissias* and *E. polychroma*. By August it starts to produce crimson flowers – if you do not like these with the yellow-green leaves, then snip them off. If you do like them, you should choose a flower of comparable colour to make a strong impact: *Monarda* 'Cambridge Scarlet' or *Phlox* 'July Glow' will both flower at the same time, and so will *Sedum* 'Sunset Cloud'. The subtlety of the succulent purplish sedum leaves would look well with the spiraea, in colour, size and contrast. A point in favour of all these spiraeas is their quality of solidly covering the ground. In fact, apart from their annual clipping, the area they occupy takes care of itself – no weeding is needed.

Some low shrubs, rather than making mounds in the border, are essentially 'edging plants'. Wall germander, *Teucrium chamaedrys*, is brilliant as a narrow ribbon all through the year and in August can be spectacular when the purple flowers open – for two weeks or more it is completely taken over by the local bee population. Used in a drift or a block in the border, it should have spring bulbs (at least 30cm/12in tall) planted through it to give an extra season of interest. As often happens with low subshrubs, it will become leggy and lose its firm shape unless you give it a clipping in spring.

## Perennial fillers

In the mixed border perennials are essential to link and infill between your chosen shrubs. They are especially useful to give a feeling of fullness while the shrubs are maturing. Some of your shrubs will flower in winter and spring, but the perennials will mostly flower in summer and autumn, so the picture will have variety and colour throughout the year. You will find other ideas about perennials in the chapter on herbaceous borders, and you can select those that harmonize with the colour scheme in your mixed border. Here is a selection of my own thoughts.

Penstemons are wonderful infillers, flowering over several weeks. Put *Penstemon* 'Sour Grapes' close beside dwarf 'Munstead' lavender: the colours of the flowers blend beautifully, and in winter the lavender will give slight protection for the penstemon. One of the best is *P.* 'Garnet', with wine-red flowers which are good companions for June-flowering bearded iris. The penstemons will follow on from the iris, whose strap-like leaves are a contrast in texture to the softer penstemon foliage. Another eye-catcher is *P.* 'Alice Hindley', with very delicate mauve and white flowers, a perfect foil and blend for *Erysimum* 'Bowles' Mauve'. We have put angel's fishing rods, *Dierama pulcherrimum*, right through them, knowing that these dislike root disturbance. (They should not be moved, nor should their leaves be cut down in winter.) They will then flower gracefully, bending over the wallflowers, and also over two *Hebe rakaiensis* nearby. These are all evergreen, though we will cut the penstemon down to their basal growth in spring. They will all help protect each other during frosty weather.

# A mixed border in mid-summer

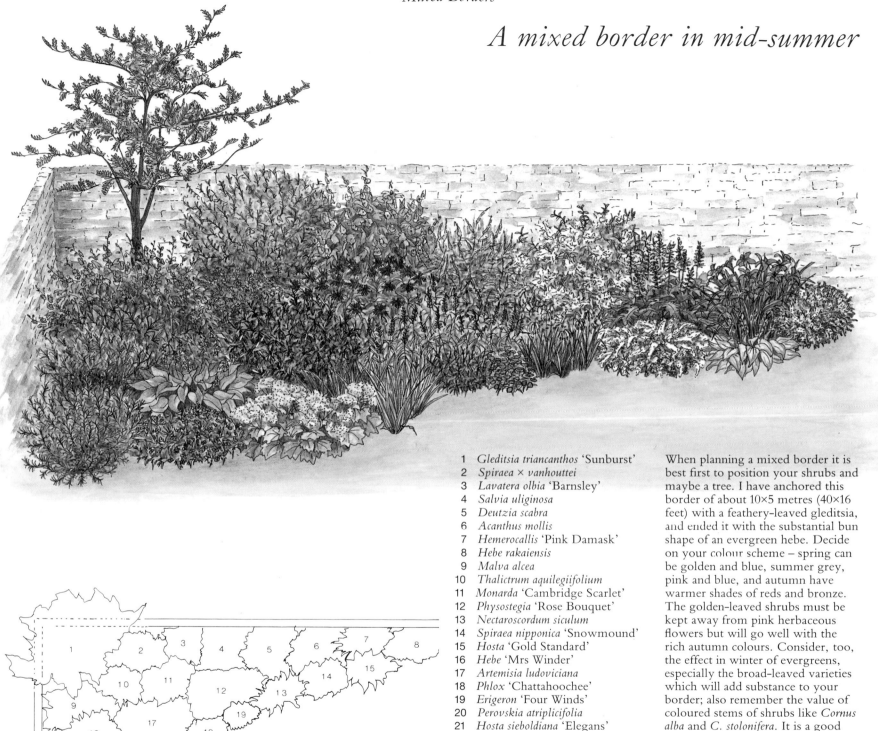

1  Gleditsia triacanthos 'Sunburst'
2  Spiraea × vanhouttei
3  Lavatera olbia 'Barnsley'
4  Salvia uliginosa
5  Deutzia scabra
6  Acanthus mollis
7  Hemerocallis 'Pink Damask'
8  Hebe rakaiensis
9  Malva alcea
10  Thalictrum aquilegiifolium
11  Monarda 'Cambridge Scarlet'
12  Physostegia 'Rose Bouquet'
13  Nectaroscordum siculum
14  Spiraea nipponica 'Snowmound'
15  Hosta 'Gold Standard'
16  Hebe 'Mrs Winder'
17  Artemisia ludoviciana
18  Phlox 'Chattahoochee'
19  Erigeron 'Four Winds'
20  Perovskia atriplicifolia
21  Hosta sieboldiana 'Elegans'
22  Iris foetidissima 'Variegata'
23  Rosmarinus officinalis
24  Geranium endressii
25  Alchemilla mollis

When planning a mixed border it is best first to position your shrubs and maybe a tree. I have anchored this border of about 10×5 metres (40×16 feet) with a feathery-leaved gleditsia, and ended it with the substantial bun shape of an evergreen hebe. Decide on your colour scheme – spring can be golden and blue, summer grey, pink and blue, and autumn have warmer shades of reds and bronze. The golden-leaved shrubs must be kept away from pink herbaceous flowers but will go well with the rich autumn colours. Consider, too, the effect in winter of evergreens, especially the broad-leaved varieties which will add substance to your border; also remember the value of coloured stems of shrubs like Cornus alba and C. stolonifera. It is a good idea to give your border an edging of low plants, including those which keep their foliage in winter – Hebe topiaria and Parahebe lyallii or saxifrage, especially 'London pride', and it is always worth tucking in plenty of hellebores.

Penstemons flower on straight, erect stems, so a rounded plant helps to contrast with their vertical structure – epimediums and hostas on one side for their leaves, and *Spiraea* 'Little Princess' on the other for its flowers. The clear pink flowers of *Centurea hypoleuca* 'John Coutts' would complement the rather narrow-leaved *P.* 'Evelyn' and the taller *P.* 'Pennington Gem'.

The evergreen perennial wallflowers have a long flowering period in spring; the only time they fail is after an exceptionally hard winter. My favourite is the well-known *Erysimum* 'Bowles' Mauve', which in its second or third year will be 60cm/24in tall and as much across. They are a good shape and their grey-green leaves and mauve flowers go well with most spring bulbs, but keep scarlet tulips away. Later in the year nearby colour will have to be supplied by herbaceous flowers which complement the wallflower leaves and thrive in full sun. My suggestions are agapanthus, dierama, hardy fuchsias, anemone hybrids, or perhaps a selection of hostas with grey leaves.

As the wallflowers can become leggy and also appreciate protection from wind and frost, a 60-90cm/24-36in shrub on the windy side of them might help. Thoughts are *Teucrium cha-*

*maedrys, Hebe rakaiensis*, cistus, skimmia or *Viburnum opulus* 'Compactum'. I also recommend as a neighbour the slightly taller *Dicentra formosa alba*; according to the specialist nurseryman John Coke, it is an altogether easier plant than *D. spectabilis alba*, flowers for longer and makes a lush spreading clump of bright apple-green leaves.

I love all these bleeding hearts for their foliage as well as their flowers. We wonder why some flowers hang their heads; dicentras hang their whole person. Pick a flower, turn it upside down, and as you carefully open it with both hands you will be entranced by the bride in the bath. She can vary from the bright red *D.* 'Luxuriant' (30cm/12in) to the pink *D. eximia* and finally the ivory-white forms mentioned earlier. The very fleshiness of their stems and leaves tells you that they will do best in a deep rich soil, so add plenty of organic material, compost or manure when you plant them.

Aquilegias, like the dicentras, have the advantage of flowering at a time when the bulbs and spring plants are over and there is little else in bloom. You can never have too many aquilegias. They are beautiful in flower and leaf, with their rosettes of tri-

foliate leaves at ground level below the 60cm/24in flower stems. They will seed themselves and their colours will always fit into the blue-mauve spectrum, so you need never worry that their presence will be jarring. It is a wise policy to save their seed and either sow it down in lines in your seed bed as soon as it ripens, or keep the seed until the spring and sow it in a seed tray indoors.

Goat's rue, *Galega officinalis*, especially in selected forms of *G.* × *hartlandii*, is well worth searching for. At one time it was one of the mainstays of the herbaceous border, but now it has become less common in gardens. I am surprised how many and how often people enquire its name (if they can't find the label). Surprising, as it has so many good qualities: a bushy plant with pretty grey-green pinnate leaves, and masses of small pea flowers in racemes in white and shades of blue-to-purple (*G.* × *h.* 'Lady Wilson' is mauvy-pink). After flowering, the seed heads turn green to dark brown.

Good companions for this galega are *Thalictrum aquilegiifolium* (1.2mcm/4ft) with *Monarda* 'Prairie Night' (90cm/36in) in front to give colour through to August, when the seed heads are attractive. A clump of astrantia in any of its varieties would complete the group. With enough space behind all these I would like to add *Aruncus dioicus* 'Glasnevin' for its erect creamy-white plumes and handsome foliage. Another bonus is that aruncus never need to be staked.

There are some plants which my garden visitors inevitably ask for in the nursery – *Euphorbia griffithii* 'Fireglow' especially. The loose heads of the small flowers are conspicuous for their bright orange-red bracts. The intensity of this colour makes it important to choose the right companions. The deep orange flowers of *Helianthemum* 'Henfield Brilliant', opening in June, if used in a semi-circle round the front, would mirror the euphorbia's brightness. Round the back, the orange-flame flowers of *Gaillardia* 'Mandarin' would have the same effect. Although the euphorbia's bracts will be fading slightly by July, there is still a hint of the colour in the midribs of the leaves. Later in the sum-mer its immediate neighbours might be some of the border phlox which come into flower in July: *Phlox paniculata* 'Prince of Orange' almost matches the euphorbia in colour; I would also use *P.p.* 'White Admiral', a variety I have found very reliable and long lived. *Artemisia splendens* or *A. stelleriana*, planted to make dense summer carpets, would be effective at the front of this combination, since grey is a wonderful standby and it can be a background to every colour, including green.

In late spring, the points of hosta leaves will be spiking through and then uncurling; like the aquilegias, they will cover over the ground where spring bulbs have finished. Hosta leaves are wonderful and can be a foil to almost every plant in the garden. They are spectacular in a mass in the distance and as a single plant.

Most of the beauty of the leaves comes from the perfect way they present themselves, with their undulating edges and ribbed and crimpled surface. They look imposing in groups, but you may have a temptation to make a medley of every kind and this would not look right – bold leaves need bold groups. If you want to grow as many varieties as you can find, then space them out in

# *A group of alpines in early summer*

1 *Uncinia clavata*
2 *Geranium sessiliflorum novae-zelandiae nigricans*
3 *Anthemis marschalliana*
4 *Milium effusum aureum*
5 *Saxifraga × urbium*
6 *Arabis ferdinandi-coburgii*
7 *Ophiopogon planiscapus nigrescens*
8 *Ajuga reptans* 'Burgundy Glow'

Even without a special alpine bed, many low growing perennials, which by the purist would be regarded as rock garden plants, can be incorporated into the front of your mixed border. Group them carefully so they do not become swamped by taller, more aggressive perennials, and make sure they have well drained soil.

---

your borders, limiting them to not more than three varieties together, and do not mix different variegated leaves together, nor the blue-grey with the plain green. Green- and yellow-leaved hostas are best matched with golden-variegated forms, grey-leaved hostas with those that have silver variegation. Being shade-lovers, the natural home for hostas is under deciduous and airy trees, where the canopy is not too heavy, allowing in rain and sunshine.

Hostas and ferns are good companions: dark green hart's tongue fern associates well with grey hostas in colour, shape and mass; and the texture of the soft shield fern, *Polystichum setiferum*, has a delicate lacy look which contrasts appropriately with *Hosta ventricosa* 'Aureo-marginata'. The fronds of the ostrich feather fern, *Matteuccia struthiopteris*, 60cm/24in tall, upright and bright green, contrast and associate well with *H.* 'Honeybells'.

## Carpeters and clump-forming plants

We all have our own individual way of gardening. My failing is my neglect of a special alpine bed, which means that low evergreen alpine and herbaceous plants have to be incorporated into the front of my mixed borders. In fact there are many alpines which, with the right neighbours, can play a small but essential part in mixed plantings.

Of the many saxifrages, those with large rosettes – London pride (*Saxifraga × urbium* and *S. × u.* 'Aureopunctata') – are especially good for the front of the border. Suddenly in early summer you notice the delicate pale pink/white flowers opening above the leathery rosettes. Both varieties make a superb impenetrable carpet and will cover the ground under a taller plant. I tried putting crocus to grow through them, but even they have had difficulty in penetrating.

To continue the evergreen theme, we have a patch of *Arabis ferdinandi-coburgii* 'Variegata' on one side of the saxifrage and *Anthemis marschalliana (A. rudolphiana)* on the other. The arabis has white spring flowers, and the leaves have the added charm of taking on purplish overtones in winter. The anthemis has finely cut grey foliage and bright yellow daisy flowers. Try planting a patch of *Ajuga reptans* 'Burgundy Glow' beside the arabis; its leaves are strikingly edged with cream and centred with rose and magenta, the blue flower spikes about 30cm/12in tall. A good little plant to offset the grey filigree leaves of the anthemis would be the unusual *Geranium sessiliflorum novae-zelandiae nigricans*, with small round brown leaves (sometimes you will find one which is bright orange).

I would like to use some clumps of low grasses behind or between these evergreen plants; they would contrast well in leaf

Low-growing plants for the front of the border.

FAR LEFT The variegated grass *Holcus mollis* 'Albovariegatus' pushes through the carpet of ajuga at Denmans. The blue flowers in May make a striking tonal contrast with the shining new leaves of the grass. Both will tolerate shade.

LEFT The hardy *Geranium sanguineum striatum (G.s. lancastrense)* is closely planted with *Campanula portenschlagiana*. Grey foliage of artemisia in the background sets them off.

and line. *Uncinia clavata* is a New Zealand sedge with yellow leaves and almost black flowers, and this would complement the geranium. Bowles' golden grass, *Milium effusum aureum*, might look well behind the London pride, and *Ophiopogon planiscapus nigrescens* would be a good backing for the ajuga.

Do not neglect the range of low erysimums. *Erysimum* 'Moonlight', only 25cm/10in tall, is a lovely soft yellow in May and June. *E.* 'Wenlock Beauty', 30cm/12in tall, flowers with an amazing combination of yellow and bronze. *E.* 'Constant Cheer' has an even greater colour variety, including violet-mauve and a tinge of amber.

The alpine phlox are mostly mat-forming, exceptionally free-flowering, trouble-free and long-lived. The *Phlox douglasii* species grow to only 10cm/4in and the *P. subulata* species to 15cm/6in. They are most suitable for the rock garden, revelling in sunshine and good drainage, but if you have no rock garden then use them in the front of your mixed border, blending their white, pink, purple or crimson flowers with your chosen colour scheme. They flower for two months, the *subulata* starting in April and the *douglasii* in May, so you can have a show of colour for three whole months. Less spectacular but always appealing are the front-of-the-border *Phlox* 'Chattahoochee'. The flowers are carried on wiry stems about 30cm/12in high and create a cloud of blue.

*Campanula carpatica* is another dwarf carpeter and its large, saucer-shaped flowers come out all summer. Combine these with the alpine phlox and mix groups of the low-growing *Erysimum* 'Constant Cheer', whose very eye-catching plum/purple and brown flowers will go well with the colours of the phlox.

If your border is long enough to continue a fringe of very low alpine perennials, then add the white *Epilobium glabellum*, which flowers throughout the summer. Leave the flower stems on and by October the whole plant – seed heads, stems and leaves – will have turned from green and white to a rich bronzy-red. Unlike its relation the wild epilobium, it does not self-sow, and so will not become invasive. Another charmer to include in this group, or rather chain, of edging plants is the summer-flowering *Erigeron* 'Four Winds'.

Polygonums are carpet-formers and best low varieties are *Polygonum affine* 'Darjeeling Red' (25cm/10in) with deep pink spikes, and *P.a.* 'Dimity' (15cm/6in) with paler pink pokers. The leaves of both turn a good crimson colour in autumn.

Almost in the same category as polygonums, as both make wonderful ground cover, are the prunellas and ajugas. They do well in shade, so you can use them right up to and under shrubs such as hebes, *Senecio* (now *Brachyglottis*) 'Sunshine', spiraeas and potentillas. The flowers of prunellas, or self-heal, grow on spikes up to 20-30cm/8-12in high, blooming in early summer. *Prunella webbiana* in its various colours – white, pale violet and pink – will continue until September. The leaves of *Ajuga reptans* in its three forms, 'Atropurpurea', 'Multicolour' ('Rainbow') and 'Variegata', are pretty even without their flowers, but do not allow them to dry out; they appreciate a wet rather than a dry summer. You can plant *Iris reticulata* to grow through all of these for a bonus in February.

I like the hardy geranium family for their long-flowering quality and their often attractive leaves. There are several front-of-the-border species – my favourites for this situation are *Geranium renardii* (30cm/12in), lovely in flower and foliage. The sage-green leaves are deeply scalloped and quilted, offsetting the May and

LEFT A narrow sunny border at Castle Ashby has been planted for lots of autumn interest, using the soft colours of *Sedum* 'Ruby Glow', the annual *Cleome hassleriana*, verbena and heliotrope. *Vitis vinifera* 'Purpurea' is climbing the south-west-facing wall.

OPPOSITE Hot colours predominate in this terrace border at Powis Castle. The long hips of *Rosa* × *highdownensis* hang in profusion with matching *Crocosmia* 'Carmin Brillant'. Add blue to the red hips and you will have the colour of the flowers of *Clematis viticella* 'Purpurea Plena Elegans' which is growing on the wall behind. Green is as important as the reds and is in contrast, keeping the whole picture together.

June flowers, white with a purplish eye and grey veins. The bloody cranesbill, *G. sanguineum* (25cm/10in), is another useful hardy plant. The leaves are deeply divided, strong green all the summer and often taking on remarkably effective autumn tints. They will make hummocks, solid and wide, and genuinely earn their keep, each established plant covering a 60cm/24in radius and bearing many striking magenta flowers. They do not bloom in such a mass as the alpine phlox but continue all through the summer and then develop the stiff-spiked seed heads from which the plant gets its common name, cranesbill. My original planting was of *G.s.* 'Glenluce' with a clear pink flower and *G.s. striatum* (*G.s. lancastriense*), a light pink with crimson veins. Innumerable seedlings have appeared, all with a slightly different but alluring character and colour.

The very low erodiums, or heronsbills, are more suitable for the rock garden or between paving on the patio, but *Erodium manescavi* (55cm/22in) will hold its own in the border in July and August. It has dense feathery leaves and lilac-pink flowers and a deep blotch on the upper two of its five petals.

To add a little permanent height and shape in between these low mat-forming perennials, a few small shrubs or sub-shrubs would give a rhythm to the planting. *Hebe topiaria* is ideal for this, and so is *Euonymus japonicus* 'Microphyllus Variegatus', which may need a slight clipping to keep it neat and firm. These dwarf shrubs will come into their own in winter, when they stand up above the green mats of the alpine perennial leaves, lending interest and structure to the border edge.

A border is forever changing through the year: bulbs appear and disappear within a matter of weeks; perennials grow up – sometimes to as much as 2m/6ft – and die down again between spring and autumn; even the shrubs, which provide a permanent framework, change their outlines. I have suggested a number of ways in which you could combine plants from season to season within a border. Other combinations and suggestions are given in other chapters, especially those on colour, but in the end a border will be your own selection of ideas, and will depend upon your soil, your climate and your own personal taste. Do always jot down in a gardening notebook any especially striking plant associations that impress you, and do not allow yourself to be intimidated by imagining that a plan would be too complicated to realize or that a planting scheme would take too long to mature.

# Ground Cover and Low-Maintenance Plants

In her garden at Winslow, Mrs Tonge makes use of every space. Ivy in variety and lamium have been planted between the steps, and other plants are allowed to self-seed, changing a formal stairway into a relaxed, luxuriant effect. The only maintenance needed is to clip the plants back occasionally – especially the lamium – to keep the treads reasonably clear. At Hidcote steps are treated in a similar way, with cotoneaster clipped and trained along the risers, and I have also seen box used like this.

Walk round your garden and notice those areas which have had little time spent on them; they may be occupied by ground cover or low-maintenance plants. There will be flat ribbons or pools of low evergreens – obvious plants like ajuga and lamium – used at the edge of the border, under shrubs and trees, under the overhang of a hedge or at the base of a wall; or plants like heathers or prostrate junipers which need little attention. Both ground cover and low-maintenance plants are very wide subjects. To a certain extent they overlap, but there are subtle differences between the two: ground-cover plants are low-maintenance in that the area of soil that they cover requires scant attention and very little weeding, whereas with a low-maintenance plant, it is the plant itself which is trouble free and demands little attention.

The expression 'ground cover' will probably bring to your mind plants such as periwinkles and monochrome ivies, which simply serve the purpose of keeping large areas of ground green at all times of the year, but there is a range of more exciting plants to choose from, many of which provide flowers as well as interesting foliage. Taller shrubs and trees with ground-hugging branches qualify as ground cover too.

Low-maintenance plants I think of more as individuals like hellebores, or perennials which do not need dividing, are long-lived and occupy their allotted space in the border for many years. These include herbaceous peonies, hostas, Japanese anemones, day lilies, ophiopogon, liriope, astilbes, crocosmias, sedums, acanthus, dictamnus, all of which dislike disturbance; they require time to settle, and for years will increase and spread slowly with minimum attention. You can use them together or plant them through your border, interspersed with short-lived plants or those which, like Michaelmas daisies and monardas, are better divided at least every other year. Whichever system I adopt when planning my planting, I try to have enough bulbs – tulips, daffodils, crocus – to infill between the herbaceous plants. In addition, there is the option of a bed planted with a colourful mixture of easily-maintained shrubs – the traditional 'shrubbery' – where the area as well as the plants requires very little attention.

**Ground cover**

The great virtue of ground-cover plants is that they will take care of themselves, without digging or dividing, not only season by season but also over several years. If initially they are planted in clean ground, this should solve the weeding problem, for annual re-seeding will be inhibited by the vigorous spread of the ground cover. A yearly tidy will improve the look, but even this may not be essential.

Grass, of course, is the quintessential ground cover – but one which requires plenty of attention. A burning question is whether to have or not to have a lawn, and if not, what could be a reasonable substitute. Grass has great ecological benefits. According to the 1948 United States Department of Agriculture Year Book, it is unparalleled in its ability to convert carbon dioxide into oxygen, thereby improving the air we breathe.

Some ground-cover plants lack horticultural interest and, used unimaginatively, may give away the fact that the owner has called in a contractor to do his planting for him. But used with skill and imagination, they can be as versatile and eye-catching as any shrub or perennial and there are always associates to add interest at different seasons. The ajugas and lamiums, for instance,

keep their main rosettes of leaves in winter, sending out longer arms and flowering shoots in spring and summer. The early bulbs are good companions for them: chionodoxas, scillas, *Iris reticulata, Anemone nemorosa* and puschkinias which come through from February to April. Used with discretion, lamiums can be some of the most useful and adaptable garden plants. Their leaves are small and attractive, their flowers vary in colour from white to darkish pink, and, provided you keep them clipped back after they have flowered, they will remain discreet.

The obvious places for ground cover are difficult areas – dry and sunless, under trees or at the foot of a north-facing wall. A bank can be very dry too, either south-facing and sun-baked or north-facing and shaded for much of the day.

After every visit to Powis Castle I have always taken home with me pictures of good planting. An early visit gave me the idea of underplanting the trunks of trees: the apple trees, set in lawn, have generous circles round them, each with its own colour theme. There is rue, golden marjoram, lamium, *Ophiopogon planiscapus nigrescens* and *Stachys byzantina (S. lanata)*.

The ground under a northerly-facing wall or hedge can be extremely dry, as well as shady, so you will have to choose your plants carefully. If it is a hedge, you will be limited to anything which can tolerate the competition from the hedge roots, for these will be taking a lot of moisture. Keep the ground cover disciplined to its place at the foot so that it does not interfere with the hedge's growth or clipping. A simple effect is best and I would use a single ribbon of the same plant in a contrasting colour to the hedge. Under a dark evergreen such as *Thuja plicata* or yew, try an ivy with golden or grey markings – *Hedera helix* 'Goldheart' or *H.h.* 'Adam'. Although the grey will not look as bright as the gold, it will keep its colour better in the shade. The only attention ivy needs is an occasional cutting with secateurs (at the same time removing dead leaves), to stop long arms from encroaching on the hedge foliage, and a firm tidy with clippers in the spring, which will encourage it to make a good thick carpet. In winter

LEFT ABOVE The golden ivy *Hedera helix* 'Buttercup' covers the ground around and climbs up an ornamental cherry, *Prunus serrula*, at Crathes Castle in Scotland. The colour of the ivy leaves and the cherry bark is in strong contrast. This makes a good year-round picture as the ivy is, of course, evergreen and the shiny cherry bark looks superb in the winter.

LEFT BELOW In the old vegetable garden at Powis Castle the venerable apple trees, still pruned well into shape, have been underplanted effectively with ground cover to make eye-catching foliage displays. The fruit trees line the main gravel path; this apple tree has a carpet of *Origanum vulgare* 'Aureum' surrounding it, the golden apples matching the origanum foliage. Other apples have grey stachys or silvery lamium at their feet.

the leaves can be very useful for smaller flower arrangements.

Under my north-west-facing yew hedge many years ago I planted twenty-five corms of *Cyclamen hederifolium* at 30cm/12in intervals. They are now a joy in August and right through until early October, the alluring scented flowers pushing their way through before the leaves appear. They scatter their seeds around generously, and now each spring we look out for the young seedlings which come through both around the parent plants and also in the adjacent lawn, often as much as three metres/yards away. We dig these seedlings carefully and put them into seed trays, which then stand in a shady place. The leaves die down in the trays, but by late autumn they will have made new foliage and the corms grown to the diameter of a one penny piece – large enough to be handled and planted in their final positions. They should send up a flower or two the following autumn. When finally you have cyclamen in all the places you want, you can leave them to increase on their own and create a wonderful carpet – a very sound reason for not moving house!

For a hedge or wall where the plants will be in the sun most of the day but where the ground – unless irrigated – will be extremely dry, your choice must be tough plants which will thrive in dry conditions. *Alchemilla mollis, Galium odoratum (Asperula odorata), Vinca minor, Campanula poscharskyana* and *C. portenschlagiana (C. muralis)* will cover the ground for you and all have attractive foliage and seasonal flowers.

In this sunny position you can have golden foliage plants which, in the shade, would often revert to green. One suggestion would be *Mentha × gentilis* 'Aurea' (ginger mint), a truly invasive plant, but kept under control by the roots of a hedge. Another plant which requires sunshine to maintain the colour of its leaves is golden feverfew; this is a short-lived perennial, but it comes true from seed and will live longer if, as soon as the white flowers fade, you cut their stems down. Leave just enough to set seed. Again I would emphasize that a ribbon planting under a hedge should be kept to a single plant.

RIGHT ABOVE *Euphorbia amygdaloides robbiae* and narcissus make a spring carpet beneath the great white cherry, *Prunus* 'Tai-haku', at Mrs Robinson's garden, Denmans, in Sussex. The euphorbia is most obliging and, given some protection from cold winter winds, will grow almost anywhere. If you cut it down at the end of the summer, you will be rewarded with new shoots which will give evergreen interest in the winter and more flowers the following spring.

RIGHT BELOW *Erythronium* 'Pagoda', whose yellow heads hang humbly above their dark shining leaves, come into bloom in late April at the same time as the flowers of the weeping cherry open. This cherry, *Prunus × yedoensis* 'Shidare-yoshino' (syn. *P. × y.* 'Perpendens'), makes a delicate veil of blossom in spring and then a curtain of foliage in summer, which turns a rich colour in autumn. The erythronium loves its place in the shade of the weeping cherry.

Never neglect the spurge family – they make good ground cover and need little maintenance, and there is a form for most situations. For shade choose *Euphorbia amygdaloides rubra* with wonderful beetroot-red young shoots which later become maroon and carry amazing chartreuse green flowers. To me they are sensational in May and invaluable to pick for a small bunch, together with grape hyacinths, blue pansies and purple honesty.

Less spectacular but undeniably useful is *E. amygdaloides robbiae*, especially where it is free to run and romp among trees and bushes. It will grow almost anywhere, in sun or shade, but does appreciate a place where it will have protection from winter wind and hard frost – under a wall would be ideal. You can watch the rather loose heads of yellow-green flowers unfold in spring, carried on the tops of strong 60cm/24in stems clothed with evergreen rosettes of dark green shiny foliage. As the flower bracts become spent and papery-brown in July or August, cut the stems to the ground, allowing the strong new growth to take over, ready to flower the following spring.

In a dry, sunless place we grow *Omphalodes cappadocica*; it has now been in the same situation for quite ten years, keeping weeds away and producing bright blue forget-me-not-like flowers in May and June. The April-flowering *O. verna* is just as satisfactory. Neither perhaps is important enough for a prominent place, but both make undemanding ground cover, with bright-eyed flowers lasting three or four weeks. *O. cappadocica* is a lower

growing but more vigorous plant, valuable for total shade.

Once a person or a plant acquires a reputation it is hard to change. So *Tolmiea menziesii* 'Taff's Gold' – the piggy-back plant – constantly surprises me: usually sold as a house plant, it has been reliably hardy here for several years and creates a completely weed-proof carpet. Choose the form with a yellow variegation to the leaves – the plain green-leaved variety is very dull.

A rather neglected ground-cover plant is *Hacquetia epipactis*, which makes a tight clump with yellow-green flowers surrounded by apple-green bracts. It is not a showy plant, but useful in shady, dry conditions. If you have an acid soil, then try planting *Galax urceolata* (syn. *G. aphylla*); it has shining evergreen round leaves that turn bronze in autumn and winter. A clump-forming plant, you can increase it readily and spread it into a ribbon under your hedge. The white flowers come densely on 20cm/8in spikes in late spring. Another choice would be *Waldsteinia ternata*, which will create a carpet of overlapping leaves after a year and produce its small yellow buttercup-like flowers in late spring. These are just a few suggestions. Always remember to be patient, for good ground cover will take a season or two to join up and become an effective carpet.

A bank is not the easiest place to work on, so you will probably want to reduce the upkeep to a minimum. If mowing is difficult because the gradient is steep, ground-cover plants are the obvious answer. After the ground has been cleared, my first

OPPOSITE LEFT A well drained, south-facing bank is treated dramatically in John and Caryl Hubbard's garden. A carpet of thyme sweeps down to a narrow but well-filled bed in which purples, pinks and silver blend together and the plants provide a rich storehouse for bees when they are in flower. In the foreground *Penstemon* 'Garnet' and *P.* 'Purple Bedder' are mixed with *Verbena* 'Sissinghurst' and *V.* 'Silver Anne' and the decorative grey-leaved *Convolvulus cneorum*.

OPPOSITE RIGHT *Dianthus* 'Sops in Wine', each petal with a white finger mark and white rim, grows here through variegated thyme. Together they make a sweet-scented cushion on a stone path at Westwell Manor in Oxfordshire.

RIGHT A complete ground cover at Denmans is created by mounds of flowering evergreens, cleverly planted so that they taper from the *Daphne pontica* at the back to the thin strip of *Ajuga reptans* at the front, with heathers in shades of pink in between. This collection of plants has the added dimension of scent which comes from the daphne and the purple sage to the right.

piece of advice would be to put flat stones in strategic places up the bank, embedding them as horizontally as possible so they become stepping stones when you are planting and tidying. Or you could make a diagonal path, slightly cut into the bank, which would ensure the gradient was reasonable, and give you easier access to the plants.

A south-facing bank will dry out quickly, and this will limit your choice. The most satisfactory planting might be a single main ground cover, with spring bulbs for extra interest. Heathers could be your answer. You may well become an erica addict, and use them in many situations. All callunas and ericas are evergreen, so will keep their interest in winter. I like them planted in large enough drifts of a single variety, to make an effect that is calming, not agitating.

Only those which flower in winter and early spring are lime-tolerant: *Erica carnea, E. × darleyensis* and *E. erigena (E. hibernica)*. Choosing between varieties of these, you can have flowers from November to April in colours ranging from white (*E. × darleyensis* 'Silberschmelze' and *E. carnea* 'Springwood White') through pink (*E.c.* 'Springwood Pink') to madder-carmine (*E.c.* 'King George').

With an acid soil the whole range of heathers, flowering for most months of the year, is open to you. These include *Calluna vulgaris* 'Beoley Gold', *C.v.* 'Gold Haze' and others with outstanding golden foliage.

Between your heathers, plant a single variety of narcissus – my choice is 'Trevithian', a lovely lemon-yellow jonquil flowering in April, or the snow-white, scented *Narcissus* 'Thalia'. The taller pheasant-eye narcissus, *N. poeticus recurvus*, is later-flowering and fragrant. All will increase over the years and require no work.

A bank of thyme is both beautiful and scented, and will last for years with little attention, but I would only recommend it for a small bank as you may find that bald spots need replanting. To remedy this, peg down pieces of thyme; when they have rooted you can use them as infills.

A carpet of *Euphorbia cyparissias* could work well on a bank where it will not encroach and swamp other plants. It spreads by a mass of underground runners, outdoing any neighbours. Remember that it dies down in autumn and that the new growth does not start until March; in winter this patch will be dull, and I would only use it on a bank which is not visible from the house. In April and May the stems, with their narrow grey-green ferny leaves, will carry their typical euphorbia flower heads of a lovely lime green. They would make a good picture growing together with white or blue flowers such as mertensia, bluebells (*Hyacinthoides non-scripta*), ericas, *Lithodora diffusa* (*Lithospermum diffusum*) 'Heavenly Blue', omphalodes, or the dwarf *Rhododendron* 'Blue Diamond'. I should like to plant *Acanthus spinosus* – an equally tough competitor – among them: the contrast of dark

green and grey-green would be exciting. Or you could combine the euphorbia with a spot planting of Mount Etna brooms, *Genista aetnensis*, whose narrow leaves and sparse habit make it an excellent wind-resistant shrub.

Lavender, helianthemums (rock roses) and santolina create a ground cover with a lighter touch. All like a sunny, well drained site, but all require an annual cut-back, the lavender and rock roses after flowering and the santolina in early spring in order to keep it tidy. These can be used on a bank close to the house, extending the flower garden, or beside the swimming pool where you wish to create a feeling of sunshine and warmth.

*Geranium procurrens* is an effective summer ground cover. It is herbaceous, so disappears totally in winter, but each spring will start to send out shoots many metres/yards long, which form extra roots as they travel. You could plant them at the top of the bank, or in the middle if the bank is high, as their natural habit is to grow down rather than up. With them you should have spring bulbs to cover the ground until the geraniums take over and produce a continuous succession of black-eyed purple flowers from July until the first frost.

Another, rather similar, thought is to use the golden-leaved hop, *Humulus lupulus aureus*, planting this at the bottom of your bank – it will find its way up, probably rooting as it goes. In a warm place it will make clusters of hops which are useful for picking and bringing indoors for autumn decoration. Take off the leaves and the hops dry well. As it is an herbaceous plant and will die down to the ground in autumn, daffodils could be naturalized on the same bank for spring interest.

In considering the habit of plants, several other climbers are quite adaptable to clambering up or down a bank. *Rosa* 'Paulii' and *R*. 'Paulii Rosea' are vigorous trailing shrubs with white or silky pink flowers (the white is more vigorous than the pink). They have strong thorny growth forming a really dense ground cover, each individual plant spreading up to 3.5m/12ft. I would recommend planting them midway up the bank.

The ideal clematis for ground cover is *Clematis* × *jouiniana*, a sprawling sub-shrub which will dramatically take over an area at least 3.5m/12ft square. The leaves are coarse but the small flowers are remarkable for their scent. In autumn cut it back to the main stem, leaving only .5m/1-2ft, and the ground can then be filled with early bulbs. For March we have *Narcissus* 'Tête-à-Tête', 15cm/6in tall and increasing in number every year, and for April chionodoxas. There could be a later-flowering narcissus as well – *N*. 'Baby Moon' or *N*. 'Tittle Tattle' which, like many narcissus, will multiply for years.

Much as I like the everlasting pea, *Lathyrus latifolius*, it is difficult to find the right home for it, because it is so rampant, with

ABOVE Rock roses – helianthemums – line the paved path at Barnsley House in a variety of colours. They make a vivid carpet when they come into bloom in May, and last for a full month. They are then pruned hard to keep them in good shape, and to make sure they have time to produce plenty of young new growth on which they will flower the following year.

OPPOSITE LEFT *Vinca major* 'Variegata' is one of the best ground covers and can be kept in check by clipping it hard back in winter. Here it is growing under golden hop, *Humulus lupulus aureus*, a perennial which climbs vigorously and will completely cover an arbour.

OPPOSITE RIGHT This shady border in Gwen Beaumont's garden, The Gables House, in Somerset, is backed by a high boundary wall. The green hosta makes a bold feature, flanked by the variegated-leaved form of the common yellow flag iris, *Iris pseudacorus* 'Variegata'. This theme of rounded shapes alternating with spikes and spires is carried out through this border, so well filled that it has become trouble-free. The old pump still works so that the flag irises and hosta can easily have the water they enjoy.

roots that travel even under paths and seeds that ripen, scatter and germinate everywhere. It could well be the ideal plant for a sunny bank, where it can rampage at will. I have seen it growing on a bank and up through the hedge along a lane in France.

Contrary to what you would imagine, a bank with a northerly aspect is easier to clothe with plants than one which is very sunny, because most spreading plants like the protection of shade to keep their roots cool and their leaves looking fresh. Of course the three obvious ground coverers – *Hypericum calycinum, Lamium galeobdolon* and the green forms of *Vinca minor* and *V. major* – could be used, and effective they will be; but it is a sin to be dull, whatever your task, so think further.

We can divide our thinking between plants which will spread and eventually take over the area, and others which will form large clumps. *Symphytum grandiflorum* makes a carpet which is difficult ever to eradicate, but it does its job well, completely smothering any weeds and in spring providing attractive racemes of tubular creamy flowers with a narrow red edge. It only requires a winter tidy. *Tellima grandiflora* is much less coarse and needs help in spreading by dividing the clumps in winter; eventually it will become a thick carpet with attractive scalloped leaves turning shades of bronze and purple in winter. *Pachy-*

*phragma macrophyllum* is also best increased by division in autumn. I am surprised by how little it is used: it will always create an interest in early spring – at crocus time – when the white cress-like flowers open.

I would like to see shrubs planted among both the symphytum and the pachyphragma. *Prunus laurocerasus* 'Zabeliana' is an evergreen, low and obliquely branched, and the narrow shiny leaves look well spreading over the ground cover. *Cotoneaster franchetii*, although not evergreen, has the same effect. Different but extremely eye-catching, fountains of vivid white stems of *Rubus cockburnianus*, the Himalayan whitewash bramble, would also be exciting here.

## Low-maintenance plants

Whereas ground-cover plants tend to occupy extensive and difficult places and are usually evergreen, minimum upkeep plants can feature in any part of the garden, including mixed and herbaceous borders. When you are planning these borders, it is wise to keep an eye to the future so that you will not find yourself having to do major upheavals, sometimes every autumn. This is when low-maintenance plants are useful. Whereas some are relatively short-lived, others improve with age, rather than deteriorate,

when they are left undivided. But I am not advocating that you should not use plants such as delphiniums and asters, which need a lot of attention, for they include some of the most beautiful perennials which are essential ingredients of summer borders.

Herbaceous peonies – have we not all seen and coveted them? – dislike disturbance. In fact, they will take two years to settle back into a flowering routine after replanting, so choose their position and their neighbours carefully. Once planted, all they require is an annual mulch of farmyard manure or leaf mould in autumn and a bonemeal feed in spring. Their wonderful double flowers may need staking if they get wet and heavy with rain, and for

tidiness you can control their leaves, which often turn a rich bronze and crimson in autumn. When the young stems first push through the soil they are the same shade of crimson as velvety red Barnhaven Courichan primulas, which look perfect beside them. You can leave the primulas in the ground, and the peony foliage will protect them from the sun in summer. At the front of this same picture, add a carpet of *Ipheion uniflorum* 'Wisley Blue', only 15cm/6in tall, whose star-shaped flowers appear in March and April.

Ideal for this low-maintenance bed are the Madonna lilies, *Lilium candidum* and also *L. regale*. They appreciate shade around their base, so plant them close beside tall blue delphiniums or monkshood. The only time you will not have colour is late August onwards, so add clumps of tall perennials at the back, such as *Aster novae-angliae* 'September Ruby'. Now you have a mixture of minimum-upkeep plants – peonies, primulas and ipheion – with asters to divide and lilies to mulch and keep slugs away from each spring.

Another combination I like, using only low-maintenance plants, is *Hydrangea sargentiana* (2m/6-7ft) backing *Acanthus spinosus* (1.2m/4ft) and *Anemone hupehensis japonica* 'September Charm' (45cm/18in) or *A.* × *hybrida* 'Queen Charlotte' (80cm/32in). These will be flowering together in August or September, so you should add midsummer plants in front – *Campanula lactiflora* 'Pouffe' (25cm/10in), with lavender-blue flowers in June and July, and a patch of *Heuchera* 'Palace Purple' to round it off.

The hardy geraniums are a wonderful family; the only work they require in order to emerge strongly again in spring is a tidy when their foliage dies back in winter. *Geranium sanguineum* and its cultivars are low-growing, forming carpets only 30cm/12in high. You can add spring crocus or *Puschkinia scilloides (P. libanotica)* close up to each plant. The geraniums flower almost continuously throughout the summer, and in autumn the leaves turn a lovely mixture of green, bronze and crimson, contrasting well with late-winter-flowering crocus species. *G. endressii* 'Wargrave Pink' (40cm/16in) has clear pink flowers and a softer, larger leaf than *G. sanguineum.*

I use *G. pratense* 'Mrs Kendall Clark' (60cm/24in), the best form of the field cranesbill, in large drifts in my borders. They are interplanted with tulips; when these are over and the geraniums have finished flowering we cut them down close to the ground, and add penstemons or nicotianas. The geraniums will make new leaves of a lovely green to encircle them. Although this scheme involves upkeep, it certainly covers the ground.

Another good low-maintenance picture can be made with *Hemerocallis* 'Bonanza', rich orange day-lilies with brown throats. Interplant them with pale yellow hollyhocks (the seed for mine came originally from Giverny, the painter Monet's garden in France) and both bronze and green fennel. They all have an ascending character, but the effect will be softened by the light fennel foliage. For later colour, plant *Gaillardia* 'Mandarin', which is orange with a mahogany centre, and will flower into September. The fennel is trouble-free and will seed itself, the hollyhocks are long-lived once established, but gaillardias and day-lilies, though long-lived, must be cut down in autumn. The important thing to keep your picture crisp is to dead-head the day-lilies every morning.

OPPOSITE LEFT In the walled garden at Ablington Manor in Gloucestershire, Robert Cooper has made an oak pergola, each pillar with a climbing rose and a clematis to give interest from spring through to summer. This picture shows the young shoots of the peonies coming through and exactly matching the burgundy red Barnhaven Courichan primulas and contrasting with the blue grape hyacinths. The primulas were all grown from seed from the Barnhaven nursery.

OPPOSITE RIGHT By May the peonies are in full bloom. Later a mass of delphiniums and many lilies come through the peony leaves. This is a perfect example of successional interest achieved with the minimum amount of work once the beds are planted.

ABOVE At Tintinhull in August a mass planting of Japanese anemones with *Lilium* 'Golden Clarion' has evergreen bergenia leaves and *Aster divaricatus* covering their feet.

RIGHT In a shady north-facing border beside her house at Minster Lovell, Jill Parker has chosen hostas, including 'Thomas Hogg', and ferns in variety to establish a low-upkeep foliage picture with hellebore, epimedium and alchemilla.

OPPOSITE At Tintinhull, *Rosa* 'Nathalie Nypels', *Nepeta nervosa* and *Geranium sanguineum* 'Glenluce' spill on to a stone path. These densely packed borders frame the vegetable garden on either side, and the luxuriant ground cover makes a fitting contrast to the bare earth between the rows of vegetables nearby.

The foliage of hostas and epimediums makes them good companions, and both will tolerate dry shade. On the other side of the hostas you could plant evergreen hardy ferns such as *Polystichum setiferum divisilobum* or the lady fern, *Athyrium filix-femina*. You must cut the fern fronds to the ground in March, and new fresh fronds will unfurl just as the hosta leaves start to appear.

Ferns are trouble-free by nature – you may leave the clumps to grow in girth over the years, but they are not difficult to dig and divide if you wish to do so. They are fascinating plants and once you start collecting them you will want more, both for picking and for their use in the garden. The elegant arching behaviour of their fronds, sometimes sweeping the earth, sometimes sweeping upwards, always makes an interesting contrast to dark yew or box and to large-leaved hostas.

Hostas and grey-foliage plants can be used in so many situations that it is hard to go wrong with them. Hostas associate well with low conifers, the *Juniperus horizontalis*, *J. squamata* 'Blue Carpet' and *Picea glauca* 'Albertiana Conica'. I have a patch of grey *Stachys byzantina* (*S. lanata*) surrounding an old specimen of *Santolina pinnata neapolitana*, with a juniper behind them. All have been there for quite twenty-five years and have had the minimum of attention. The santolina is clipped hard back every spring and the stachys is divided every three or four years.

## Rose bed underplanting

Shrub roses, so called because they do not need the drastic pruning of Hybrid Tea roses, are becoming increasingly popular. A single Hybrid Tea or even a small group of them looks out of place in the shrub border – each individual bloom is too big and blowsy to associate well with the flowers of graceful shrubs. As the Victorians did, and when space allows and taste demands, Hybrid Teas should have beds of their own. But both old and modern shrub roses fit in admirably with other border plants. They do not need pruning to their stumps or bare bones each winter, their stems are graceful and often arching and many have attractive hips to add to the autumn effect.

I suppose there are two schools of thought regarding their associates. The purists insist that roses must stand alone; others believe that there is plenty of scope – and space – for underplanting them. Your type of soil must always be considered and, most importantly, the type of roses grown. Obviously you cannot underplant small and miniature roses or modern shrub roses which are grown as ground cover, but I think that Hybrid Tea, Floribunda and Polyantha roses – growing to 1-1.5m/3-5ft – look better with a planting round them, preferably no taller than 30cm/12in. And with beds of shrub roses, such as the Hybrid Musks 'Buff Beauty' and 'Penelope', and many of the modern

LEFT ABOVE A pleasing combination of pinks in a rose border at Powis Castle which is thickly underplanted with *Diascia vigilis* and grey festuca.

LEFT BELOW At Westwell Manor, a bed of shrub roses has a ground cover of *Geranium macrorrhizen* 'Ingwersen's Variety'. This is a strongly scented geranium which flowers before the roses. The surround of clipped box balls gives an original effect and a change from straight edging.

OPPOSITE ABOVE In the late Humphrey Brooke's garden a rich medley of blending red and pink roses is underplanted for carpeting ground cover with hardy geraniums.

OPPOSITE BELOW The grey leaves of *Lychnis coronaria* make an excellent foil for this shrub rose, while its pink flowers blend with the paler colour of the 'Bourbon Queen'.

shrub roses, like 'Cerise Bouquet' or 'Frühlingsgold', which grow even taller, I do like an underplanting.

One of the first things I remember about the garden at Barnsley was the unusual display of violas in my mother-in-law Linda's rose beds. These were full of Poulsen roses, introduced from Denmark in 1924 and producing large open clusters of single or semi-double flowers – pink, bright cherry-red and rich crimson – on long, strong stems, altogether 1.25m/4ft tall. The pansies were not huge-faced, but smaller and more delicate, closer to *Viola* 'Arkwright Ruby', *V.* 'Belmont Blue' and *V.* 'Huntercombe Purple', and to others with many-coloured and amusing faces, like *V.* 'Jackanapes' and *V.* 'Ullswater'. Linda's violas lasted for years and were a constant source of delight to my young family who loved picking different 'faces' to put into a vase on the nursery table. Some seeded themselves, and no doubt the gardener took cuttings of others. And so they went on. Much later, when I took over the garden, I moved the rose beds elsewhere and the violas were scattered, but for the last forty years I have been cogitating about how best to complete the look of a rose bed.

It is well to consider a few golden rules. First, I think it is essential in a rose bed for the underplanting to be of a single species. This is not the occasion for a tapestry effect – the roses must always take the leading role. Second, you are adding another layer in order to hide the knobbly lower stems of the roses and to clothe the bare soil, so the ground cover must be quite low. Third, I recommend that, although possibly evergreen, it should either be cut back sufficiently or its edges lifted back to allow an autumn mulch or manuring to be put round the roses. I have always found well-rotted horse manure much the best for this – best for the rose and for the gardener, as it does not blow around. Fourth, choose a plant that is sufficiently interesting in flower or leaf while the roses look like dead stumps; if the two are in flower at the same time, the colours must be complementary.

In illustrations of Edwardian rose gardens you will notice that the beds are usually edged with neatly trimmed box – the box acting as a frame round each bed and as a pattern for the whole picture. This is especially effective when the ground next to the rose bed is paved, as it softens the hard outline. In fact, giving the beds an evergreen framework is a good alternative to infilling with ground cover. Other conventional edgings to use are lavender or santolina in any of their varieties, or *Teucrium chamaedrys* (wall germander).

Silver-grey foliage plants combine well with roses, and several are right for the margins of the beds, where they can spill out over the paving or the gravel (but not the grass). Real spreaders, but not invaders, are *Cerastium tomentosum*, *Stachys byzantina (S. lanata)* and *Veronica cinerea*, the last with short pale blue spikes in July. *Nepeta × faassenii* is a more usual edging plant and coarser than the cerastium and veronica.

Rather more controlled are the many dianthus, but as you will

be using them for their grey foliage I would choose the small-flowered varieties, selecting them for their neat leaves and tidy habit rather than for their flowers. Outline your beds with them, adding a few extras between the front of the border roses to relieve the straight-line effect. Auriculas make a good outline too. If you treat them well, each plant will increase in size and remain for several years; you can propagate them by pulling off a few side shoots carefully and rooting them in well drained compost. They come in wonderful rich colours, with grey-green leaves, but as they flower in April and May you need not be concerned about matching their colours with the roses.

In Mrs Biddulph's garden at Rodmarton Manor, in Gloucestershire, I have seen *Limnanthes douglasii* encircling a bed of yellow roses; around white roses they would be equally effective. I am assured that they are perennial, keeping their green leaves all through the winter and flowering in April and May. By August the top growth is pulled off and very soon new shoots appear. Another piece of useful information I had from this same garden is that a continuous edging can prevent the birds scratching the horse manure used on these beds on to the paved paths.

The plants I would choose to make complete cover on the beds would be *Viola labradorica purpurea* and *V. cornuta* (for taller roses as these violas will climb if given the chance), *Lamium maculatum* 'Beacon Silver', *L.m. album* and *L.m. roseum*. After flowering, clip each plant right back, leaving just the new shoots. This way the plants stay neat under control and provide a constant supply of young leaves.

*Campanula carpatica* and *C. portenschlagiana* (syn. *C. muralis*) both make a trouble-free carpet of green leaves with blue-to-purple flowers no higher than 30cm/12in from June to August. With white roses I would also like to have the hardy *Geranium sanguineum* – the crimson-to-magenta flowers might be too strong for pink or yellow roses. I have also seen *G. endressii* used effectively with taller shrub roses.

Different thoughts are plants which flower in the spring: when the roses put on leaves and then flowers they will have disappeared below ground. Winter aconites, *Eranthis hyemalis*, push through the soil with their yellow flowers in February; these are quickly followed by their leaves, then by May all trace of them has gone. The same is true of crocus. You could make a dramatic carpet of the aconites and crocus through your rose beds – but, if you do so, I would advise putting the manure on early and not too thickly, to allow the bulbs to come through. Add another helping of manure in April when the bulbs are over. Simpler would be a carpet of forget-me-nots to flower in April and early May, pulling them out as soon as they are over and allowing seedlings to appear and be thinned out in the autumn.

One last golden rule. When you are working on your rose borders, take care that you do not disturb and wound the rose roots with your fork; this is so easy to do, and has dire results, as unwanted suckers may shoot from the wounds.

## Shrubberies

If you are a weekend gardener and must keep your work to a realistic minimum, or if you have a large garden with parts quite far from the house where you do not want to spend too long working, a straightforward shrub border, with no underplanting, is an ideal solution. It requires a different approach. Once planted, it should involve minimum upkeep, but first you must make sure the ground is clear of perennial weeds. In the autumn the bed should have a mulching when the soil is damp. This mulch will help keep the soil moist the following summer, and will prevent seedlings from germinating, eliminating most of the weeding. What to mulch with is the question. Your choice could be peat, pulverized bark, mushroom compost, spent hops, leaf mould or straw – and probably will depend on whichever is easiest to get. Each has its drawbacks and its advantages. Whatever mulch you choose, discover the most economical way of getting enough – buying in bulk is best and cheapest.

When you are choosing the plants for your shrub border, consider their different characteristics. Some shrubs are a natural ground cover and are also low-maintenance, as I have already explained. Plants such as the horizontal junipers, *Lonicera pileata* and *Cotoneaster microphyllus* cover the ground with their spreading evergreen branches and these require no pruning to keep them shapely. Choose some of these, but remember that they are basically green, and that you will want to include colour in the whole picture, for instance with spring blossom such as *Spiraea* 'Arguta' and forsythia, or with summer flowers like *Kolkwitzia amabilis* and tree peonies. For autumn colour *Acer japonicum, Viburnum opulus* and *Euonymus alatus* all change dramatically in October. If you like berries for flower arranging *Viburnum opulus* will again be useful, and you could choose the variety, *V.o.* 'Fructu-luteo' for yellow berries, and the varying colours of the berrying forms of pernettya. Do not forget the charm of coloured stems in winter months.

The diversity of these different features will give you a pattern of heights, shapes, density and movement. Whereas in an herbaceous border, as long as you have a colour scheme in mind, you can build up vignettes one by one to create the whole pattern, in a shrub border it is the overall effect which must be considered; the important shrubs should be positioned first, forming either a backing or, if the border is free-standing, a spine. For this reason, rather than writing a description, I have devised a plan.

# A shrub border in the spring

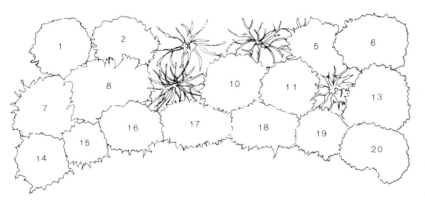

1 *Cryptomeria japonica* 'Elegans Compacta'
2 *Ligustrun lucidum* 'Aureovariegatum'
3 *Cotinus coggygria* 'Notcutts Variety'
4 *Buddleja davidii* 'Dartmoor'
5 *Photinia × fraseri* 'Robusta'
6 *Osmanthus × burkwoodii*
7 *Hebe speciosa* hybrid
8 *Spiraea* 'Arguta'
9 *Cornus alba* 'Sibirica'
10 *Rhamnus alaternus* 'Argenteovariegata'
11 *Choisya ternata*
12 *Philadelphus microphyllus*
13 *Ligustrum ovalifolium* 'Aureum'
14 *Gaultheria procumbens*
15 *Cistus* 'Silver Pink'
16 *Sarcococca humilis*
17 *Santolina chamaecyparissus*
18 *Juniperus communis* 'Repanda'
19 *Euonymus fortunei* 'Emerald 'n' Gold'
20 *Rhododendron impeditum*

In this border of about 9×3.5 metres (about 30×11 feet) I have tried to use enough coloured twigs and evergreen shrubs to give a sufficient background effect for winter – and for picking – and then to follow on with spring and summer flowers and finally to bring a splash of autumn colour. It is important to keep your border well mulched to minimize weeding, though the low-growing evergreens should also help.

# Woodland, Wild Areas and Damp Sites

Woodland, wilderness and often water gardens are places apart, separate from the rest of the garden. They have a different appeal, a quieter ambience and atmosphere, and demand a different treatment. Rather than carefully chosen colour schemes and a tutored look, these wilder areas have an overflowing of careless rapture, and a mingling of colours. In woodland, entwining branches of honeysuckle and climbing roses overhang carpets of spring bulbs, violets, hardy geraniums, ferns, foxgloves and shade-loving lilies.

Woodland and wilderness gardens may have streams running through them, adding an extra element among the trees with sound and movement and often wildlife. Gardens near the house are sometimes created around a stream or a mill-leat, and the moisture banks of the water covered with moisture-loving plants. Gardeners who are lucky enough to have natural water running through their gardens can grow those plants, both small and bold, which thrive in damp conditions.

Nowadays there is something of a fashion for wild areas with carefully thought-out mixtures of seeds of grasses and wild flowers. Thanks to the enthusiasm and experiments of private individuals, which has led to the marketing of seeds by commercial growers, you can buy mixtures of flower seeds especially suited to woodland, field, hedgerow or moist banks round a pond or stream.

Of course, there is little new in gardening – most things have been tried before! I am thinking of the flowery mead – a natural garden before the lawn mower was invented and flower beds became important – so well illustrated in Frank Crisp's book *Medieval Gardens*. These are idealized in embroideries such as the Unicorn Tapestries, woven about 1500 and now hanging in the Cloisters Museum in New York. These meadow gardens would be lovely to sit in – there are trees for shade, but not closely planted as in a wood: hawthorn and hazel, medlars and walnuts, apples and peaches, with wild cherry, *Prunus avium*, planted in the centre. The ground is carpeted with wild strawberries, sweet violets, daisies, periwinkles, wallflowers and marigolds, pansies and primroses, carnations and forget-me-nots, aquilegias, stocks, gilliflowers (*Matthiola perennis*), *Lilium candidum* and wild orchids. Many of these are scented, all of them symbolic. Although it would require special maintenance to keep the grass under control and give the flowers a space to breathe, this is very practical planting – no need to dig over and weed – and all of the flowers are in our present-day seed catalogues.

Francis Bacon in early Stuart times had contemporary thoughts about wild flowers. In his essay 'Of Gardens' he wrote that a large garden should have a heath 'to be framed, as much as maybe, to a natural wilderness', and 'set with violets, strawberries and primroses', 'to be here and there, not in any special order'. He recommended 'little heaps, in the nature of mole-hills', where wild thyme, pinks, germander, periwinkles, daisies, cowslips, strawberries and 'sweet-williams red' would grow. Among the flowers there should be standards of roses, holly, redcurrants, gooseberries, rosemary, bay, and sweet briar.

Miriam Rothschild was the pioneer in England in encouraging us to become more aware of the disappearance of wild flowers from our verges and hedgerows through mowing and spraying. Starting in her own county, Northamptonshire, she has done much to persuade local councils to refrain from cutting their

ABOVE At Denmans in Sussex, where Mrs Robinson has lived since 1947, many of the trees and shrubs she planted have reached maturity. The distinctive horizontal tiered branches of *Viburnum plicatum* 'Mariesii' have been allowed full rein here and contrast well in contour with the trunks of the ornamental trees.

FAR LEFT Spring bulbs make a carpet of green, yellow and white – white bluebells, small yellow narcissi, and white daisies, normally regarded as a weed, but here cherished under an apple tree.

LEFT Winter aconites, *Eranthis hyemalis*, can make a golden carpet in February. Here they nestle close to the trunk and roots of a horse chestnut tree. Bees love them for their early pollen, and I love them to pick for my table.

Woodland, Wild Areas and Damp Sites

verges until after the wild flowers have bloomed and re-seeded. We can already see the start of the resurgence of our wild flowers as we drive along country lanes. In her garden at Ashton Wold she has an experimental meadow garden and also grows individual wild flowers in the walled vegetable garden to use as a source of seed. Her book, *The Butterfly Gardener* (London, 1983), shows us the way to create meadow gardens for ourselves, with special emphasis on plants which attract butterflies. If you do not have a place for a meadow, then the edges of garden paths, where gravel and grass meet, provide another habitat for flowers and butterflies.

Following in her footsteps and originally advised by her, HRH The Prince of Wales is also a pioneer in this experimental field, and is now perfecting his own technique and style. In his High-grove paddocks he has sown samples of combine-harvested wild-flower seed together with a mixture of carefully selected native species. In summer there is a spectacular array of coreopsis, poppies and cornflowers on each side of the drive.

In America, especially in Texas, Lady Bird Johnson has spear-headed the planting of native wild flowers along the miles of broad highway verges. Their very quantity is breathtaking.

Pathways through the wild garden are important. Not only do they give you a purpose, as well as structure and change of height, but they make possible a series of focal points to catch as you turn each corner. Use shrubs to create different shapes: *Viburnum plicatum* 'Lanarth' and the beautiful *Cornus controversa* 'Variegata' will provide horizontal branches stretching out in layers. *Pyrus calleryana* 'Chanticleer', the river birch (*Betula nigra*) and *Prunus* × *hillieri* 'Spire' will form pyramids. If you want evergreens then choose *Juniperus scopulorum* 'Skyrocket' or columns of fastigiate yew for a very narrow effect, *Chamaecyparis lawsoniana* 'Pembury Blue' for a grey effect, or *C.l.* 'Lane' for a gold one.

Remember that this kind of 'natural' gardening will inevitably have its untidy moments, and the effect will be spoilt if it looks too well cared for. Its appeal lies in the skill of the creator – there should be impressions rather than bold statements, allowing scenes to unfold rather than be curtain raisers. You must curb yourself from adding just one more shrub, for it may be a distraction rather than a helpful addition. It should be restful to the eye and to the mind, with a sheltered seat to catch the evening sun. Finally, when you have wandered to its edge your eye should be able to travel on and enjoy the scene beyond.

## Woodland plants

Woodland flowers have a special appeal. They are humble and often – like bluebells – they hang their heads; they are never garish, often hiding among ferns and fallen leaves. Then there are the flowers of the trees themselves: hazel catkins and the often-overlooked, tiny red flowers on parrotia – inconspicuous unless you are looking for them – and the more showy maple and lime flowers, and the black flowers of the oaks.

But by woodland flowers, I really mean the carpeting flowers – wild and cultivated, perennials, bulbs and shrubs. One of the first to appear, in early spring before the trees become green, are patches of winter aconites, *Eranthis hyemalis*; they can flood the ground, their golden faces pushing through in frost and snow, their neck ruffs fringed green, conspicuous to the earliest bees searching for pollen. Beside them the stinking hellebores, *Helleborus foetidus*, should be growing in generous drifts where the sun can catch the light on their drooping lime-green bells and serrated fingered leaves. They may be low-key plants, but they become so special in January when little else excels.

You may become a snowdrop snob, turning up their faces and dropping the names of all the species – *elwesii, atkinsii, fosteri* – but another way to enjoy them is in an extravaganza, in great white sheets, multitudes of singles, doubles, short and tall, growing round tree trunks and framing the rigid stems of *Daphne laureola*, a daphne which loves a limestone soil in woodland. A circle of waxy green bells is protected by a whorl of dark green leaves. Early as they flower, in February and March, it is not too early for the bees to be about and to ensure a crop of seedlings through the garden.

As March moves on, the first daffodils 'that come before the swallow dares', will open planted in drifts of one species, one colour between the tree trunks. Even earlier the pale primroses will entice us to pick and enjoy their honey scent. For those with eyes to see and with children to help them enjoy the garden, all the different hose-in-hose and Jack-in-the-green primroses will be coming through. The pin-eyed and thrum-eyed can provide the earliest lesson in botany, teaching how flowers are fertilized and sometimes cross-pollinated and hybridized.

Carpets of violets, once introduced, will establish themselves rapidly. Have you seen how the ripe seeds are literally catapulted out to a far distance where they can germinate and form a new colony? To start a carpet of wood anemones you should buy and plant in autumn a large quantity of their small, inexpensive tubers. They are *Anemone nemorosa* – a lovely name for a wonderful spring plant, flowering before the trees make too heavy a canopy. Put them in great drifts, white, deep crimson and pink, around your low-growing azaleas in acid soil or viburnums in alkaline soil.

Bluebells, *Hyacinthoides non-scripta*, love a dappled shade and should be planted round the dramatic white trunks of silver

ABOVE The Rococo garden at Painswick in Gloucestershire has recently been restored to its eighteenth-century glory – guided by the contemporary painting by Thomas Robins. Snowdrops have been allowed to naturalize over the years, creating sensational carpets in spring.

RIGHT An incredible carpet of March-flowering *Narcissus bulbocodium*. As with many other flowers, their heads turn to the light, so they look happy under deciduous trees or on a grassy bank where there is plenty of moisture available in spring.

OPPOSITE ABOVE and BELOW Mown grass paths lead through the woodland at Abbotswood in Gloucestershire, where white and blue *Anemone blanda* and blue *Scilla messeniaca* make a millefleur carpet under the canopy of deciduous trees. It is an ideal woodland garden – large enough to make a brilliant effect in contrast to the areas of formal planting at Abbotswood which were originally designed by Gertrude Jekyll and Sir Edwin Lutyens.

birch, or the ghost-like, whitewashed stems of the bramble *Rubus cockburnianus*. White, blue and green are in perfect harmony, and the rubus stems arch over, reflecting the graceful curve of the bluebells weighed down by the tubular flowers.

Next in the year come the orchids: the first to appear in the woodland are the early purple *Orchis mascula*, with rich magenta splashes on both its flowers and leaves. They are difficult to transplant, for they depend on the presence of a mycorrhizal fungus in the soil for their food, so if you have them established they must be nurtured – do not pick them or you will be spoiling their chance of increasing. The green-flowered twayblade, *Listera ovata*, probably the most common of British orchids, starts to push through in April; then you see two leaves, 'ribbed and chamfered' as Gerard described them in his *Herball* of 1597, and by the end of June and into July the yellow-green flowers on slender 50cm/20in stems will be maturing. These need nurturing too – do not pick them or mow them down.

One of my spring delights is the mixing of purple with char-treuse – a perfect combination in the hand and in the garden or

ABOVE Martagon lilies (the Turk's cap lilies) are best grown in partial, not deep, shade and naturalize well.

LEFT ABOVE At Knightshayes in Devon, a wonderful woodland garden has been developed on an acid soil. White foxgloves and blue *Meconopsis betonicifolia* have seeded themselves and make a beautiful combination.

LEFT BELOW Hybrid erythroniums are easy to grow in a woodland setting. Flowering in April, they come into bloom before the leaves of deciduous trees cast shade. *E.* 'Rose Beauty', a hybrid of *E. revolutum*, and *E.* 'White Beauty' are both free-flowering; later their well-mottled leaves make an attractive ground cover.

OPPOSITE ABOVE The light catches the hanging white flowers of Solomon's seal at Jenkyn Place, Hampshire, where they are well sited against the dark background of a hedge.

OPPOSITE BELOW *Trillium grandiflorum* – of which this is the pink form, *T.g.* 'Roseum' – flowers in spring. They are ideally suited to cool shady woodland. They are very hardy, and their thick rhizomes can be divided once a clump is established.

woodland. The special deep-mauve-flowered honesty – its leaves often mottled with deep purple – and the wood spurge, *Euphorbia amygdaloides*, together make a picture to excite and remember. Look at them closely, and you will discover how wonderful they are – two common flowers, but memorable when combined.

As the weeks progress, so will the shade in your woodland, and your planting must be adapted to this, using aquilegias, *Geranium sylvaticum*, digitalis, ferns and above all lilies. In dappled shade white flowers will shine. Tall spikes of foxgloves look wonderful towering over hosta leaves and ferns, but to keep the strain white, care must be taken to cut off the offending pink and purple flower stems before the bees begin their work and cause havoc to your colour plans. On the edge of your woodland, where sunshine will reach for some of the day, hardy strong-growing *Achillea ptarmica* 'The Pearl' will do well.

I love white with grey and white with green, but mixed in with too heavy a hand among hot colours it can become disastrous – the contrast is too strong. Used sparingly and with tact, white will lighten a dark corner, looking like stars in a night sky. *Erythronium* 'White Beauty', which loves to be tucked in under overhanging branches, and Solomon's seal (*Polygonatum* × *hybridum*) are both for the woodland or for the shady border. Do remember that many flowers are versatile and will grow in different situations, but try to give them the conditions they like most. You must aim at a not too dense canopy of leaves, branching up some of the trees in order to let in light. Then there are the more specific needs: shade-loving trilliums must have an acid soil, with plenty of leaf mould, to survive and excel. Once you have seen them growing wild, you will long for them in your woodland garden, and you will have the same feelings about *Sanguinaria canadensis*. If you are lucky enough to be given a plant of the double form – as I was by John Treasure several years ago – put it in a west-facing border among other treasures; it is far too precious to risk in the woodland.

One early May I had the privilege of walking with Bill Frederick through his woodland garden in Delaware. Bill is an enthusiast and one of the great plantsmen of our time, and half an hour with him taught me far more than I could possibly have learnt from reading books or catalogues. It is seeing the plants growing which makes the lasting picture, and I wrote in my diary that day, 'My impression which came through clearly was Bill's cleverness with colour combinations.' Like me he loves the yellowy green chartreuse colours of spring, combining woodland euphorbia with the purples and claret of berberis and maple leaves. In his woodland drifts of blue *Scilla siberica* and *Trachystemon orientalis* were flowering together, the large hairy leaves

of the latter taking over the ground after the scillas have faded.

Lovely Virginia bluebells, *Mertensia pulmonarioides* (syn. *M. virginica*), 50–70cm/20–25in tall, were flowering beside the unfolding leaves of *Rodgersia podophylla*. The mertensia leaves turn yellow and disappear as the rodgersia spreads itself; they are good companions, both liking a moist rich peaty soil and half-shade. Early oriental hellebores lined the paths and *Crocus tommasinianus* was coming up in drifts with pink *Claytonia virginica*.

There were epimediums and dicentra, both plants which have beautiful leaves. They will flower and flourish in the woodland, but also make good neighbours in a border where the sun does not beat down all day long. Drifts of violets, and three different hardy geraniums were flowering: *Geranium phaeum*, the mourning widow, a shade lover with sombre purple flowers; *G. macrorrhizum*, a wonderful ground cover for sun or shade, with lilac-pink flowers and aromatic, almost evergreen leaves which take on a rustic look as the winter weather becomes cold; and *G. procurrens* which does well in sun or shade and is an ideal plant to be allowed a free hand. Its natural habit is to remain prostrate, but

RIGHT Everything in this wild area at Vann is self-sown on the weald clay: *Fritillaria meleagris*, lady's smock, buttercups and *Lamium galeobdolon*.

BELOW A spectacular stand of white foxgloves rising from a clump of grey-leaved *Hosta sieboldiana* in the woodland at Knightshayes.

OPPOSITE A carpet of woodland plants at Vann in May: *Azalea pontica, Hosta fortunei*, ostrich ferns, *Rheum tanguticum*, wild garlic, *Symphytum grandiflorum, Petasites fragrans*.

given a chance it will clamber through and drape itself over low bushes. *G. sylvaticum albiflorum*, another woodlander, though I did not see it in Bill's garden, has just the right amount of pure white flowers standing 90cm/36in above the mounds of divided leaves.

Hostas were coming through that day, and Bill explained to me that *Hosta ventricosa* is both tough and slug-resistant – great qualities in a woodland where things are left to take care of themselves. At that moment I was thinking how at home William Robinson would have felt in this woodland, where *Podophyllum peltatum*, the May apple, growing in a dampish spot, were just opening their Christmas rose-like flowers. *Trillium grandiflorum*, the white wood lily, were budding up, and the delicate pink pea flowers of *Lathyrus vernus* were also enjoying rich woodland soil. Later the wild foxgloves, *Digitalis purpurea*, and the tall white, evening-scented *Nicotiana sylvestris*, would be among the star performers, with patches of colchicums.

There are other moments in woodland gardens that stand out in my memory. Two occurred in gardens that I visited many years before gardening became a dominant theme in my life and my mind was ready to absorb impressions.

The first was in August, walking round a small lake surrounded by trees in a garden in Oxfordshire, where the owner had consciously given every star plant the right background. As we turned the first corner there, standing alone, was a wonderful specimen of *Aesculus parviflora* grown as a front-row shrub backed by tall trees whose lower branches had been taken off. On another side of the lake was a whole bank of white willow herb. Both were in full bloom – the chestnut with long spikes of white flowers with red anthers, and the fireweed, *Epilobium angustifolium* with 1.2m/4ft white spires and fresh green leaves. It was the mass of this epilobium reflected in the water which was so impressive.

The second was in mid-April in another Oxfordshire garden, Bampton. The woodland was magical to me. This, I believe, was the day when I learnt that, although detail is all-important, I must learn also to look in a wider sweep at the general, or total, effect. The narcissus were planted in drifts of one variety, and so were the anemones, backed by *Euphorbia amygdaloides robbiae* and forget-me-nots. There were dog-tooth violets and snakeshead fritillaries. The main flower colours were in swathes, but the more refined *Fritillaria meleagris*, with their delicate nodding heads – some white, some purple – were left amply surrounded by green. Their own leaves are grass-like, and the effect is enhanced by similar kinds of foliage, rather than heavy-textured, large leaves which would detract from the delicate appearance of the fritillary flowers.

Paths through woodland can be defined by shade-loving ferns. In spring they are lovely as their fronds unfurl, and by August they are fully grown and at their best in shape and texture. Grow them with spring bulbs and wood anemones, trilliums and lilies. Most lilies like to have their heads in the sun while their bulbs and lower stems are shaded. I like to see *Lilium auratum*, which flower in July and August, pushing their strong stems through the foliage of rhododendron bushes.

## Moisture-loving plants

Never having owned a garden with a stream, boggy ground or a place where plants which like damp but well drained soil grow best, I have never had a chance to use those which have '*aquatica*' or '*palustris*' (meaning of marshes) as their species name. If suddenly I did have this opportunity, it would open up a whole new world to me. For from the spectrum of suitable plants one can achieve a variety of contrasting leaf forms, colour effects and combinations at least as great as in your mixed borders.

I would start with notes and lists to give me ideas and possibilities for my venture. You may say that you can get these lists in books, but there is always something special about your own list – it reflects your personal preferences.

Each plant would have its height, colour and months of flowering noted and, just as important, its general habit – leaves large, feathery, evergreen, spiky, rounded. As in any other situation in the garden, I would have to consider whether it liked full sun, dappled shade or full shade; and its preferred type of soil must also come into my thinking.

At this stage you must also decide how important this part of your garden will be to you: will you want to work there often, or is it just to be a place where you will walk and enjoy the wilderness as well as the plants?

People without experience of woodland or stream gardens may well think that these areas, once planted, will take care of themselves. Treated in a certain way they can, but if you are a real gardener you will have other ideas. To quote Frances Pumphrey in *The New Englishwoman's Garden*, 'This water-cum-wild garden is definitely my favourite bit of the garden, even though it was horrendous to make and is tedious to maintain. It is hard work . . . do not for a second believe that a wild garden will look after itself. Just turn your back and see what happens.'

For sites in and near ponds and streams, or on boggy ground, the degree of damp-tolerance of plants is vital. In catalogues, you will often read that a plant needs moist but well drained soil, a somewhat enigmatic description meaning that the moisture should be moving through the soil, not standing or stagnant. The roots of some plants can literally drown if they are in water-

ABOVE Moisture-loving plants are grouped handsomely together in the stream garden at Brook Cottage, Mr and Mrs David Hodges' garden in Oxfordshire. Iris, *Primula florindae, Aruncus dioicus* and lysichiton form a green scene punctuated with white and yellow flowers.

OPPOSITE Mirabel Osler has used moisture-loving plants together with roses to create summer-long interest in her old Lower Brook House in Shropshire. The roses, red 'Tuscany Superb' and climbing pink 'Albertine', mingle with *Alchemilla mollis*, euphorbias, hellebores and sisyrinchium.

LEFT At Stancombe Park in Gloucestershire, Mr and Mrs Basil Barlow have been working on their garden, creating formal and colourful borders round the house and restoring the woodland walk down to the bog garden and the lake with its early nineteenth-century Greek temple. This part of the garden gives the right opportunity for growing ferns, *Primula florindae* and grey-leaved cardoon.

LEFT BELOW These bright *Primula japonica* growing at the Royal Horticultural Society's gardens at Wisley are the selected form *P.j.* 'Miller's Crimson' – they are among the most striking and ornamental of moisture-loving plants for a cool position.

OPPOSITE A view of the pond at Brook Cottage. Mrs Hodges has covered the banks with a profusion of plants. In the foreground *Alchemilla mollis* is looking its best, and the clumps of *Euphorbia griffithii* 'Fireglow', now lovely green mounds, have lost their startling red. *Primula florindae* echo the colour of the alchemilla flowers. The various forms of *Iris laevigata* are opening their flat heads, their leaves in contrast to the bold foliage of *Hosta sieboldiana* 'Elegans'. Bowles' golden grass, *Carex elata* 'Aurea', enjoying the damp, has made a significant clump, and so have the *Mimulus* 'Wisley Red'. In the border beyond there are evergreens and a copper beech hedge. The pond was dug out twenty-five years ago and the overflow contributes to the moisture of the primula garden further down the hill.

logged soil or standing water – they cannot breathe – while others require the extra moisture to survive and flourish.

Here, then, are some of my suggestions for plants which could be worked into a tapestry of colour and shapes. Astilbes, which will flower in July and August, are wonderful grown in drifts on the water's edge. You could make a rainbow effect with white through pale pink, then to a deep pink using *A.* 'Deutschland' (white, 50cm/20in), *A.* 'Irrlicht' (white with dark foliage, 50cm/20in), *A.* 'Pink Curtsey' (bright pink, 60cm/24 in), *A.* 'Fanal' (deep red, 40cm/18in – front), *A.* 'Purpurlanze' (rose-purple, 120cm/48in – behind) and finally, *A.* 'Snowdrift' (white, 60cm/24 in).

Beside the astilbe, have a large-leaved plant such as *Darmera peltata (Peltiphyllum peltatum)*, the naked stems of which come through in April, opening with flat heads of pink flowers; later, by June, the parasol-like leaves will be 90-100cm/36-40in high. A planting of spikes – red *Lobelia cardinalis, Iris laevigata, I. ensata (I. kaempferi), Polygonum bistorta* and *Lysimachia clethroides* – in association with round-leaved plants – *Ligularia dentata* 'Othello' or 'Desdemona' – would make a good contrast. *Caltha palustris*, the marsh marigold, in its single and double forms, will provide a shining and golden-yellow reflection to the edge of a stream or pool in April and May; the seed heads are attractive too.

For scent, grow the creamy-white flowers of *Filipendula ulmaria* 'Aurea'; if you cut the flower heads down in good time, you will have a new flush of yellow foliage in autumn. Keep these away from your astilbes for colour – they are better neighbours for hemerocallis and *Iris sibirica*, yellow *Lysimachia punctata*, hostas with gold in their leaves and *Primula florindae*, the yellow primula which will tolerate an alkaline soil.

The plant that makes me feel most covetous of gardeners with a stream and acid soil is the spectacular *Primula japonica*. I remember especially admiring these candelabra primulas one year in Scottish gardens I visited. Their flowers vary widely in colour, from 'Miller's Crimson' to 'Postford White' and from the pink, salmon and orange of Bressingham Strain to the scented, light primrose *P. sikkimensis* and *P. bulleyana*, with its bold orange spikes.

Several plants that grow in normal herbaceous beds do noticeably better in damp soil which does not dry out in summer. *Angelica archangelica* will make flower spikes 2-2.5m/7-8ft tall. *Thalictrum aquilegiifolium, T. flavum glaucum (T. speciosissum)* and *Eupatorium purpureum*, though good in your regular border, will appreciate the damp and so will *Artemisia lactiflora* and *Campanula lactiflora*. The large-leaved *Rheum palmatum* 'Atrosanguineum' and *Inula magnifica* both survive in my border but would become twice the plants given more moisture.

# A stream garden in mid-summer

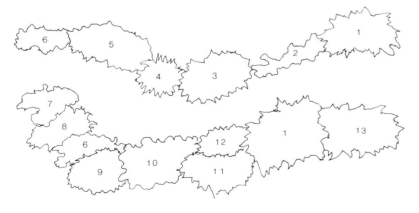

1　*Rheum palmatum* 'Rubrum'
2　*Primula japonica*
3　*Astilbe* 'Fanal'
4　*Leucojum aestivum*
5　*Ligularia przewalskii*
6　*Caltha palustris*
7　*Lysichiton americanus*
8　*Astilbe chinensis pumila*
9　*Gentiana asclepiadea*
10　*Ligularia dentata* 'Desdemona'
11　*Lysimachia clethroides*
12　*Lobelia cardinalis*
13　*Hosta sieboldiana* 'Elegans'

A stream side can be made exciting, using plants which excel with that extra moisture available to help them grow to their full stature and best flowering. Maybe you will want a whole sweep of June primulas or July astilbes to give a dramatic effect – but here I have chosen to use small groups of waterside plants beside the stream. Exciting shrubs could be planted under the canopy of trees I imagine might fringe the stream.

There are many other plants of this type to add to your lists. *Gunnera manicata* needs both plenty of space and plenty of water. Plant the handsome grass *Miscanthus sacchariflorus* beside the gunnera to match it in height. All the readily available miscanthus are lovely on the water's edge, their waving plumes reflecting in the water. Narcissus will grow in soil which is moist but not too wet. The summer snowflake, *Leucojum aestivum*, likes to be near water and the selection 'Gravetye Beauty', which will reach 75-90 cm/30-36in, must never be allowed to dry out if you want it to form large clumps. The snakeshead fritillary, *Fritillaria meleagris*, grows wild in wet meadows, and although it survives in dry grassland there is a greater chance of its seeds germinating in a damp situation where the seedlings will not dry out.

I have never grown the two helleborines which need a damp and shady place: *Epipactis palustris*, the marsh helleborine, and *E. gigantea*, the false lady's slipper, with sombre brown and green flowers with orange markings and a purple heart. They should be associated with more choice plants such as *Gentiana asclepiadea* (40cm/15in), the willow gentian which flowers in late summer

ABOVE LEFT *Zantedeschia aethiopica* are much more hardy than we often think. They flourish when their roots are well covered with water in a pond or lake and in a damp area protected from the severest frosts. This well-known arum lily or lily of the Nile is beautiful with its great white spathes and deep yellow spadices, and even after the flowers are over the broad spear-shaped leaves are a handsome feature.

ABOVE RIGHT *Iris sibirica* are best grown in moist soil in full sun but they will flower in a dry situation. *I.s.* 'Cambridge' is a fairly new variety. The falls are marked in the centre with yellow or white veining – a decorative feature. They bloom in early summer and are followed by mahogany brown seed heads, useful for dried winter arrangements with honesty and evergreen leaves.

and carries on until the *Schizostylis coccinea* open in the autumn.

The lovely white arum, *Zantedeschia aethiopica*, which grows naturally in marshy places, is hardier than we may believe, especially if it is planted with its tubers below water-level so that they are protected from severe frost. They are spectacular in summer if grown in a mass, as at the edge of the lake in the famous garden of Pusey House, Oxfordshire. Another memory I have is of a group of them growing in a small, circular, formal pool in the late Lord Buchan's garden. Here, he told me, they were planted half a metre/18 inches deep, in fact below the level of ice danger.

Probably one of the most spectacular streamside plants is *Lysichiton americanus*, which grows in wet mud. The bright yellow arum flowers start pushing through in early March and continue in flower for several weeks – but remember that the leaves will become enormous, up to 1.2m/4ft long, so you must not plant any treasures too close to them. The Asiatic variety, *L. camtschatcensis*, has pure white flowers and is slightly smaller in all its parts. Both these lysichitons prefer a peaty soil.

There are shrubs for your pool and stream bank too. Among the most spectacular for winter interest are *Cornus alba* with their coloured stems, sealing-wax red to golden, and *C. stolonifera* 'Flaviramea' with striking yellow stems. The willows will thrive even in swampy sites; with most you will get a better display of catkins if you keep them pollarded regularly.

Two of Britain's native shrubs do well in moist situations, *Viburnum lantana*, the wayfaring tree, and *V. opulus*, the guelder rose, with its persistent, translucent red berries. *V.o.* 'Xanthocarpum' has clear golden fruits. Planted together, these make a good bank of colour in the autumn.

Just as in the rest of your garden, the scale of your planting will depend upon the size of your lake, pool or stream. A lake or large pool with a view from a distance will call for a bold planting with a backdrop of interesting trees. A stream will meander, so you will meander too, looking at plants as individuals. Here you will be able to use choicer plants which merit a close scrutiny. Always suit your planting to the situation.

OPPOSITE The heavy weald clay edging the pond at Vann in Surrey is too sticky to dig, so ground cover has been allowed to take over; this part of the garden is cleared once a year, but it is impossible to eradicate the wild garlic. In the foreground, *Rodgersia podophylla* leaves emerge brown and then turn green; beside it is the sensitive fern, *Onoclea sensibilis*.

ABOVE Ferns, wild garlic and kingcups grow at the edge of the pond at Vann. The ostrich fern, *Matteucia struthiopteris*, increases by stolons right into the water and has excellent brown 'seed heads' all winter; here its fronds are emerging out of a generous clump of wild garlic.

ABOVE RIGHT At Vann the red stems of *Cornus alba* 'Sibirica' are a good choice for winter effect. They are growing above the pond on a bank of clay some 1.4m/4½ft high, riddled with honey fungus from an oak bole too heavy to lift out. It is an area of low maintenance, where the grass is cut four times a year.

RIGHT The bog arum, *Lysichiton americanus*, likes to be by water. The yellow flowers, which unfortunately have an unpleasant scent, push through in early spring, making spectacular ribbons of colour once established. The leaves, which develop later, are shaped like paddles and can become as large as 1m/40in long and 30cm/12in wide; they are good weed suppressors.

# Tubs and Containers

Whatever size your garden, tubs and containers can play an important part, both in summer and in winter. Here at The Old Rectory, Burghfield, Mrs Merton has used *Verbena* 'Kemerton', *V.* 'Silver Anne', *Pelargonium* 'Mme Crousse' and *P.* 'Lady Plymouth' for leaf effect, *Fuchsia* 'Preston Guild' and *F.* 'Igloo Maid', *Argyranthemum* 'Rollason's Red' and grey helichrysum to give a surrounding enclosing effect. With a generous infilling of plants they make their own supports, but it is often wise to add bamboo canes when the initial planting is made.

Grouping plants in containers needs the same skill as creating a successful mixed border. You must know your plants, their rate of growth, the colour of their flowers and their cultural needs. Whatever your containers, they should harmonize with their surroundings. They can clothe a terrace, bringing extra colour, incident and architectural effect. Large terraces need boldly planted Versailles-type tubs, probably containing just clipped standard bay or Portugal laurel, *Prunus lusitanica*, which will remain for several years. Intricate planting would be too fussy and the incident would be lost. By contrast, a sunny, much frequented sitting area must have a wealth of well planted pots and tubs, chosen especially to give evening scent and attract the butterflies. For perfection these will be changed twice a year, so that they have a winter and spring look followed by a summer and autumn display.

At Powis Castle large clay pots stand dramatically on top of the walls and balustrades flanking the steps. Another clever use of containers there is within a series of alcoves set within a high retaining wall, where the surrounding brickwork creates a frame for each flower picture. Gertrude Jekyll was splendid at growing plants in pots and tubs at her home at Munstead Wood. She used banks of hostas behind *Francoa ramosa*, all in pots, and stationed containers of hydrangeas and geraniums in strategic places – on steps leading from one area of the garden to another, framing seats and vistas.

In my garden I have two different aspects of container planting – one on a verandah facing west, where the prevailing wind is quite wicked in winter time. Here we put box shapes, balls or pyramids into Italian clay containers in order to reinforce the architectural effect of the verandah pillars and steps. Species crocus around the box provide pollen for the first February bees and, to break the austerity, we add a few trailing periwinkles or variegated ivy. In recent winters, with little frost, there has been no trouble with pots cracking, but nevertheless we avoid those with narrow necks as they do not allow for expansion. Well-cast clay pots with wide tops should not crack.

Where you have containers set in plenty of garden space I think that it is best to concentrate on plants you do not – or cannot – grow in the borders. One great advantage of plants in pots is that you can give them the acid or alkaline soil they need, and with careful planning you need not move them around too often. But it is clever to leave enough space between your 'fixtures' to drop in lilies, tobacco plants, mignonette, snapdragons and trailing nasturtiums.

In our verandah pots we have chosen a yellow, white and grey theme for the last two years. The white daisy, *Leucanthemum vulgare*, has been the centrepiece, and we have surrounded this with the bright yellow *Bidens ferulifolia*; for infilling, cuttings of *Helichrysum petiolare* 'Limelight' soon grow into good-sized plants. Do be generous with numbers and always remember that with so many plants in one container they will all be competing for nutrients and need regular feeding. Just as important, keep deadheading.

Our tubs along the terrace are half-barrels with a diameter of 60cm/24in. I really enjoy filling these, and try to plant the winter/spring display by mid-October in order to allow the bulbs to root and have a good start. We use our own home-made mixture, consisting of compost, peat and perlite (3:2:1). We lay a

A late summer visit to Powis Castle in North Wales is always rewarding. Here are three examples of planting in containers.

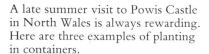

ABOVE LEFT AND RIGHT These old lattice clay pots are free-standing on a balustrade overlooking a spectacular drop of terraces and the Welsh mountains beyond. *Fuchsia* 'Mrs Popple' and *F.* 'Eva Boerg' predominate, but a mingling of soft pinks with strong reds immediately catches your attention and blends with the ageing on the pots.

RIGHT Set in a niche, *Melianthus major*, *Fuchsia* 'Thalia' and scarlet nasturtiums (*Tropaeolum majus* 'Hermine Grashoff', a very old and scarce variety which has to be propagated from cuttings) create a Mediterranean effect against the mellow, 300-year-old high brick wall. Each year the combination of plants changes.

few handfuls of drainage crocks, then 5-7.5cm/2-3in of soil. To give immediate interest which will carry on all winter, we put in a standard holly or a box pyramid, firmed in and well staked against the winter wind. Then the bulb planting begins. We put these in layers: first about a dozen tulip bulbs, all of the same variety. More soil is added and then some narcissus, more soil again and a selection of ground-cover foliage plants like ajuga, vinca, arabis or sedum – something with a small leaf. There are still *Iris reticulata* and species crocus to add, and we pop these in between the ground cover before making a final fill-up of soil. This planting lasts from mid-October to mid-May – seven months – so it must look good.

The success of the summer display varies. Over the years we have decided on a pale mauve, slightly double ivy-leaved pelargonium for its toughness, for the generous way in which it flowers and for the fact that its growth gives a solid appearance. If we have saved enough of these over the winter I like to plant one in the centre and three more around the edges of the barrel. The spaces will be filled with scented-leaved geraniums, grey helichrysum and *Pelargonium* 'Lady Plymouth', a good choice with her attractive white variegated leaves.

Steps into the house are the ideal site for making a display. If you like really bright colours, then a collection of hybrid begonias will create a show all summer. Fuchsias make some of the best container plants because of their non-stop flowering and graceful habit. Last year we discovered the virtue of *Verbena* 'Silver Anne' too: it flowers all summer – in fact into the winter until frost puts a stop to it – and its arms spread out far and wide. Our plants have survived through the last two winters. Distinctive and colourful in their own right, none of this trio needs a companion.

I have always wanted auriculas in my garden but since I do not have the well-drained raised bed that they would like, we have given them a permanent home in wooden barrels, which also have a central standard holly. They thrive there and are close to eye level so that we may enjoy their beautiful colours and textures. Another recent and surprising success has been *Buddleja davidii* 'Dartmoor', planted two years ago in a tub because I could not find a good home for it. Now it is dramatic, with a beautiful growth habit, and it makes a strong feature by the house, especially in August when the red admiral and peacock butterflies are about. Other such plants enjoyed best as individuals are *Brugmansia suaveolens (Datura s.)*, oleander, citrus trees and, of course, the wonderful agapanthus with huge blue heads loved by bowler-hatted Edwardian head gardeners.

Recently I had a very exciting experience at the Seattle Flower Show on the north-west coast of America, where a stand with plants for container gardens set up by Karen Kienholz Steeb captured my imagination. Her expertise lay in the way each group of containers represented one of the four seasons. I cannot do better than to quote her, for she expresses my own feelings: 'A container garden is an expression, a statement of style and warmth. It is an outdoor bouquet in a durable vase. It can be composed of spring bulbs, summer annuals, autumn pansies and evergreen shrubs.' I was tempted by these large skilfully displayed, brim-filled containers, each a 80cm/30in cube filled with at least three different plants. It was not until I tapped them that I realized that they were made of polyurethane – they were for all the world like majestic clay pots. They conveyed the feeling of the unfolding of the months, like a panorama of the year seen through a picture window. I would like to try a theme along these lines, each season joining hands with the next. They may have an infilling of bulbs and easy annuals. Here, I would like to pass on some ideas taken directly from Karen's stand since it was so full of good ideas for busy gardeners who have little spare time and want year-round, interesting displays.

One simple yet sophisticated winter scene included *Carex buchananii*, an eye-catching foxy-red grass with narrow arching leaves curling at the tips, lovely through the whole year, surrounded by primroses and silver-leaved thyme. The carex would also look well with *Euonymus fortunei* 'Emerald 'n' Gold' and *Santolina chamaecyparissus*. Another winter scene included two low-growing conifers, *Juniperus horizontalis* and *Chamaecyparis obtusa* 'Nana Gracilis', with *Nandina domestica* for vertical lines, santolina for a contrast of grey and for its rounded shape, and *Mahonia aquifolium* for the beauty of its winter leaf colour and berries. A third combination for winter had the shiny green-leaved *Prunus laurocerasus*, golden euonymus, nandina, photinia and *Carex buchananii*.

Moving on to spring, the sweet-smelling sarcococca and *Polystichum setiferum divisilobum* were grouped with primroses and the lovely *Nandina domestica* 'Meyers Red'. For another spring planting the background was *Euonymus fortunei radicans*, with pink tulips, winter-flowering pansies and violas (Johnny-jump-ups). Choose your own favourite tulips: mine would be the lily-flowered 'Mariette' or 'White Triumphator', 'Angélique' (an early double, 35cm/14in high) or 'Peach Blossom' (only 30cm/12in tall but sturdy). There are many lovely winter-flowering pansies, too. The violas are at their best in May, while the euonymus will continue to look good all year. If you were to add a few species crocus and replace the tulips with pelargoniums and grey *Helichrysum petiolare* 'Limelight', the container would then be handsomely planted for many months.

Moving from spring to summer, the late-flowering pink tulip

157

'Toronto' was generously planted between a grey-green euonymus, a pale mauve heliotrope and the pink daisy *Bellis perennis*. Other summer choices had tradescantia and geraniums mixed with *Leucanthemum vulgare (Chrysanthemum leucanthemum)*, and the container was edged with the annual *Browallia speciosa* 'Blue Troll' (an alpine campanula would have the same effect). Another had *Phormium tenax* 'Purpureum' as a central feature and the blue browallia used again in profusion.

Your thoughts need not be restricted to purely decorative planting. I know I would want to introduce a few vegetables. Cherry-sized tomatoes make smallish bushes and would be a good decorative crop, or you could be bold and have a container of eggplants. I would also concentrate on vegetables with attractive foliage, the only drawback being that you would be picking them. Try planting a container with the French 'Merveille des Quatre Saisons' lettuce, its huge leaves tipped with ruby-red,

acting as the centrepiece for other green-hearted lettuces and yellow zucchinis or amusing 'Patty Pan' or 'Sunburst Yellow' scallop squash. By the time you cut your lettuces the courgettes will have taken over.

Then there are the cutting or salad bowl lettuces which form loose rosettes rather than heads; with these you can harvest the individual leaves. 'Lollo Rosso' is a loose-leaf Italian variety with crinkly, densely ruffled leaves in a deep crimson with an icy green heart. I grow oak-leaved lettuces, both green and red, as edging in my vegetable garden, and they would look well round the rim of a large pot with red-stemmed rhubarb chard in the centre. The Swiss chard with white stems could couple with corn salad or radicchio chicory. Not long ago the seeds of these more unusual leaf vegetables were hard to get, but now many seed firms sell them. You can also experiment with flower and vegetable combinations. Black or very dark purple tulips would look

wonderful piercing through pale green early 'Tom Thumb' lettuces and a summer tub with a standard rose or *Viburnum opulus* 'Compactum' underplanted with salad bowl lettuce. Pansies, tagetes and nasturtiums all combine well with the vegetables, and one success could lead you on to further experiments.

If you have no garden but must have growing plants in your life, you can still have the satisfaction and joy of planting and watching them develop and flower by using containers. You may have just a tiny paved area in front of a town house, or a 'cat-run' at the back, or, smaller still, only a window sill. With any of these you can still 'garden'; it simply has to be on a different scale and with smaller dimensions. You will need plenty of imagination, skill and an eye for detail.

Let us start by thinking of the smallest of all the possibilities – a window box, or even just a collection of pots on a kitchen window sill. There are a few imperatives to be borne in mind.

Different types and sizes of containers can all be put to good use. You can still find old clay pots which are frost proof.

OPPOSITE You can never have too many well-filled pots, however small your garden. Steps into the house make an ideal place for this summer display, with *Pelargonium* 'Roi des Balcons Rose' (syn. *P.* 'Ville de Paris'), *Diascia vigilis*, *Fuchsia* 'Checkerboard', and *Pelargonium* × *fragrans* and *Salvia rutilans* for scented leaves.

ABOVE LEFT A most original idea using *Heuchera* 'Palace Purple' in a beautiful dark purply-brown ali-baba pot. It would be nice to bring this indoors in winter.

ABOVE RIGHT Wooden barrels will last for many years, especially if they are raised slightly to allow moisture to escape. Growing in a 45-cm/18-in half barrel, *Diascia stachyoides* (syn. *D. flanaganii*) surrounds and climbs through a standard variegated rhamnus, generously lending its flowers to this evergreen shrub.

# A cross-section of bulb-filled tub

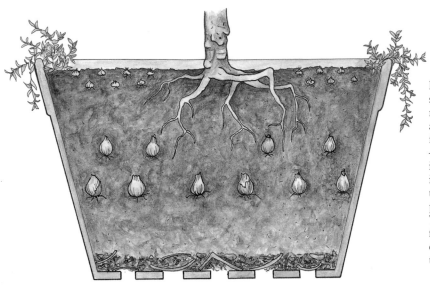

Filling our tubs in late autumn for spring display is always an exciting moment. We now have a routine, always dominated by the inevitable fact that twice – or even three times – the number of bulbs will be inncorporated than might be imagined. Earliest to flower will be the species crocus, then the paperwhites, then the 'Peeping Tom' narcissus, then an April-flowering daffodil, followed by elegant lily-flowered white or pink tulips. There must be a central feature for winter interest, and vincas or violas to give a touch of green as well as colour in the winter.

The cross-section shows the depth at which you should plant the bulbs and corms.

Window boxes must be firmly fixed; they also must have adequate drainage holes – one every 25-30cm/10-12in in a trough-shaped box – covered either with broken crocks (pieces of broken clay flower pots) or small flat stones to prevent the soil from clogging up the holes. Put a layer of clean gravel or pebbles on the bottom, then start adding your compost.

Wooden boxes may seem old-fashioned today in our plastic world. You can buy plastic window boxes which are extremely light; they are not very attractive but can be dropped inside the wooden boxes and have the advantage of being easily lifted out and put on a working surface for refilling. There are now also polyurethane containers which simulate stone, metal, wood or clay; they are realistic, and, again, very light, so make handling much simpler. A good way of fixing these boxes is to have a simple, open framework of narrow (say 2-3cm/1in) metal strips made and attached to the sill, and the box slotted into this.

If you live in a town or city, you will probably have no option but to go to a garden shop and buy bags of peat-based compost. These contain added slow-release fertilizers which are essential to the well-being of the plants but only effective for perhaps three months. Peat itself has no food value, so you must consult your garden centre and buy a slow-release fertilizer as a future back-up to give the plants the nutrients they require.

Watering is all important, even for plants such as herbs which generally need only a little water. Keep in mind the fact that, depending on positioning and the direction in which the wind is blowing, the rain may not reach the window box. So, rain or no rain, the watering must be watched. Plants are not like garden furniture – they will deteriorate without correct care.

Herbs are particularly suitable for a window box. The most useful in the kitchen are parsley, chives, thyme and marjoram, small plants of sage in its grey or purple form, and for an extra element of height a fennel plant (*Foeniculum vulgare*). Keep picking the feathery leaves of the fennel to encourage new young growth and they will look beautiful appearing through the sage. These herbs are all hardy. If you can find a plant of prostrate rosemary, *R.* × *lavandulaceus*, also known as *R. corsicus* 'Prostratus', this could go near the outside and be allowed to hang down. If you want to brighten the scene with a few colourful bulbs or annuals, put species crocus round the fennel, chionodoxas or scillas by the sage, and winter-flowering pansies by the chives. As the chives push through you can keep the pansies in check.

Most plants, herbs included, require as much light as possible: to achieve more on a shady window sill I would get mirrors fixed on the side walls of the sill to reflect all the available sun and light. Silver foil would be adequate but less attractive. You could also double the number of your pot plants by attaching metal fitments to the wall with slots to carry firm wire baskets.

Ideas often seem simple until you start to carry them out; then problems somehow arise! You can lift a sash window and reach your plants on the sill outside, but if you have latched windows which open outwards you will have a problem. The only solution in these cases is to keep your plants indoors: here they will do better in pots, preferably clay, with each one planted individually. Make sure the pots have good drainage by covering the bottom with crocks. This is of the utmost importance, especially for herbs, which in the wild grow in well drained soil in sunny places where their aroma is at its strongest. If you choose to have herbs, I would have as many as possible, allowing some to form flower heads and keeping others more compact so that they produce the maximum number of aromatic leaves for cooking. Chives and thymes can be planted in shallow pots (10cm/4in deep), sage and rosemary in taller (16cm/6in) pots, and basil, coriander and summer savory grown as annuals. Borage is a biennial and best bought as a well grown plant.

Next let us think about balcony gardens. For me, they always bring to mind stage sets in which each plant has its own important role, either as static background scenery or as a moving player. Here the backdrop and containers must be carefully arranged and chosen for both beauty and usefulness. If you are at all concerned about the weight on the balcony being too heavy, call in an architect or surveyor before making your plans. I

ABOVE LEFT Be generous with spring-flowering bulbs. First come the *Iris reticulata* and crocus, then the narcissus and tulips. A central evergreen feature – holly or box – gives winter interest.

ABOVE CENTRE Pretty Italian clay pots have withstood many hard frosts. They are now filled for summer with *Helichrysum petiolare, Pelargonium* 'Lady Plymouth', white *Argyranthemum frutescens* and yellow *Bidens ferulifolium*.

ABOVE RIGHT A medley of pots of mostly scented plants in a sunny courtyard. A standard lemon-scented verbena is in full flower, and has satellite pots of freesias and *Gladiolus callianthus* which will flower later. *Ipomoea* 'Heavenly Blue' provides morning glamour.

RIGHT The colour theme in this clay pot filled to overflowing by Mrs Merton is green, white and grey. The plants used so successfully are variegated myrtle, *Helichrysum petiolare* 'Limelight', white verbena, white pelargonium and daisies.

Three different conceptions of planting in containers – in an old lead urn with elegant handles, in a traditional clay pot and in a container created to line steps under a yew hedge.

ABOVE LEFT Tubs should never be conceived in isolation – their background and positioning are as important as their content. At Knightshayes, the planting of blue *Felicia amoena* and grey helichrysum reflects and softens the strong shapes, rounded and square, of its clipped yew neighbour, while the colours harmonize with the urn.

ABOVE RIGHT As at Powis Castle, visitors will be struck by the originality of Mrs Merton's ideas. At the top is *Tanacetum ptarmiciflorum* and *Verbena* 'Hidcote Purple'; then come *Pelargonium* 'White Boar' and *P.* 'Lord Bute', *Fuchsia* 'Tom West' and *Senecio bicolor cineraria* with a skirt of grey helichrysum and a fringe of *Pelargonium* 'Barbe Bleu'.

OPPOSITE A summer planting of fuchsias and *Helichrysum petiolare* 'Limelight' brightens the feet of the evergreen hedge. This full planting in a rather unexpected place shows how containers can so easily add extra interest.

would choose to have my doorway opening inwards to allow maximum space outside.

Any wall space on either side of the balcony must be put to maximum use. For tidiness fix an appropriately designed trellis painted the same colour as the wall. For the base of the trellis you should buy containers large enough to accommodate a clematis and a rose, and other plants to cover their lower stems.

Square or rectangular containers which will fit neatly together make the best use of limited space; you can keep your best round pots to go as a pretty skirt around the straight sides of those behind. A long polyurethane trough at the front of the balcony, carefully chosen to look authentic, is a good solution for any weight problems. If you don't have to worry about weight, you could attach hanging baskets, which are easy enough to water and deadhead, to the base of the railing.

A balcony garden should be *multum in parvo*, each detail a jewel of perfection and every individual plant worthy of its place – never a distraction, too dominant in character, too brilliant in colour, or having leaves that are out of scale with its neighbours'. The balcony must have some colour through the summer, and trays of your favourite annuals can be bought and varied from year to year. Look at your curtains and try to echo their colour scheme in your planting, so that the room and balcony will become united when the windows are open. You could even choose your plants first and have curtains to match.

A balcony makes a wonderful scented garden too: think how lovely to open the doors on summer days and have the scent of the flowers coming into your room. For permanent planting choose lavender, santolina, the curry plant (*Helichrysum italicum*) and *Daphne odora*, and use more tender shrubs as summer interest. These you may have to buy every year unless you have a good friend with plenty of glasshouse space who would over-winter them for you. My first favourite for scent is *Aloysia triphylla (Lippia citriodora)*; it is quite easy to look after in the winter as long as it is kept under cover and never watered until March or early April to start it into new growth. The scented-leaved geraniums are essential, my two favourites being *Pelargonium* 'Mabel Grey' and *P. tomentosum*. Both make good-sized plants – if you want to fit one or two into tiny spaces, then *P. × fragrans* and *P. radula* are smaller and just as fragrant. A pair of clipped *Myrtus communis tarentina* make an elegant addition.

My advice for either a balcony or, on a larger scale, a paved garden, is to have evergreen foliage shrubs for year-long interest, interspersing these with the inevitable flower colour – some of the shrubs will flower anyway. Remember that tall plants can give a small space an added dimension. Bamboos, for example, can look magnificent in containers, giving an upright accent. I like *Sinarundinaria nitida (Arundinaria n.)* for its purple stems; though reaching 3m/10ft in open ground, it remains lower without its freedom; *A. viridistriata* (now correctly *Pleioblastus auricoma*) needs less space and has broadly striped yellow leaves. In a paved garden with a pool, these would give structure and reflect well.

Phormium may be treated in the same way, using its firm vertical leaves as a foil and contrast to rounded shrubs. The red-purple lobed and palmate leaves of a small Japanese maple, *Acer palmatum* 'Atropurpureum', could echo the red margins of *Phormium cookianum* 'Tricolor'. On the other side of the phormium I would like to have *Spiraea japonica* 'Goldflame': the cream of the young spiraea foliage would pick up the white stripes of the flax.

For year-round interest choose a repeat-flowering rose and an autumn-flowering clematis and underplant these with bulbs and

pansies for spring and *Galtonia candicans* for summer. Hostas look extremely good in containers, and for interest before the leaves unfold I would underplant these with tulips or narcissus.

Wherever you are going to put your pots or containers, my advice is to do some thoughtful reading first. Use reliable plant catalogues which give the information you need and take these along with you when you go buying – it is all too easy to collect a basketful of alluring looking plants in small pots from a garden centre and put them as a mixed bunch into a large container with no consideration of their behaviour in a few months' time. Make a list, and do not be tempted by last-minute substitutes unless they will really serve your purpose. Bear in mind the importance of colours, shapes and textures on a small scale, and your contained garden could be as rewarding and bring as much pleasure as any on a larger scale.

# Index

NOTE: Page numbers in **bold type** refer to captions to the illustrations

pansy 41, 124, 137, 158, 163; winter-flowering p. 157, 160
*Parahebe lyallii* **113**
Parker, Jill **130**
*Parrotia* 139
parsley **25**, 160
*Parthenocissus henryana* 79, **82**; *P. quinquefolia* **42**
*Passiflora caerulea* (passion flower) 79
*Pelargonium* 157, **161**; *P.* × *fragrans* **159**, 163; *P. radula* 163; *P. tomentosum* 163; *P.* 'Barbe Bleu' **162**; *P.* 'Lady Plymouth' **154**, 157, **161**; *P.* 'Lord Bute' **162**; *P.* 'Mabel Gray' 163; *P.* 'Paul Crampel' 18; *P.* 'Roi des Balcons Rose' (*P.* 'Ville de Paris') **159**; *P.* 'White Boar' **162**
*Petiphyllum peltatum* (= *Darmera peltata*) 148
*Penstemon* 16, 32, 62, 69, **91**, 103, **111**, 112, 129; *P.* 'Alice Hindley' 65, **105**, 112; *P.* 'Catherine de la Mare' 62; *P.* 'Charles Rudd' **115**; *P.* 'Evelyn' 20, 29, 65, 114; *P.* 'Garnet' 112, **125**; *P.* 'Hewell's Pink' 65; *P.* 'Hidcote Pink' 29; *P.* 'Pennington Gem' 114; *P.* 'Purple Bedder' **68**, **91**, **125**; *P.* 'Rich Ruby' **11**, 65, 112; *P.* 'Snow Storm' 99; *P.* 'Sour Grapes' 69, 112; *P.* 'White Bedder' **68**
pergolas 75
*Periploca graeca* 79
periwinkle 120, 137, 154
*Perovskia atriplicifolia* (Russian sage) 62, 108, **113**; *P.* 'Blue Spire' 109
*Persicaria* SEE *Polygonum*
*Petasites fragrans* **144**
*Petunia* 62, 65
pheasant berry (= *Leycesteria formosa*) 81, 85
*Philadelphus* 55; *P. coronarius* 'Aurcus' 32, 33, **34**, 36, **99**, 103; *P. microphyllus* **135**; *P.* 'Belle Etoile' **102**; *P.* 'Manteau d'Hermine' 60, 103
*Phlomis* 37; *P. fruticosa* 99; *P. russeliana* **23**, **100**, 108
*Phlox* 18, 65, 67, 103; *P. douglasii* 117; *P. paniculata* 'July Glow' 112; *P.p.* 'Prince of Orange' 115; *P.p.* 'White Admiral' 65, 115; *P. subulata* 117; *P.* 'Chattahoochee' 101, **111**, **113**, 117
*Phormium* 11, 93, 101; *P. cookianum* 'Tricolor' 163; *P. tenax* 93; *P.t. purpureum* 93, 158; *P.* 'Dazzler' 85
*Photinia* 157; *P. davidiana* **42**; *P.* × *fraseri* 'Robusta' **135**
*Phuopsis stylosa* **22**
*Phygelius* **95**; *P. aequalis* 'Yellow Trumpet' 79, **82**; *P. capensis coccineus* 85
*Phyllitis scolopendrium* **82**
*Physostegia* 'Rose Bouquet' 99, **113**
*Picea abies* 'Nidiformis' 110; *P. glauca* 'Albertiana Conica' 131; *P. pungens* 'Glauca' **31**
piggy-back plant (= *Tolmiea menziesii*) 124
*Pileostegia viburnoides* **82**
*Piptanthus nepalensis* **111**
Pitmuies, House of (Tayside) **16**, **72**, **111**
*Pittosporum tenuifolium* 'Purpureum' 33
*Pleioblastus auricoma* 33, 72, 163
poached egg plant (= *Limnanthes douglasii*) 38, 134
*Podophyllum peltatum* 144
*Polemonium* 20, **89**; *P. caeruleum* 33, **68**, 69
polyanthus 80, 89, 111; Courichan p. 41, **54**, 128, **129**
*Polygonatum* × *hybridum* 50, **137**, 142, **142**
*Polygonum affine* **107**; *P.a.* 'Darjeeling Red' 117; *P.a.* 'Dimity' 93, 117; *P.*

*baldschuanicum* 80; *P. bistorta* 20; *P. b.* 'Superbum' 57, **58**, **89**, 93
*Polystichum setiferum* 116; *P.s. divisilobum* 20, 102, 129, 157
poppy **16**, 18, 38, **48**, **91**, 139; oriental p. **19**, 67, **97**, 103, **105**; species p. 38; Welsh p. (= *Meconopsis cambrica*) 33, **34**, 41
Portugal laurel (= *Prunus lusitanica*) 154
*Potentilla* 11, 62, **115**, 117; *P. anserina* **25**; *P.* 'Elizabeth' **34**, **100**, 108
Powis Castle (Powys) **69**, 72, 76, **100**, **118**, 122, **122**, **132**, 154, **156**
primrose 20, **92**, 137, **137**, 139, 157
*Primula* **92**, 99, **150**; *P. bulleyana* 148; *P. florindae* **146**, 148, **148**; *P. japonica* 148, **148**, **150**; *P.j.* 'Miller's Crimson' 148, **148**; *P.j.* 'Postford White' 148; *P.* × *polyantha* Gold Laced **54**; *P. sikkimensis* 148; Barnhaven hybrid p. 43, **52**, 128, **129**; drumstick 51; *P.* 'Guinevere' **49**
privet, golden (= *Ligustrum ovalifolium* 'Aureum') **34**, 37, **89**, **95**, 98, 108, **135**
*Prunella* 117; *P. webbiana* 117
*Prunus* 45; *P. avium* 137; *P. glandulosa* 107; *P.* × *hillieri* 'Spire' 139; *P. laurocerasus* 157; *P.l.* 'Zabeliana' 127; *P.l. lusitanica* 154; *P.l.* 'Variegata' 98; *P. serrula* **122**; *P. tenella* 38, 50; *P.t.* 'Fire Hill' 107; *P.* × *yedoensis* 'Shidare-yoshino' (*P.* × *y.* 'Perpendens') 48, **123**; *P.* 'Tai-haku' **123**
Pyrford Court (Surrey) 13
Pugh, Mrs **7**
*Pulmonaria* 110, **137**; *P. angustifolia azurea* 110; *P. saccarata argentea* 110; *P. vallarsae* 'Margery Fish' 110
*Pulsatilla vulgaris* 103
Pumphrey, Frances: *The New Englishwoman's Garden* 146
*Puschkinia* 120; *P. scilloides* (*P. libanotica*) **47**, 48, 129
Pusey House (Oxfordshire) 152
*Pyracantha* **82**; *P. atalantioides* 75, 80, **82**; *P. rogersiana* 75, 80; *P.r. flava* 80; *P.* 'Mohave' 80
pyrethrum 67
*Pyrus calleryana* 'Chanticleer' 139; *P. salicifolia* 'Pendula' **30**

quince, flowering 75

Reiss, Mrs Phyllis 69
Renoir, Auguste 15
*Rhamnus alaternus* 98; *R.a.* 'Argenteovariegata' 98, **135**
*Rheum palmatum* **8**; *R.p.* 'Atrosanguineum' 29, 50, 148; *R.p.* 'Rubrum' **150**; *R. tanguticum* **144**
*Rhododendron* 60; *R. impeditum* 101, **135**; *R.* 'Blue Diamond' 125
*Ribes sanguineum* 'Brocklebankii' 103
*Ricinus* 70; *R. communis* 29
*Robinia pseudoacacia* 'Frisia' 36, **37**, 108
Robins, Thomas **140**
Robinson, Mrs **123**, 137
Robinson, William 62, 144; *The English Flower Garden* 96
rock rose (= *Helianthemum*) 19, 22, **62**, 110, 112, 125, **126**
*Rodgersia pinnata* 21; *R. podophylla* 143, **153**
Rodmarton Manor (Gloucestershire) 134
Roper, Lanning 99
*Rosa* (roses) 9, 11, **14**, 16, 20, **22**, **26**, 29, 61, 62, **82**, 89, **132**, 162; *R. filipes* 'Kiftsgate' 77; *R. gentiliana* **84**; *R. glauca* (*R. rubrifolia*) **72**; *R.* × *highdownensis* **118**; *R. multiflora*

'Grevillei' (Seven Sisters r.) 83; *R.* × *odorata* 'Mutabilis' (*R. chinensis* 'M') **106**; *R.* 'Aimée Vibert' 76; *R.* 'Albertine' 146; *R.* 'Blairii Number 2' 76, **77**; *R.* 'Blush Noisette' 76; *R.* 'Bobbie James' 76, 77; *R.* 'Bourbon Queen' **132**; *R.* 'Buff Beauty' 131; *R.* 'Cécile Brunner' 107; *R.* 'Cerise Bouquet' 131; *R.* 'Climbing Etoile de Hollande' 76; *R.* 'Climbing Lady Hillingdon' 76; *R.* 'Dearest' 84; *R.* 'Dimples' 65; *R.* 'Everest' 65; *R.* 'Fantin-Latour' 107; *R.* 'Félicité Perpétue' 77; *R.* 'Francis E. Lester' 76; *R.* 'François Juranville' 77; *R.* 'Fru Dagmar Hastrup' **78**; *R.* 'Frühlingsgold' 131; *R.* 'The Garland' 77; *R.* 'Gloire de Dijon' 76; *R.* 'Golden Showers' 76, 79, **82**, 84; *R.* 'Guinée' 76; *R.* 'Helen Knight' **75**; *R.* 'Iceberg' **14**; *R.* 'Lady Hillingdon' 83; *R.* 'Lavender Lassie' **30**; *R.* 'Madame Alfred Carrière' 76; *R.* 'Madame Hardy' **106**; *R.* 'Madame Isaac Pereire' 107; *R.* 'Maréchal Niel' 77; *R.* 'Maigold' **23**; *R.* 'Mermaid' 77; *R.* 'Nathalie Nypels' **130**; *R.* 'New Dawn' **95**; *R.* 'Paul's Lemon Pillar' 76; *R.* 'Paulii' 76; *R.* 'Paulii Rosea' 126; *R.* 'Penelope' 131; *R.* 'Pretty Jessica' 107; *R.* 'Rambling Rector' 77; *R.* 'Saint Cecilia' 107; *R.* 'Snow Carpet' 103; *R.* 'Souvenir de la Malmaison' 107; Sweetheart r. 84; *R.* 'Tuscany Superb' **146**; *R.* 'Veilchenblau' 19, 77, 84; *R.* 'Wedding Day' 77; *R.* 'Wife of Bath' 107; *R.* 'Zéphirine Drouhin' 76, **76**, 107; climbing 76-7; New English 108; Poulsen 131; shrub 65, 131-4, **132**
*Rosmarinus* (rosemary) 161; *R.* × *lavandulaceus* (*R. corsicus* 'Prostratus' (prostrate r.) 160; *R. officinalis* **113**
Rothschild, Miriam 137; *The Butterfly Gardener* 139
royal fern (= *Osmunda regalis*) **8**, 102
*Rubus cockburnianus* 127, 141; *R. phoenicolasius* **42**
*Rudbeckia* 15, 29, 62, 107; *R. laciniata* 71; *R.* 'Marmalade' 62
rue 37
runner bean 75
Russian sage (= *Perovskia atricipifolia*) 62, 108, 113
*Ruta graveolens* 12; *R.g.* 'Jackman's Blue' 78

Sackville-West, Victoria 108, **109**
sage 32, **37**, 41, 110, **125**, 160-1
Sales, John 29, **70**
*Salix alba* 'Britzensis' (*S.a.* 'Chermesina') 96; *S. integra* 'Hakuro-nishiki' 41
*Salvia* **26**; *S. fulgens* 19; *S. involucrata* 'Bethellii' 84; *S. nemorosa* 65, **76**; *S.n.* 'East Friesland' 20, **26**, 112; *S. officinalis* 'Icterina' **25**, 37; *S. o.* 'Kew Gold' **25**; *S.o.* 'Purpurascens' 33; *S.o.* 'Tricolor' 33; *S. patens* 18, 111; *S. pratensis haematodes* 62; *S. rutilans* **159**; *S. sclarea turkestanica* 62, 72; *S.* × *superba* 37, **91**; *S.* × *s.* 'Superba' **115**; *S. uliginosa* 107, **113**
*Sambucus racemosa* 'Plumosa Aurea' 33
*Sanguinaria canadensis* 142
*Santolina* 23, 29, 37, 43, 62, 110, 125, 132, 162; *S. chamaecyparissus* (*S. incana*) 20, **21**, 29, 37, 57, **60**, **92**, 111, **135**, 157; *S. pinnata neapolitana* 12, 111, 131; *S. rosmarinifolia* (*S. virens*) 111
*Sarcococca* 157; *S. humilis* 101, **135**
*Saxifraga* 51; *S. umbrosa* 'Variegata' 99; *S.* × *urbium* 79, **113**, 116-17, **116**; *S.* × *u.*

'Aureopunctata' 99, 116; scabious 108
*Schizostylis coccinea* **14**, 61, 152; *S.c.* 'Tambara' 61; *S.c.* 'Viscountess Byng' 61
*Scilla* 48, 55, **91**, 102-3, 120, 160; *S. messeniaca* **140**; *S. mischtschenkoana* (*S. tubergeniana*) 48; *S. siberica* 48, 142; *S.s.* 'Spring Beauty' **47**
Seattle Flower Show 157
*Sedum* 62, 120, 157; *S. spectabile* **26**, 62; *S. telephium maximum* 'Atropurpureum' 62, **68**; *S.* 'Autumn Joy' **105**; *S.* 'Ruby Glow' **118**; *S.* 'Sunset Cloud' 112
*Senecio* **61**; *S. bicolor cineraria* (*Cineraria maritima*) 99, 162; *S. monroi* 105; *S. viravira* (*S. leucostachys*) 29, 37, 62; *S.* (now *Brachyglottis*) 'Sunshine' 29, 32, **35**, 43, 50, 79, 96, 99, 117; *S.* 'White Diamond' 62
shape 20-1, 37
Shasta daisy (= *Leucanthemum* × *superbum*) **21**, 62
shrubberies 134, **135**
*Sidalcea malviflora* 'Rose Queen' 20, 29
silk vine (= *Periploca graeca*) 79
*Sinarundinaria nitida* (*Arundinaria n.*) 163
*Sisyrinchium* **146**; *S. striatum* 84, 101
*Skimmia* 114
*Smilacina racemosa* **92**
snow in summer (= *Cerastium tomentosum*) 29, 99, 133
snowberry, variegated (= *Symphoricarpos orbiculatus* 'Foliis Variegatis') 32, 48, **91**, 108
snowdrop 11, 15, 48, **49**, 80, 102-3, **137**, 139, **140**
soft-shield fern (= *Polystichum setiferum*) 20, 102, 116, 129, 157
*Solanum crispum* 'Glasnevin' 84-5, **85**
Solomon's seal (= *Polygonatum* × *hybridum*) 50, **137**, 142, **142**
*Sorbus* 16; *S. pohuashanensis* 41
southernwood (= *Artemisia abrotanum*) **25**, **115**
*Spartium junceum* 90
*Sphaeralcea munroana* **30**
spider plant (= *Cleome hassleriana*) 29, **118**
spinach 29
*Spiraea* 82, 117; *S. japonica* 'Goldflame' 12, **32**, 32-3, 60, 108, 112, 163; *S.j.* 'Little Princess' **91**, 112, 114; *S. nipponica* 'Snowmound' 112, **113**; *S.* × *vanhouttei* 102, **113**; *S.* 'Arguta' 32, **38**, **89**, 90, 134, **135**
spurge (= *Euphorbia*) 16, 20, 37, 110, **137**, **146**; wood s. 142
squash, scallop 'Patty Pan' 158; 'Sunburst Yellow' 158
*Stachys* **8**, **14**, **122**; *S. byzantina* (*S. lanata*) 20, **21**, **23**, 29, 32, 37, **41**, 43, **91**, **92**, 99, 108, 122, 131, 132
Stancombe Park (Gloucestershire) 148
*Statice latifolia* 96
Steadman, Keith 83
Steeb, Karen K. 157
Steeple Aston (Oxfordshire) **19**
*Stipa gigantea* 72
stock 137
stream gardens **150**
summer savory 161
summer snowflake (= *Leucojum aestivum*) 56, **56**, **92**, 98, 150
sunflower 16
Sweden, James van 12
sweet cicely (= *Myrrhis odorata*) 99
sweet pea 75-6, 78-9
sweet William **16**, **111**

## Author's and Photographer's Acknowledgments

I would like to thank all the garden owners who kindly allowed their gardens to be photographed for this book; and I am specially grateful to Anne Dexter, Peter Healing, Penny Hobhouse and John Malins, Kathleen and David Hodges, Caryl and John Hubbard, Andrew Norton, and Margaret Ogilvie for helping me to identify particular plants in their gardens. **R.V.**

Very grateful thanks to the many garden owners who welcomed me to their gardens. Some wonderful gardens are only represented here in microcosm, with a few leaves and a flower or two standing for a whole vista. My special thanks to: Barbara Ackroyd, Basil and Gerda Barlow, Gwen Beaumont, Meg and Jeff Blumson, the late Humphrey Brooke, Martin and Mary Caroe, the late Mrs Clutterbuck, Robert Cooper, Anne Dexter, Caroline Eckersley, Joe Elliott, Connie Franks, Lucy Gent, Thomas and Anthea Gibson, Brian Halliwell and The Royal Botanic Garden Kew, Mr and the Hon Mrs Peter Healing, David Hicks, Kathleen and David Hodges, John and Caryl Hubbard, Briony Lawson, John Malins and Penelope Hobhouse, John and Eve Meares, Ralph and Esther Merton, The National Trust [Buscot Park, Hidcote Manor, Knightshayes Court, Mottisfont Abbey, Powis Castle, Tintinhull House, Sizergh Castle), The National Trust for Scotland (Crathes Castle, Malleny), Andrew Norton, Margaret Ogilvie, Mirabel Osler, Mr and Mrs Paice, Sir Peter and Lady Parker, Norrie and Sandra Pope, Steve and Iris Pugh, Joyce Robinson, John Sales, Lady Saye and Sele, Mrs Shuker and Mrs Pollitt, Mr and Mrs Smalley, Dr James Smart, Mrs M. C. Stanley, Gladys Tonge, John Treasure, and Rosemary Verey – last alphabetically but first in every other way; her garden at Barnsley House has inspired not only a large proportion of the pictures, but has had an influence on many of the other gardens that appear in the book, not least my own. **A.L.**

## Publishers' Acknowledgments

*Horticultural consultant:* Tony Lord
*Designer:* John Laing
*Illustrator:* Valerie Price
*Picture Editor:* Anne Fraser
*Indexer:* Douglas Matthews
*Production:* Nicky Bowden
*Associate Art Directors:* Tim Foster, Caroline Hillier
*Editorial Director:* Erica Hunningher